Praise for *Blink* and Ted Dekker's Previous Novels

"Ted Dekker is the most exciting writer I've read in a very long time. *Blink* will expand his fan base tremendously. Wonderful reading . . . powerful insights. Bravo!"

—TED BAEHR
President, *MOVIEGUIDE®* Magazine

"Cloaked in the mystery of Saudi Arabia, this tale woven by Dekker is compulsively readable. Written with an arresting hybrid of suspense and love, *Blink* casts a sweeping light on a surreal world where the future is buried by the past. Saudi Arabia was my home for twelve years. Dekker has an uncanny ability to capture the true essence of the world's most mysterious land in this hauntingly beautiful story. You will be astonished."

—JEAN SASSON
New York Times Best-selling Author of
Princess: A True Story of Life Behind the Veil in Saudi Arabia

" . . . knock-your-socks-off storytelling."

—ROBERT LIPARULO
New Man magazine

"Someone recently asked if I would be interested in reading the hottest new fiction writer on the market. I asked who that might that be, expecting a writer along the lines of John Grisham or Stephen King. Instead, I was introduced to *Blink,* the new novel by Ted Dekker. They were right. . . . Ted Dekker has caused me to miss some serious sleep the past three nights! Dekker is awesome. I will own everything he writes."

—TOM NEWMAN
Film Producer and Founder of Impact Productions

"Dekker is an emerging powerhouse among fiction writers. *Blink* is a thrilling tale that grabs your attention immediately and is near impossible to put down."

—LARRY J. LEECH II
Christian Retailing

"[*Heaven's Wager* is] genuinely exciting . . . fast-paced . . . spine-tingling . . . "

—*Publishers Weekly*

"Well, well, well, guess what I've found? A fiction writer with a rare knack for a compelling story, an expansive reservoir of clever ideas, and a unique wit that makes me laugh."

—FRANK PERETTI
Best-selling author of *This Present Darkness* and *The Oath*

" . . . page-turning, action-packed suspense and adventure."

—*Lifewise Magazine*

"[*Blessed Child* is] superbly written and deeply captivating."

—*CBA Marketplace*

"[*Thunder of Heaven* is] a real page-turner . . . scenes read like the best of David Morrell . . . his description is upsettingly precise."

—*Booklist*

"Ted is a great weaver of stories that are believable yet tinged with the mystery of the unseen."

—TIM WAY
Senior Book Buyer, Family Christian Stores

blink

TED DEKKER

A Division of Thomas Nelson Publishers
Since 1798

visit us at www.westbowpress.com

Published by WestBow Press, a division of Thomas Nelson, Inc., P.O. Box 141000, Nashville, Tennessee 37214.

Library of Congress Cataloging-in-Publication Data

Dekker, Ted, 1962–
Blink / by Ted Dekker.
p. cm.
ISBN 0-8499-4371-X (SC)
ISBN 0-8499-4511-9 (Rpkg)
1. Muslim women—Fiction. 2. Middle East—Fiction. I. Title.
PS3554.E43 B586 2002
813'.6—dc21 2002008734

Printed in the United States of America

05 06 07 08 RRD 5

acknowledgments

THERE ARE A HANDFUL of people who invariably influence the final draft of any novel tremendously, some through harsh words and others through kind words. Both are welcomed and deeply appreciated, though not necessarily with equal grace, I'm afraid. I would like to thank the following people from the bottom of my heart. I suppose they can try to guess which category they fit into.

Phil Strople, my dearest friend. Tim Graham, a true genius who was as strange as I was back then, with one marked difference—he was much smarter. Carl Medearis, who perhaps understands and loves our Arab brothers more than any one I know. Debbie Wickwire, Mark Sweeney, Laura Kendall, David Moberg, Ami McConnell, Allen Arnold, Jennifer Willingham and the rest of the Publishing team who have believed in my stories from the beginning, when the rest were still seeing through a glass darkly. (Please, no need for panic; I am not implying that my words are even modestly inspired, regardless of what my five-year-old daughter thinks.) Erin Healy, my editor, who is brilliant and truly worthy of a much better writer than I. My friends Mitzi, Cheryl, and Laurel, who subjected me to their opinions of the rough draft. Actually, this time it was quite painless. LeeAnn, without whom I could not write at all. God bless you all.

TED DEKKER

prologue

THE HEART OF HISTORY beats in the Middle East, that plot of ground surrounding the holy city of Jerusalem. It was there along the Euphrates in a garden called Eden that history began. And it will be there in a land called Israel, a stone's throw from that same garden, that history will end. The Middle East was the birthplace of Abraham and Isaac and Ishmael. It was the birthplace of Christ. And it was the birthplace of Mohammed.

What happened in history happened because of what first occurred in this small corner of the world. And what happens in the future will happen because of what first occurs in the Middle East. It has always been so; it is so now; it will be so, until the end.

Everyone knows this.

But not everyone knows that what happens in the Middle East itself will be largely shaped by what happens south of Jerusalem, in the great desert land known as the Arabian Peninsula. The motherland of Mecca, the birthplace of Islam. Saudi Arabia.

And what happens to Saudi Arabia will largely depend on what happens to the royal family that rules the land, the House of Saud.

And what happens to the House of Saud will largely depend on the fate of one woman, a princess in the House of Saud.

Her name is Miriam and this is her story.

But what happens to Miriam will depend entirely on what happens in a land far from her own. In America. To a very uncommon man who has absolutely nothing in common with Miriam.

His name is Seth and this is his story too.

1

THEY CALL IT THE CRADLE of Islam. A land covered by a white sand that hides vast reserves of black oil. A country where wealth is measured by the number of palaces a man owns. A kingdom ruled without a constitution, by a king and a thousand princes who hold all the positions of power. A society that guards dark secrets covered up with rubies and diamonds and black veils. A world stuck in time like a fairy tale gone awry.

The country is Saudi Arabia and it is heaven and it is hell, depending on the name of your father. Depending on your loyalty to the religion. But mostly depending on whether you were born male or female.

Miriam was born the latter, the daughter of a prince named Salman bin Fahd, and today the sounds of hell floated through the palace, mocking the thousand or so female guests who'd gathered for her friend Sita's wedding.

Miriam swept the purple velvet drape to one side and gazed through the window to the courtyard. The marble palace had been completed just last year and was easily the grandest of her father's residences. She hadn't visited all of them, but she didn't need to. Prince Salman bin Fahd had four wives, and he'd built each of them three palaces, two in Riyadh, and one in Jiddah. All four wives had identical dwellings in each location, as was the common practice, although to say his wives *had* the palaces was misleading. *Father* had the palaces, and he had wives to put in each.

This, Salman's thirteenth palace, he'd built solely for special events such as today's, the wedding of his friend Hatam.

Outside, the sun glinted off a spewing fountain in the center of a large pond. Bright red petals from two hundred dozen roses flown in from Holland blanketed the water. Evidently the groom, Hatam bin Hazat, had heard that his young new bride liked red roses. Upon seeing the extravagant display two days earlier, Sita vowed never to look on another red rose in her life.

Dozens of Filipino servants crossed the lawn, carrying silver trays stacked high with every imaginable kind of food prepared by eighteen chefs brought in from Egypt. Roast almond duck, curried beef rolled in lamb flanks, liver-stuffed lobster—Miriam had never seen such an extravagant display of food. And this for the women only. As at all Saudi weddings, the men would never actually see the women. Custom required two separate ceremonies for the simple reason that women attended weddings unveiled. The true path of Islam forbade a man from seeing the face of a woman unless she was a family member or tied very closely to his family.

Sounds of music and drums and gaiety drifted through the window, but really they were the sounds of death. Miriam once told her mother that a Saudi woman dies three times during her span on earth. She dies on the day of her first menses, when she is forced to don the black veil and slip into obscurity; she dies on the day of her wedding, when she is given as a possession to a stranger; and, most mercifully, she dies when she finally gives up her ghost. The statement had earned her a slap.

Best be a good woman and accept your fate.

The women in Miriam's life had always said that. The whole world seemed to say that. Miriam had studied in America for three months one summer, and she found that even the Americans said that, not about themselves, of course, but about foreign women. *Best be a good woman and accept your fate.* Not in so many words, of course, but those few who took the time to hear her stories just attributed the horrors to cultural differences. What Saudis called social pressure, Americans called political correctness, and questioning another's cultural practices was clearly not politically correct.

Perhaps if the Americans knew Saudi history better, they would rise up in outrage and wave that flag of human rights they took up now and then. But after her brief exposure to the Americans, she doubted they wanted to hear the truth.

Miriam let her mind drift over the events that had placed her and her friend Sita here, in this magnificent palace, where they awaited the ceremony that would end Sita's life as she knew it.

The kingdom's first king, Abdul Aziz bin Saud, conquered Riyadh in 1902. He was in his early twenties then, and he swung his sword until he ruled most of the Arabian Peninsula. The four kings since his death in 1953 were all his sons. But when Miriam looked down history's foggy halls, she decided it was the king's women, not his sons, that truly delighted Aziz. He'd shown his appetites by taking over three hundred women as wives and perhaps over a thousand slaves and concubines as lovers, often sequestering them in a windowless basement. To keep other lovers out, he said.

Yes, Aziz liked his women. But he'd often treated them as animals, and to Miriam's thinking the treatment had stuck. Women were barred from a host of activities common to men. Driving, for example. Driving gave the female too much freedom and required skills not natural to the woman, men said. Neither was a woman allowed to give testimony in a dispute, other than the word of the last man she had spoken with. Evidently a woman could no better steer her tongue than she could steer a car. Women were muzzled with black hoods and held captive in their own homes by husbands who ruled with iron fists.

It was a kind of death.

Today it was her friend Sita's turn to die.

Miriam took a deep breath and bit her lip. In one sense, weddings did represent life. They were the one time when thousands of women gathered and shed their black *abaayas* and veils for colorful dresses. For a few days, the nonperson of the Saudi culture could become a real person, allowed to be viewed by other real persons before being forced back into their abaayas. Like many daughters of royalty, Miriam had received a classic English education in Riyadh and at every opportunity experimented with Western ways and clothes, everything from jeans to bathing suits. But here in the kingdom, those opportunities were few and never in the public eye.

"I can't believe it's actually happening," Sita said from the sofa.

Miriam let the curtain fall back in place and turned around. Sita sat like a small doll dressed in lace and pink. Her eyes were round and dark—so very sad. Miriam and Sultana had rescued Sita from a flock of aunts busying her for the final marriage ceremony and brought her here, to this room they'd dubbed the piano room for the white grand piano sitting to their right. The carpet, a thick Persian weave with a lion embroidered at the center, swallowed their feet. Evidently someone liked big cats; the walls of the room formed a virtual zoo of cat paintings. It wouldn't be her father, Salman; the old bull didn't have a creative hair on his head.

Sita's lips trembled. "I'm scared."

Sultana, the third in the inseparable trio of friends, ran her hand over the younger girl's hair. "*Shh, shh.* It won't be the end of the world. At least he's wealthy. Better to marry into palaces than into the gutter."

"How can you say that?" Sita was squeaking in desperation, and Miriam felt her own throat tighten. "He's old enough to be my grandfather!"

"He's younger than my sister's husband," Miriam said. "Sara's husband was sixty-two when he snatched her from the cradle. I understand that Hatam bin Hazat is no older than fifty-five."

"And I'm *fifteen!*" Sita said.

"And Sara was fifteen too," Miriam said. She'd always considered the tradition of old men snapping up young girls cruel, but in the face of Sita's unavoidable predicament, Miriam desperately wanted to offer hope.

"What about Haya?" Miriam continued.

That got silence from both of them. Her father, Salman bin Fahd, had taken Haya as a bride two years earlier when Miriam's mother died. Fine enough, except that his new bride was only thirteen at the time. As was customary, the thirteen-year-old girl took over the duties of the wife in their household, even though she was younger than those under her charge. Miriam had been nineteen.

At first the notion had infuriated Miriam. But one look at Haya's trembling lips after the wedding changed her heart. The girl was terrified, a condition that only grew worse when Father ignored his other three wives for a full month in favor of his new young bride. Haya played the submissive wife and survived the ordeal.

But Sita was not Haya.

Miriam looked at Sita's frightened face. Her friend was still a child. Seeing her round eyes, Miriam wanted to cry. But she could never cry, especially not now, just minutes before the ceremony.

Sultana looked out the window, fire in her eyes. Of the three, she was perhaps the boldest. She was twenty-three and barren. But she was married to a good man who treated her well and turned a blind eye to her outspoken resentment of their society's ills. Both Sita and Miriam found her and her candor welcome companions. The three had formed a tight bond of friendship, and if the group had a leader, it was Sultana. She'd been to Europe with her husband many times, and although her black veil imprisoned her, too, she was never physically mistreated or forced beyond her will like so many women.

"Haya was two years younger than you," Miriam said.

"*I'm* not Haya!" Sita returned.

"This is ridiculous and you know it, Miriam," Sultana said softly, casting a glare.

Miriam sat next to Sita and stared at Sultana. "Of course I know it. But it's also unavoidable. What do you suggest, that she just walk out of here and make a run for it?"

"I saw him," Sita said softly.

Miriam glanced up, shocked. Sultana's mouth fell open. It was highly unusual for a man or a woman to have seen the one they were to marry before the actual wedding.

"You *saw* the groom?" Sultana asked. "You saw *Hatam?*"

Sita nodded, her face wrinkled in distress.

"How?" Miriam asked. "What is he like?"

"Two weeks ago, at the *Souq* Market." She looked up and her eyes flashed. "He's a pig!" She turned to the side, crying. "An elephant! He'll kill me."

Miriam knew she should say something, but words escaped her. She'd never seen Hatam, but her younger brother, Faisal, once joked about him being a large man. Evidently, Hatam was powerful in Jiddah but few knew him in Riyadh. The marriage was tied to a business deal between Hatam and Sita's father, himself a wealthy developer.

Sultana stood and stormed across the room. At any other time she would be spitting contempt for a woman's place in Saudi society about now, telling them they should slit Hatam's throat or something absurd. But today the die had been cast. Sita would marry this pig who had paid his dowry and waited to collect his new pet. There was nothing any of them could do about it.

Sita sniffed and wiped her nose with a frail, shaky hand. She spoke quietly. "I make a vow," she said. "I make a vow today to refuse my husband. He will not touch me while I am alive."

Miriam reached out a hand. "Please, Sita . . ."

Sita rose to her feet, suddenly red in the face. "*You* do not have to marry him, Miriam. I *do*. I'm not ready to marry!" She trembled, nothing more or less than a desperate child. Miriam felt her stomach turn.

"I swear he will *never* touch me, not if I have to claw his eyes out!" Sita said.

Miriam stood. "He will only hurt you!"

"No!" Sultana said, walking back. "She's right, Miriam. This marriage is a sick perversion of the prophet's intention. If no one ever fights back, our children will face the same."

"But this isn't the time to complain," Miriam said. "This is Sita's wedding! Who will pay the price for her intolerance? *She* will!"

"And who will pay the price when the big fat pig goes after her?"

They stared at each other, silent.

"I swear it," Sita said, and Miriam did not doubt her. She might be only fifteen, but she was a fighter to the bone.

Miriam made another plea. "Maybe he's a loving man."

"That's easy for you to say," Sita snapped. "You're almost twenty-one and you're still not married. And you have this secret love with Samir. I *hate* you for it!" She turned away and crossed her arms, and a fresh tear slipped down her cheek.

"You don't hate me, Sita. You better not hate me, because you're like a little sister to me and I love you dearly."

Twenty and not married. Rumor had it that dozens of suitors had approached Father for her hand and he'd turned them all away. It was a sore subject that Miriam had warded off a hundred times with various excuses. In fact, she herself had not known the truth until Samir had confided in her just two years ago. It was the only secret she kept from her two friends. Soon enough they would know the truth.

"What is worse, to suffer punishment because you refuse your husband," Sultana asked, "or to suffer at his hand? You wouldn't know, Miriam. Salman protects you."

Heat flashed up Miriam's spine. "My father protects me? Believe me, there's no love lost between Salman and me. He doesn't know *how* to love a woman."

"Maybe, but he's still protecting you from an early marriage," Sita shot back. "So how do you know how it feels to be given away like a rag doll to an ugly old pig?"

"Both Haya and Sara were married—"

"Sure, your mother and sister were married early, but not *you!*"

The door suddenly flew open and they turned as one. "Sita!" Her mother stood in the doorway, white as a sheet. "Where have you been? They are ready!"

Then she saw Sita's tears and she hurried in, her face softening. "Please, don't cry, child. I know you are frightened, but we all grow up, don't we?" She smoothed Sita's hair and looked at her lovingly.

"I'm afraid, Mother," Sita said.

"Of course. It's a big step, but you must think beyond the uncertainty that you feel and consider the wonderful position that awaits you as the wife of a powerful man." She kissed her daughter's forehead.

"He's a wealthy man, Sita. He will give you a good life, and you'll bear him many children. What else could a woman ask? Hmm?"

"I don't want to bear his children."

"Don't be silly, Sita! It will be a great honor to bear his children. You'll see." She paused and studied her daughter tenderly. "God knows how much I love you, Sita. I am so proud of you. It seems that just yesterday you were still a child, playing with your dolls. Now look at you, how you've grown into a beautiful young woman." She kissed her again. "Now, come along. The drummers are waiting."

She slipped Sita's black veil over her face. Just like that Sita was a faceless one again, emotions covered, bundled in her black body bag, although today the body bag had been fancied up in pink for its new owner, Hatam bin Hazat, the old, fat pig.

Miriam joined a thousand other women in the great hall and watched with growing dread as the drums announced the groom's arrival. As in all Saudi weddings, the only men present were the bride's father, the groom's father (who in this case was dead of old age), the groom himself, and the religious man who would execute the marriage.

Hatam walked out alone, and Miriam nearly gasped aloud. Blubber sat like a bloated inner tube around his stomach, sloshing with each step despite his attempt to hide it under a tent of a tunic. The fat under his chin hung like a reservoir of water. To say the man was large would be a horrible miscalculation. He was an obese ape.

Beside Miriam, Sultana groaned softly. Several women glanced at her, but she ignored them. Sultana was right. This was a gross injustice, and they should rush the man and claw his eyes out before he had a chance to lay eyes on dear young Sita.

The drums beat again and Sita's mother and her aunt led her out. The black veil hid her face, but Miriam imagined she was already spitting at the obscene sight before her. A sweat broke out on Miriam's brow, and she began to mutter prayers under her breath.

Hatam grinned at his new child bride, and when he lifted the veil, a sickening glint filled his eyes. Sita stood staring at him blankly, and in her cloaked defiance, she looked more beautiful than Miriam could remember.

The ceremony lasted only a few minutes. The actual marriage had been performed hours earlier, first with the bride and then with the groom, separately, signing documents that affirmed the agreed upon dowry and terms of marriage.

Now the religious man looked at Sita's father and spoke the token words that confirmed Sita's marriage to Hatam. After a nod, he glanced over at the groom, who replied that he accepted Sita as his bride. A thousand women broke the silence, shrieking and ululating with their tongues. It was a sound meant to express joy, but today it sent chills down Miriam's arms. Hatam walked past his new bride, tossing coins to the women. Sita hesitated, then followed.

He led Sita from the room, and Miriam saw that her friend walked unsteadily, like a lamb still searching for its legs, now being led to the slaughter by this monster.

The women began to move outside where more food and celebration awaited them. Music wavered across the room again. They would celebrate for another two days after the groom departed with his new bride. Celebrate what? Sita's death? Still, it was the way it was. Like Mother used to say, the sooner they got used to it, the easier life would become.

Miriam felt like she might throw up.

2

IT WAS THREE O'CLOCK in the afternoon and, to be perfectly honest, Seth Border, although arguably the most popular man on campus, was lonely. Popular because he possessed both the sharpest mind the university had seen since its inception and the kind of all-Californian face the media loved. Lonely because he felt oddly disconnected with that popularity. Like a fish out of water.

If there was one thing he'd learned at Berkeley, it was that when the academic institution put you on a pedestal, it expected you to perform as advertised. If they wanted you to have green skin, you'd better paint your skin green, because if you came out on stage with blue skin, they'd resent you for it.

Seth stared out the small windows that ran along the top of the lecture hall, thinking he was a blue person in a green person's world. Blue, like the sky outside—another cloudless California day. He ran a hand through his shaggy blond mop and released a barely audible sigh. He glanced at the complex equation on the whiteboard behind the professor, solved it before he'd finished reading it, and let his mind drift again.

He was twenty-six and his whole life had felt like a long string of abandonments. Sitting here listening to graduate lectures on quantum physics by Professor Gregory Baaron with forty other students only seemed to reinforce the feeling. He should be doing something to snap himself out of this valley. Something like surfing.

Surfing had always been his one escape from a world gone mad, but the last time he'd seen the really good side of a wave was three years ago, back at Point Loma in San Diego, during a freak storm that had deposited fifteen-foot swells along the coast from Malibu to Tijuana.

There was nothing quite like catching the right wave and riding in its belly until it decided to dump you off.

Seth first experienced the freedom of surfing when he was six, when his mom bought him a board and took him to the beach—her way of helping them both escape his father's abuse.

Paul loved three things in life and, as far as Seth saw, three things only: Pabst Blue Ribbon. Baseball. Himself. In no particular order. The fact that he'd married a woman named Jane and had a kid they'd named Seth barely mattered to him.

His mom, on the other hand, did love her son. They had, in fact, saved each other's lives on more than one occasion, most memorably the times when his dad had confused their bodies for baseballs.

It had been during the worst of those times when Seth asked his mom if she would take him to the library. She'd taken him the very next day in the Rust Bucket, as she called their Vega. From age six on, Seth's life comprised a strange brew of surfing, reading, and being kicked around the house by his dad.

"You're special, Seth," his mom used to say. "Don't let anyone ever tell you any different, you hear? You ignore what your father says."

Her words filled him with more warmth than the sun. "I love you, Mom."

She would always swallow, pull him close, and wipe at the tears in her eyes when he said that.

As it turned out, Seth *was* more than special. He was a genius.

In any other setting his unique gift would have been discovered and nurtured from the time he was two or three. Unfortunately or fortunately, depending on your point of view, no one really understood what an exceptional young boy Seth was until he was older. Jane was a hairdresser, not a schoolteacher. Although she made sure all the other beauticians knew about her boy's quick wit, she wasn't equipped to recognize genius. And because Jane would just as often take him to the beach or the library as to the school, his reputation as a student languished.

He was nine before anyone in the academic world even noticed Seth's brilliance. A surfer named Mark Nobel who attended the

Nazarene college on Point Loma had watched him surf and insisted Seth give his surfboard a spin. By the time Seth washed back to shore, the student had left for class. Seth wandered onto the campus looking for Mark. Half an hour later he found him in the math department, wading though a calculus equation with twenty other students and a professor who seemed to be having difficulty showing them just how simple this particular equation really was.

Seeing Seth at the door, the professor had jokingly suggested that he come forward and show this band of half-wits how simple math could be. None of them expected him to actually do it, of course. But he had.

Then he'd solved another more complex equation that the professor quickly scribbled on the board. And another. He'd left the students sitting in stunned silence twenty minutes later, not quite sure how he knew what he knew. The equations had just come together in his mind like simple puzzles.

The teachers at his grade school learned of his little adventure the next day, and their attitude toward him brightened considerably. He agreed to some tests. They said that less than 1 percent of humans had an IQ greater than 135 and that Einstein's was estimated at 163. Seth's IQ was 193. They told him he had the intelligence of an average college graduate then, when he was nine, and he couldn't dare waste such an exceptional mind.

But Seth still had to find a way to cope with reality at home, which meant losing himself in the books at the library and riding the waves off the point. School simply wasn't meant to be a meaningful part of his world.

Life improved immeasurably when his dad left for good after discovering just how effectively a thirteen-year-old boy could fight back. But by then Seth had lost his taste for formal education altogether. It wasn't until he was twenty that he began to think about responding to the pressures around him who insisted he pursue a real education.

He'd selected Berkeley in part for its location—not in his backyard, where he was the strange guy who could count by primes in his sleep, but not two thousand miles away either. He thought he'd be a fish out of water at Harvard or Yale or any of the other half-dozen universities that had begged him to attend. Berkeley seemed like a good compromise.

As it turned out, it didn't matter; he was a fish out of water up here among the airheads anyway. It had taken him exactly two days on Berkeley's campus to understand that. If he was a fish, Berkeley felt like a desert.

The alienation had nothing to do with Seth not finishing high school—one day of tests settled that issue. Nor with his difficulty in understanding their preoccupation with scholastic elitism. They were not too intelligent or too advanced or too politically correct for him. In fact, he'd simply found the last three years of academia unchallenging. As much as Seth hated to admit it, he was bored. Bored with academia, bored with his own mind.

The only real challenge to his own boredom came from an unlikely source. A recruiter from the NSA named Clive Masters.

Berkeley's dean of students had set up the recruiters exclusively for Seth during his freshman year. They came from IBM, NASA, Lawrence Livermore National Laboratories, a bunch of Japanese companies. Even Sony Pictures sent a rep to meet with Seth; evidently movie magic took brains. But Clive was the only recruiter who really struck a chord with him.

"You have a gift, Seth," he'd said. "I've been watching you for ten years because it's in my job description to watch people like you. You may never work for the NSA, but I can at least insist that you finish what you've started here. Anything less might actually be a crime. And I've given my life to fighting crime, Seth. First with the FBI and now with the NSA."

"FBI, huh? Were you *born* wrapped in a flag?"

"No. I was born to be challenged," Clive said.

"Locking heads with fugitives," Seth said. "With the dregs of society. Sounds like a ball."

"There are two kinds of bad guys. The stupid ones, which make up about 99 percent of the lot, and the brilliant ones—few and far between but capable of the damage done by a thousand dumb ones. I've gone up against some of the sharpest." He paused. "But there's more to the thrill than raw intelligence."

"And what would that be?"

"Danger."

Seth nodded. "Danger."

"There's no substitute for the thrill of danger. But I think you've already figured that out, haven't you?"

"And the NSA provides that for you now?"

"I split my time between being called in on the impossible cases and finding that rare breed who can do the same. We have something in common, you and I."

"Which is why you're interested in convincing an innocent impressionable that pursuing the life of James Bond is far more attractive than sitting in a basement cell of some laboratory, breaking complex codes," Seth responded.

"I hadn't thought of it in those exact terms, but your summary does have a ring to it, doesn't it? On the other hand, solving mathematical challenges has its place. The NSA's Mathematical Sciences Program is the world's single largest employer of mathematicians. Cryptology isn't easy work. The halls down in Fort Meade are lined with some of the world's brightest."

Actually the thought of becoming this man who faced him with such a casual confidence struck Seth as refreshing. The other recruiters had virtually drooled over what he might bring their respective organizations. Clive, on the other hand, seemed to be more interested in Seth's psyche than in what he could do for the NSA.

"All I'm suggesting is that you finish here—get your doctorate in high energy physics and wow the world with some new discovery. But when you get bored—and the best always do—you think about me. I can bring spice to your life, that much I guarantee."

Clive smiled enigmatically, and Seth couldn't help thinking the man might be onto something.

"Do you surf, Clive?"

The man had chuckled. "Seth the surfer. No, I don't surf, but I think I understand why people do. I think it's for the same reasons I do what I do."

Clive reappeared every six months or so, just long enough to gift Seth with a few tasty morsels before disappearing into his world of secrecy. Seth never seriously thought he would ever follow the path Clive had taken, but he felt a connection to this man who, despite being no intellectual slouch, found no incongruity in using his brilliance to find a thrill. It was enough to help Seth slog through the months of academia.

Seth had received his bachelor's in his second year. He'd skipped the master's program and was now in the second year of his doctorate program. But three years of this stuff was wearing thin, and he was no longer sure he could stomach all the nonsense required to finish after all.

If the graduate dean, the very fellow lecturing at this very moment, Gregory Baaron, would allow him to write his dissertation and be done with it, that would be one thing. But Baaron had—

"Perhaps you'd like to tell us, Mr. Border." Seth blinked and returned his mind to the lecture hall. Baaron was staring over bifocals. "How do you calculate the quantum field between two charged particles?"

Seth cleared his throat. Baaron was one of the leading lights in the field of particle physics and had taught this basic material a hundred times. Much of his work was based on the equation now written on the board behind him. Unfortunately, the equation was wrong. At least by Seth's thinking. But because of Baaron's stake in the matter, the dean would hardly consider, much less accept, the possibility that it was wrong. Even worse, Baaron seemed to have developed a healthy dose of professional jealousy toward Seth.

"Well, that would depend on whether you're doing it by the textbook," Seth said. *Watch yourself, boy. Tread easy.*

"The textbook will suffice," Baaron said after a moment, and Seth felt a pang of sympathy for the man.

He paraphrased from Baaron's own textbook. "Solve the Lagrangian field equation. That is, apply the principle of least action by defining a quantity called the Lagrangian action, the integral of which is minimized along the actual observed path. The easiest way to set the equation up is to use Feynman diagrams and to insert terms in the action for each of the first-order interactions." Seth paused. "You studied with Feynman, didn't you? I read his Nobel-winning papers when I was fifteen. Some interesting thoughts." He paused, thinking he should stop there. But suddenly he couldn't. Or didn't.

"Of course, the whole method is problematic on both conceptual and explanatory levels. The conceptual problem is that the equations seem to say that the reality we observe is just the 'sum' of all possible realities. On an explanatory level, you have to bake in the renormalization factors to make the numbers come out right. That's hardly the sign of a really good predictive theory. Putting both problems together, I'm inclined to think the theory's misguided."

The professor's face twitched. "Really? Misguided? You do realize that the calculations of this method accord well with reality, at least in the world most of us live in."

"The *calculations* may work, but the implication bothers me. Are we really to believe that of all imaginable futures, the real one—the one we actually experience—is simply the weighted sum of all the others? Is the future merely the product of a simple mathematical formula? I don't think so. Someday this theory might look as outdated as a flat-earth theory." *That was too much, Seth.* He felt his pulse quicken.

Baaron stared at him for what must have been a full five seconds.

"The principle of least action is widely accepted as a basis for calculation," he finally said. "And unless you think you've outwitted a few hundred of the most brilliant mathematical minds in the country, I don't think you've got a leg to stand on, Seth."

The condescension in Baaron's voice at that last word—*Seth*—as if he were his father commanding him to go stand in the corner for questioning his recollection of baseball history, pushed Seth over a foggy cliff. He'd been here before, jumping off the same cliff, and never fail, the experience proved not only unsatisfying, but painful.

The knowledge of this fact didn't stop him.

There were over two hundred stadium seats in the hall, sloping from the podium up to a sound booth, and although only forty were filled, the occupant of every one turned their eyes Seth's way. He slipped his hands into his pockets and palmed the superball at the bottom of his right pocket.

"To have doubted one's first principles is the mark of a civilized man," Seth said.

"So now I'm not only outdated, but I'm uncivilized?" Baaron walked to the podium wearing a smirk. "This from a man who hardly knows the difference between a dinner jacket and a tank top. From where I'm standing, your reasoning looks pretty ugly, Mr. Border."

"Nothing has an uglier look to us than reason, when it's not on our side," Seth said. "Big ideas are so hard to recognize, so fragile, so easy to kill. Don't forget that, all of you who don't have them."

Baaron turned his head. There might have been a barely audible gasp in the auditorium, Seth wasn't sure. Maybe the air conditioning had just come on. *You're digging yourself a grave, Seth.*

"Watch your tongue, young man. Just because you have a natural talent does not mean you've conquered ignorance."

On the other hand, he was already in a hole. "Ignorance. To be ignorant of one's ignorance is the disease of the ignorant. And we all know that nothing is more terrible than ignorance in action—"

"You're stepping over the line, Mr. Border. You have a responsibility that comes with your mind. I suggest you keep your wits about you."

"Wit? He who doesn't lose his wits over certain things has no wits to lose."

Someone coughed to cover a chuckle. The professor paused.

"This is quantum field theory, not psychology. You think you're cute, drudging up your wit? Why don't you engage me on the point, boy?"

"I've learned never to engage in a battle of wits with an unarmed person. Sir."

Baaron's face went red. He'd lost his cool with Seth once, when Seth had come to class barefoot, dressed in surf shorts, and toting a surfboard. He'd hollowed out the board and cemented his laptop into it so that the whole contraption became his computer. The exchange had gotten ugly when Seth had expounded on the superiority of surfing over education before a howling class.

Nobody was howling now.

"I am not someone to toy with!" Baaron said, jowls trembling. "You're in no position to mock me. We have standards at this institution."

Baaron was right and Seth knew it as well as he knew this could not end well.

"Please, sir, don't mistake my simple review of literature as disregard for your authority. I'm merely saying what our most brilliant scholars have said better before me."

"This has nothing to do with literature!"

"But it does. Rather than tackle your noteworthy intellect with my own, I'm afraid I've stolen from others. In fact, not a word I've spoken has been my own." He paused and Baaron just blinked.

"The first quote was from Oliver Holmes. Then George Savile from the seventeenth century. Then Bronson Alcott and Gotthold Lessing and finally Johann Wolfgang von Goethe." Maybe that would bail him out. "Perhaps you should file a complaint against the lot of them. They are far too imaginative to associate with the tiny minds of this institution anyway."

Seth blinked and took a slow breath. Then again, maybe not.

Graduate Dean Gregory Baaron suddenly turned and walked out the side door without another word, leaving the lecture hall to a stunned silence. Seth glanced at the clock on the wall—five minutes to the hour. For a moment nobody moved.

He regretted his words already. Why did he do this? Why hadn't he just answered Baaron's question and left it at that?

A book slammed closed. One of the students vacated the back row and slipped out the rear entrance. The rest just sat there. Matt Doil, a forty-five-year-old engineer from Caltech, twisted in his chair near the front. He flashed a grin and shook his head.

"You're not serious about the least action principle being outdated, are you?"

The others were looking at him again. He cleared his throat. "Shut up and calculate, wasn't that what Feynman told students who wanted to know what his method really meant?"

They all knew it was.

"Show us," Doil said.

"Show you what?"

"An alternative."

Seth considered that. Why not? He'd done as much damage as he could possibly manage already. He might as well redeem himself in some small way.

"Okay."

He stood, walked to the stage, and picked up a whiteboard marker. It took him thirty seconds to complete a complex calculation he knew they would all understand. He finished the last stroke, stabbed the board with the marker, and turned around. To a student they were glued to him.

"What does this equation behind me tell me about the forces at work on this marker?" He held out the white stick between his thumb and forefinger, as if to drop it.

"That when you drop it, it'll bounce," someone said.

"Or that when you drop it, it'll roll," Matt said.

"But that's meaningless, isn't it?" Seth said. "What if I decide not to drop the marker at all? The numbers on the wall behind me tell us that the future is calculable as the sum of all possible futures. But I don't think it is. I think the future's beyond our calculation. And I think the future's singular. That there's only one possible future, namely the future that *will* happen, because it's known by a designer."

They looked at him with blank stares. Trying to communicate some of the ideas that popped in his head was often more complicated than the ideas themselves. Language had its limits.

"What if I did this?"

He turned, changed several numbers on the board, erased the solution, and extended the equation by eight characters with a new solution. He dropped the marker in the tray and stepped back. It was the first time even he had seen the new equation actually written down.

He cleared his throat. "Makes the world much simpler, but also much more interesting, don't you think?"

"Does that work?" It was Matt.

"I think so," Seth said. "Doesn't that work?" Of course it did. He turned to the class. They were wide-eyed. Some were writing furiously. Some still didn't get it.

Matt rose, eyes fixed on the board. "You're . . . that *does* work! That's impossible."

Seth suddenly felt awkward. He'd just rewritten a small part of history, and for some reason he felt naked. Abandoned. Like he had no business being here on the stage for everyone to look at. He belonged in a basement somewhere. Back home in San Diego.

He turned and walked off the stage, through the same door Dean Baaron had used.

3

MIRIAM FACED WEST toward Mecca and dropped to her knees in her room while the muezzin's noon prayer call from the minaret down the street still wavered. It was said that Mohammed disliked the church bells of his day, so he insisted on a vocal call to prayer. Miriam thought he was right—a bell was far too harsh.

She had gone into the mosque only once, with Sita and Sultana in a dare of rebellion. Even though Mohammed had not prohibited women from entering the mosque, he strongly encouraged them to pray in their rooms at home. Saudi Arabia had gone one step further and prohibited a woman's presence in a mosque except on certain occasions, and then only in Medina and Mecca.

She recited the first sura of the Qur'an without thinking about the words. Although she was a woman, she had taken a keen interest in the holy book, at one point thinking to become a hafiz, the coveted title of one who'd memorized all 114 suras of the Qur'an. Of course, that would have been impossible: She was a woman. But the poetic nature of the Qur'an was like music to her mind and she found it pleasing. The word *Islam* meant "surrender"; the word *Qur'an* meant "recitation." Miriam preferred the latter. Her faith was not compelled by understanding the words of Mohammed, but by repeating them. They said that a good memory, not superior judgment or analytical thinking, was the virtue of a good Muslim theologian. So then, if she could recite as well as a man, couldn't she be a great theologian?

Miriam stood and rearranged the pillows on her bed. Her room was decorated in purple because Salman had decided many years ago that it should be, despite Miriam's insistence that she despised purple.

Her declaration that he best leave decorating to women with good taste earned her a slap. She'd thought of him as her father then and felt true regret at the statement.

Now she knew better. Her real father, Sheik Abu Ali al-Asamm, would never force his will over something so insignificant. The sheik, the infamous Shi'i warrior of the eastern province, was a revolutionary who attended matters far more important than bossing around a houseful of women.

Her true father's image filled her mind. Samir had told her the truth two years ago. Twenty years earlier, the sheik surreptitiously pledged his loyalty to King Fahd in exchange for the king's adoption of Miriam into the royal bloodline. Such a trade wasn't unheard of when it came to keeping the peace in the desert. When Miriam finally married and had a son, her blood father, the sheik, would have an irrevocable claim to royal blood. The sheik had placed Samir in Prince Salman's villa as a chauffeur to secretly watch over her as part of the agreement, unbeknownst to Salman.

The revelation was as thrilling as it was scandalous. Imagine it: Miriam, the daughter of the state's most feared enemy! She had often thought she could actually feel her true father's blood flowing through her veins, urging her to fight for freedom.

She headed for the main living room, where Haya was preparing the servants for Salman's breakfast. Like most men with multiple wives, Salman rotated villas every day, so that he was with each woman only every fourth day. It was the one true blessing of many wives. Miriam was certain that neither she nor Haya could survive if Salman were to come every day.

Haya slid across the room toward Miriam, frowning. She wore a brilliant blue dress and strings of pearls that stood out nicely against her creamy neck. A shame that no one beyond these doors would ever see her so beautiful. The image of Haya stood in complete contrast to the abaayas hanging like black specters on the rack behind her. Once, in Spain, Miriam had watched the movie *Star Wars*, the only Western movie she'd ever seen. When the villain, Darth Vader, appeared on screen that first time, cloaked in black, she'd gasped aloud. Saudi women looked like villains in Western movies! If she'd hated the abaaya before then, the sentiment had turned to loathing in the theater that day.

Haya had applied a touch of makeup, something she did only when Salman came. The terror that had blackened her eyes every time he'd visited when they'd first married was gone. Now she was fifteen, a growing woman in all respects, and the horror had been replaced by a resentment that spilled over to affect them all.

"He'll be down in a few minutes," Haya said. "I don't want you around."

"Don't worry. I wouldn't subject myself to the agony of it."

Haya looked at her with a blank stare. The phone rang.

Miriam crossed to the door, eager to find Samir on the grounds or in the garage. She slipped into her black abaaya, pulled on her veil, and stepped outside. The garage stood detached, twenty meters from the entrance.

Like all males outside the family, Samir was prohibited from seeing her face, and indeed he hadn't . . . except on three occasions. The first of those times skipped through Miriam's mind as she walked for the garage.

It had been three years ago, in the late afternoon, just after she turned seventeen. She'd been in the back lawn walking with her sister, Sara, when Samir ran out to tell them that their mother was waiting for them in the car. Just then a goose leapt from the pond and rushed at Miriam for no apparent reason. The white bird's honks had been loud and startling. Panicked, she'd spun to flee.

Unfortunately, in spinning she tripped on her sister's foot. Samir rushed forward to chase the goose away, which he did easily enough. But in her fall, Miriam's veil flew off. She was on her feet and staring at a stunned Samir before she realized her face was bare. For what felt like an eternity, neither moved. Samir gazed at her face as if he'd arrived in heaven and was seeing his first angel. Something deep in Miriam's soul changed with that look. In his eyes, she was a person. Not because of her beauty, but because in that moment she had become more than a black sack among a million other black sacks.

Samir had fallen madly in love. Seeing the look in his eyes, she could not resist loving him in return. So had begun a forbidden romance that took them, on two separate occasions, to Spain, where they slipped away from the family and spent hours staring into each other's eyes and talking about love. On the second occasion he had told her about her true father and the adoption. He had also vowed to love her forever and marry her, no matter the consequence.

"Miriam."

His voice jerked her from her memories. "Samir . . ."

He stood in the shadows of the garage, and her heart swelled at the sight of him. He wore the traditional white cotton *thobe,* but in her mind she pictured the strength of his arms and chest under the garment. His dark hair swept over milky brown eyes. Miriam glanced back at the villa and walked into the shadows, her heart pounding as much from the impropriety of it as from her love for him.

"No one saw you?" he asked.

"No. And how is my love?"

"Please, keep your voice—"

"Don't be a mouse. No one can hear." She was surprisingly bold, wasn't she? Perhaps Sita's wedding had emboldened her.

He grinned. "If you think I'm a mouse, then you don't know what a lion is."

"A lion? I will turn you into a lamb. I miss you terribly, Samir. When can we go away again?"

She still wore her veil, and in a way it gave her courage to know that not even he could guess her expression.

"I'm setting it up," he said. "Next month. To Spain again. Maybe this time we will stay."

"Stay? Don't tempt me if you can't deliver."

"Nothing can keep this impossible love I have from stealing you away forever."

She desperately wanted to lift her veil for him. To see his eyes widen at seeing her mouth and eyes. The thought made her hands tremble.

"I am crazy for you," he said.

"Crazy? Where did you hear such a silly saying?" She rather liked it.

"An American movie. Do you like it?"

"It is very expressive, isn't it? Crazy. And I am crazy for you, my lion."

Samir grinned like a child. After a moment he looked away. "You've been called by your father."

She blinked under the black covering. "My father?"

"Yes. The sheik must see you. Today."

Miriam's head swam. She'd seen the sheik on three occasions. Each time Samir had taken her beyond the city under the pretense of shopping, and instead she met with Al-Asamm in a Bedouin tent. They had been wonderful, dizzying experiences, and the thought of going now sent a butterfly through her belly.

"Today?"

"This afternoon. Can you?"

"Yes. How—"

"Tell them you will go shopping, and I will take you again. After noon."

"I was supposed to meet Sultana at ten in the Souq."

"Then I will tell her that you'll be there later. The timing's perfect."

She hesitated. "What does he want?"

"You're his daughter; I imagine he wants to see you."

The rear door to the house suddenly flew open. Salman stormed out, stopped, and eyed them for a moment.

"Get in my car, Miriam. We have to go."

Haya hurried out behind him, her black abaaya flowing.

Miriam glanced back at Salman. "Go? I didn't—"

"Don't question me!" he snapped. "Get in the car. Samir, you will stay." Something was wrong. Salman used an angry voice frequently, but there was something else in his voice now. An edge that made Miriam's belly feel light.

"In the car!" he said.

"It's okay," Samir said under his breath. "Go."

Miriam broke from her stance and hurried for the large black Mercedes parked in the space reserved only for Salman's cars. She opened the rear left door and slid in next to Haya, who refused to return her questioning look.

"What's happening?"

Salman slammed his door. "Silence."

They left the villa and wound down streets in absolute silence. They both knew that defying a direct order would bring a price. Miriam could only sit and wait quietly. She pursed her lips and closed her eyes behind the veil. One day, if she were given the opportunity, she would slap Salman for being a monster.

They passed a large white mosque, and she watched the men walking through its gates. No women, of course. Islam was supported by five pillars; simple and beautiful and, unlike the *shari'a* laws, they did nothing to shackle the women. Five pillars: The *Creed:* "There is no God but Allah and Mohammed is the messenger of Allah." *Daily prayers,* upon rising, at noon, in midafternoon, after sunset, and before retiring. The annual forty-day *Ramadan* fast. The *Hajj pilgrimage* to Mecca. *Almsgiving* to the poor.

And a sixth to some, the *Jihad,* as the situation warranted, to "spread Islam or defend against infidels." This last pillar would be denied by most Muslims, but clearly, it propped up Saudi Arabia as much as the rest. The House of Saud had been birthed in the Wahhabi sect, a puritanical strain of Islam firmly rooted in the Qur'an rather than the post-Qur'anic ijma' and qiyas. Like Mohammed himself, the Wahhabis had made good use of the sword. As had the generals who'd led the Jews into their promised land. Joshua. In some ways, Islam wasn't so different from Judaism.

Only when they were almost there did Miriam know their destination. Salman pulled into the driveway of an expansive villa, covered in bougainvillea. They were at Sita's house.

A dread seeped into her bones. Sita was away on her honeymoon, in the custody of her new husband. Why were they here?

Salman opened his door. "Get out! Remember what you see today. It will teach you obedience." He walked for the courtyard, robe swirling at his feet.

The morning was deathly quiet. Miriam followed Salman and Haya through an archway that opened to the green grounds she and Sita had played on so many days as children. An old swing set built of oak sat unused beneath several tall trees to their right. Palms swayed gently in a light morning breeze. Still no sound. If any from the family were here, there was no sign of it.

Salman led them around the side of the house, which was odd—they would always wait to be greeted at the front door. They walked around the corner, toward the pool.

Miriam saw them then. Six people standing on the pool's apron. Sita's family. Her mother, her father, her two younger siblings, five and eight. And Sita.

Sita was veiled in black, standing with her arms at her side. What could this possibly . . .

Miriam stopped, frozen to the concrete. The person standing next to Sita's father was no relation to Sita; she saw that now. A tall thin man dressed in white. The religious police of Saudi Arabia, the *mutawa.*

Images of public beatings and humiliations flashed through Miriam's mind. The shari'a was a hard law to follow, but the mutawa were exceptionally gifted in enforcing it. In that instant, fixed with dread, Miriam knew her friend had kept her vow. She had refused her husband and would now pay a price.

Oh, dear Sita! For a fleeting moment Miriam thought about running to her friend, taking her hand, and fleeing for the fence with her. But Sita's father, Musa, was a good man, despite his decision to marry his daughter off to Hatam. The punishment would be his decision, not the mutawa's alone. Surely it would be reasonable.

Miriam forced her feet forward. The gathered family watched them in silence. Although Miriam could not see through the veils to the eyes of Sita or her mother, she could feel their gaze, like razors on her skin. They came to the edge of the pool, across the span of water from Sita and her family, and stopped.

For a moment no one spoke. Miriam looked at Sita's father. His face was drawn with deep lines, hardened like stone. It wasn't yet hot, but sweat glistened on his brow. The mutawa shifted on his feet, and his sandals scraped the concrete.

"These are all the witnesses?" he asked quietly. His face was bony and dark and Miriam desperately wanted to scream at him. *Leave us, you man of terror!* But she stood still with the rest.

Sita's father dipped his head barely.

A soft whimper floated across the pool. Sita or her mother, Miriam could not tell. She ached to say something. To beg for lenience on behalf of her friend. *It will be all right. If they beat her, her wounds will heal. If they cut off her hand for refusing to touch her husband, she will still live free of that pig.* Surely the man had divorced her already. He would never live with this stain on his name.

And neither would Sita's father.

"There is no God but Allah," the mutawa said, "and Mohammed is the prophet of Allah. No man shall escape his wrath. It is for our love of Allah and his prophet and all that is written that we have gathered, lest we become a people who defile God."

Sita stood motionless, unlike the fiery child Miriam knew. Nausea spread through her stomach. The mutawa were known to drug a victim on occasion, to prevent a struggle, but usually only at stonings and the more severe punishments. If they were going to beat her . . . "Let it be known on this day that this woman has defied her husband's rights and injured him bodily. For a woman to do this is no different than murder. She has made a mockery of God and of Islam and must be punished in accordance with the law of God. So be it."

A tremble had come to the father's upper lip. Still no one moved. Miriam had seen a beating once, a horrid occasion. But it was filled with anger and yelling, not this silence.

The whimper came again—Sita's mother—and this time it lingered and then grew to a soft quivering wail. The children pressed into her cloak and began to whimper.

The mutawa lifted his chin and muttered something Miriam couldn't understand. He closed his eyes. "You have heard from God. Do what you must do."

Eyes still fixed directly ahead, Musa took his daughter's arm. A guttural wail shredded the air. Sita's mother suddenly grabbed her daughter's other arm.

"No!" she moaned. "You can't do this! She is my daughter!" A chill of terror ripped through Miriam's chest. The youngest child began to scream.

Sita's mother pulled at her daughter desperately. Sita looked like a rag doll about to be pulled apart. Her head lolled on her shoulders.

"Take me, I beg . . ."

The mutawa's hand cracked against her face, stilling the cry and sending her reeling backward. Miriam cried out involuntarily. She took a step to the side, but Salman's hand gripped her elbow and squeezed it like a vise.

"Sita!" Miriam cried.

"Shut up!" Salman jerked her arm hard enough to pull it from her socket. She felt pain spread down to her elbow.

Sita turned her head toward Miriam.

Oh, dear Sita! What are they doing to you!

Sita's father was trembling from head to foot now. The mutawa gave him a nudge toward the steps. Musa blinked and then stiffly led his daughter to the steps and into the water. Sita followed like a lamb. The clear blue water soaked Sita's abaaya jet black. She stood next to her father, veiled, waiting in submission for her baptism.

It occurred to Miriam that she had stopped breathing. An unearthly silence settled, punctuated only by the pounding of blood through her ears. Long fingers of horror immobilized her, smothered her. What happened next unfolded without fanfare, like a dream, distant and disconnected from reason.

Musa took the docile child by the head and shoved her under the water.

Miriam jerked and Salman's grip tightened. *Stop it! You can't do this to my friend!* Miriam was screaming it, but the screams refused to reach past her throat.

Sita's abaaya floated around her like a black cloud. Musa's face trembled red. His eyes swam in tears and he stared directly ahead. Miriam's mind spun in dizzying circles. What she was seeing here was not part of reality. This father was not holding his fifteen-year-old daughter under the water in this pool she'd splashed in as a small child. It was all a horrible vision from hell that would end at . . .

Sita began to struggle.

Her legs kicked from her white underdress; her arms flailed to the surface and splashed madly. It sounded like a stranded fish in the tide. Her veil floated up, and for the first time since her friend's wedding Miriam saw Sita's face. Her brown eyes were wide and round. A wide band of gray tape had been strapped over her mouth.

The father stared directly ahead, eyes bulging with terror, arm trembling with exertion. His mouth suddenly parted and he began to scream.

But he held his daughter down.

Musa had chosen the drowning.

Miriam's world erupted with blinding panic. She spun to her right, breaking free from Salman's grip. She had to save Sita. She had to run and get some help! She had to dive in and pull her to safety!

Her head exploded under Salman's fist, and the horizon tipped to one side. A groan, low and unearthly, broke from her throat. She began to fall. She hit the concrete hard, inches from the edge of the pool.

Under the water, Sita stopped struggling.

The father was still screaming, long terrifying wails past twisted lips. The mutawa was staring ahead, emotionless. It was not the first time he'd overseen a father drowning a wayward daughter; it would not be the last.

Sita's round lifeless eyes stared up through shimmering water. Miriam's world went black.

4

KHALID BIN MISHAL BIN ABD AL-AZIZ. That was his name—Khalid, son of Mishal, who was son of the first king, Aziz. Prophetic, Khalid had always thought, begging him to make his bid for the throne. Technically he was a royal nephew; his father's brother was now King Fahd. Although the first king, Aziz, had sired forty-two sons, the kingdom required only so many kings. To be precise, four since the death of Aziz, all of them his sons. That left thirty-eight of his sons less fortunate.

And time was not merciful; the king's sons now grew too old for a crack at the throne—Khalid's father was seventy-eight to his fifty-eight. If they weren't too old, they had undeniably become far too liberal. It was time for Saudi Arabia to be returned to her great calling as the world's protector of Islam.

It was time for a new king.

Khalid sat on red pillows with his own son, Omar bin Khalid, and Ali, the director of transportation. Like the others, Khalid wore the traditional *ghutra* headdress topped with a black circular *igaal.* They reclined in a room that looked like a Bedouin tent in deference to their heritage, but which was actually a room in Khalid's palace.

Omar picked up a glass of scotch and sipped at the amber liquor. Alcohol was illegal in Saudi Arabia, of course, but most of the royal homes were well stocked and social drinking was the norm. Khalid himself did not touch the stuff, but every man was entitled to his vices. Omar had never let this one interfere with his better judgment. Few men could consume life so ravenously and yet remain so disciplined as his son. Brutal, passionate, wise, brilliant—qualities that would make a good king one day. But he would have to wait his turn.

"It takes great discipline to be a great leader," Khalid said. "The country is faltering."

"There's a difference between talking privately about changing things and intending to do so," Ali said. "Look at Al-Mas'ari. He was forced to England with his band of dissidents. Usama bin Laden and his Reformation Committee—we all know what happened to him. The government won't just welcome change for the sake of—"

"I'm not asking them to change," Khalid said. "If there is a cancer, you don't persuade the cancer to *change.* You cut it out. That was both Al-Mas'ari's and Bin Laden's problem. Neither had the resources to cut it out. We have no further to look than back at our first king, Aziz. What was it he said? 'The Arab understands two things only: the word of Allah and the sword. The word of the Qur'an is supreme, and the sword is how the word is carried out.' Aziz understood some things. Do you know that he carried out over 40,000 public executions and 350,000 amputations? Under Aziz your chance of having a hand cut off was nearly one in ten. That kind of resolve, my friend, is what this nation needs. And I have it."

Ali just stared at him. They had talked about returning the anemic monarchy to the fundamentals of Islam a hundred times, but always in theory. Khalid had waited until now to bring the man into full confidence.

"What do mean, you *have* it?" Ali asked.

Khalid smiled. "You think we have been talking all these months for nothing? Let me ask you a question. If a man in my position were to have the full support of the ulema and twenty top-ranking princes and the undeterred ambition to overthrow the king, could he do it?"

Ali glanced at the door—they all knew that talk like this could earn death. He studied Khalid's face. "No," he said. "Even with the princes and religious scholars, it's not enough to make it stick."

Khalid smiled and nodded. "Honest. Very good. I will remember that when this is over."

Omar chuckled from his perch on the pillow and threw back the last of the scotch in his glass.

"You're right," Khalid said. "Overthrowing a government is not the same as making a new one stick. But what if a man in my position also had the full support of the Shi'i minority in the eastern provinces?"

"That would not be possible. They are Shi'i; we are Sunni."

"Anything is possible when such great power is at stake. You should know that. Indulge me for a moment."

Ali hesitated. "Then, yes." He shifted his eyes in thought. "It could be done." Eyes back on Khalid. "But still, how could a man in your position, a prince of Wahhabi royalty, possibly gain the support of the Shi'i?"

Khalid stood and walked to a bowl of fruit. He picked up a piece of *nanka,* a yellow sweet fruit imported from Indonesia. "Through the sheik, of course," he said and pushed the fruit into his mouth. If there were a leader among the four million Shi'i living in the eastern parts of Saudi Arabia, it was Al-Asamm, and to call him *the* sheik was enough.

"The sheik? Al-Asamm? He hasn't flexed his muscles in ten years. And he's not a friend to the House of Saud. What do you hope—"

"Actually, he hasn't flexed his muscles in nearly twenty years, my friend. Have you thought about that? The token demonstration now and then, but not like he was once known to."

"That doesn't make him a friend. He's Shi'i, please!"

"The Shi'i are a passionate people. Look at Iran—they know how to overthrow. We wouldn't give them too much power, of course, but they do constitute 15 percent of Saudi citizens. We will give them a voice."

"And how in the name of God do you propose to approach Sheik Al-Asamm?" Ali waved his hand. "It'll never work."

"Yes, it will," Khalid's son said, speaking for the first time.

They both looked at Omar.

"Yes, it will," Khalid agreed. "Tell him why it will work, Omar."

Omar regarded his father and Ali. He'd been in numerous meetings like this one, plotting and gathering support for his father's plan. Now, less than a week away from the actual coup attempt, it was becoming his plan. Not because he had conceived it, but because without his role, the plan would fail. And one day, he would become king himself, after Father was either killed or died. The reign of the kingdom was built on blood, he thought. Blood and marriage.

"It will work because I will marry his daughter," Omar said.

His father faced Ali. "You see? It will work because my son will marry Sheik Al-Asamm's daughter." He grinned.

"What daughter? How does that help?"

"Oh yes, I'd forgotten," his father said. "You aren't aware of his daughter, are you? *I* wasn't even aware of his daughter until a year ago. But now I am, and now I've decided that she is the solution to all of our problems, my friend."

Ali blinked.

Omar chuckled. "The reason Sheik Al-Asamm has remained relatively quiet over these past twenty years is because our dear King Fahd took a cue from his own father by buying the sheik's allegiance," he said. "King Fahd adopted Al-Asamm's daughter in exchange for loyalty. Her name is Miriam. Fahd's son Salman has raised her as his own. She was an infant then, and her adoption created a bond, but it's marriage and the bearing of a son that will create the truly inseparable bond. King Fahd insisted that she wait until she reach twenty-one to marry—evidently he wasn't in a rush to weaken his bloodline. She is now three months from turning twenty-one."

Ali stood. A faint tremble shook his sleeves. "Salman's daughter Miriam is really the daughter of the Shi'i sheik? Abu al-Asamm? They are Shi'i; we are Sunni. The king would never—"

"Thus the secrecy," Omar said. "The king may be weak-willed, but he's no idiot. And when she marries into the royal family in the next few months and has a son, Al-Asamm will be linked to the throne by blood. At least that was Fahd's plan."

"You're saying that the Shi'i sheik's daughter Miriam will marry one of the royal cousins and link the sheik to royal blood?"

"Yes. A decent plan from an old goat."

His father cast him a side glance. Omar had no plans to undermine his father, but the unspoken threat of death would always hover over any king. Now it was Fahd. Next week it would be his father.

"How does your marriage to Miriam benefit this plan?" Ali asked. "You are the chosen cousin to complete this bond—"

"No, not chosen," Omar said. "I will marry Miriam without the king's knowledge. I will marry her before Fahd's choice has the opportunity."

"How is that possible?"

Omar smiled. "Sheik Al-Asamm may have agreed with Fahd, but there's no love lost between the two. We've been negotiating with him for several months now. You see, if his daughter marries a cousin according to his agreement with King Fahd, the sheik will be rewarded with royal lineage. If, on the other hand, his daughter marries *me,* we will give him royal lineage *and* a position of power in our government. That is our agreement. A far better choice, don't you think?"

"So—"

"So his daughter Miriam will marry Omar in a secret ceremony," Khalid said. "In exchange, he will support our coup. I will give him governorship of the eastern province."

Ali stared unblinking.

Some would argue that Sheik Al-Asamm had no right to give his blood daughter's hand in marriage when he'd already given her to the king in adoption. But there was more than one religious scholar among the ulema who would disagree. The sheik was still Miriam's blood father—blood always superseded a written agreement. How the king had missed the possibility was a wonder. Even Al-Asamm had been surprised by Khalid's suggestion. Khalid's plan was a brilliant stroke, perhaps given by Allah himself.

They were telling Ali everything now, without assurance the man would go along. But they'd done the same with two dozen ministers and all but the minister of education, Ahmed, had supported the plan. Ahmed had died within the hour—a tragic accident.

Omar stood and picked up an apple. He bit deeply into its crisp flesh. "We need your support, Ali. Your position is critical to our plans. We need the airports."

The minister of transportation swallowed. He spoke very softly. "This talk is treasonous. You are beheaded for treason in this country."

"Today what we've said is treason; in one week your speaking to my father in such a way will be treason," Omar said.

Ali glanced at Khalid and then back. "You have Sheik Al-Asamm's *full* commitment?"

"Would we be talking to you if we did not? I will take his daughter Miriam as my wife in four days' time."

"And then?"

"Two of our generals have Shi'i blood. If we have Al-Asamm, we have them. We will take care of Fahd the day after the wedding. I will be king in one week. We will be a fundamentalist state within the month."

Ali looked at Khalid and they stared each other down. Slowly Ali's expression of shock curved into a faint, knowing smile. "Then you have my support." He paused, studying Khalid's face as the prospect sunk in. "You have my full support." He dipped his head. "There is no God but Allah."

Omar took another bite. Just like that the man had switched his loyalties from the reigning king, Fahd, to Omar's father, Khalid. They all knew why, of course. If Ali refused in any way, he would pay dearly. Power always came down to fear of death in the kingdom. The brutality of the system had confused Omar as a child, but by the time he turned twelve, he accepted it as the truest way. A thief learns not to steal by losing his hand; a wife stays obedient by watching stonings; a king holds power by swinging his sword.

A bell rang near the tent door. "Come."

A thin man dressed in white walked in, dipped his head. Omar felt his pulse quicken. The mutawa was Abdallah—one of the most feared and influential in Riyadh. He crossed to the table and looked at them without speaking.

"Well?"

The man cleared his throat. "It is done."

The corner of Omar's mouth twitched. "The girl is dead?" he asked.

"She was drowned an hour ago, as you suggested."

They stared at the mutawa in silence. Stonings were fairly common; drownings not so, although it made little sense—a stoning was far more painful and took much longer. Better to drown and be done with it.

"Thank you, Abdallah," Khalid said. "You may leave."

The man lowered his head and left.

"What was that?" Ali asked.

"That was the judgment of Allah," Omar said. "And that was a message to my dear bride, Miriam."

5

SETH CROSSED THE NORTH FIELD and angled for Berkeley's Department of Philosophy. His corduroys bunched slightly over worn sandals as he stepped through the grass. To his right a dance squad performed flips in short skirts. The Faculty Club stood beyond them, bordered by a manicured glade. He'd been in the place on four occasions, each time for an event that required his attendance—receptions in honor of his awards, mostly. Like the one scheduled on Thursday evening. The American Physical Society and the American Institute of Physics had named him something or other of the year, and, like it or not, the graduate dean had been obligated to acknowledge the award. Thinking about it now, Seth wondered what would happen if he didn't show. He wasn't feeling too social after yesterday's fiasco with Baaron. Two hundred faculty all dressed to the nines with champagne glasses raised and no one to toast.

"Seth!"

He turned to see Phil—a third-year undergraduate who was the epitome of a nerd with glasses, pocket protector, and pimples to boot—run up behind him. Phil was among half a dozen down-and-outers that Seth felt truly at home with.

"Hey, Phil." He slipped his hand into his pocket and rolled the superball between his fingers.

Phil slapped an open crossword magazine in his hand. "You ready?"

"Sure," Seth said. "Let me see it."

Phil held the page up, displaying a four-inch-square crossword puzzle. Seth made quick mental notes of the puzzle's pattern—black squares, white squares, numbers. Category: GOOD MARKS.

"Okay."

Phil pulled the puzzle back and glanced ahead. "So where you going?"

"Meeting with Dr. Harland. You?"

"To the cafeteria. Okay, ready? Seventeen across, ten letters, clue—*expropriate.*"

"Commandeer," Seth said.

Phil flipped a page, checked the answer, and continued. "Good. Twenty-four across, seven letters, clue—*horse back in the pack.*"

Seth considered the clue for a second. "That would be also-ran, Phil," he said in his best game-show voice.

"Never heard of it," the younger student said. "Three down, four letters, clue—*subdues.*"

"Three *down?* Tames."

"Final answer?"

"Tames, Phil. It has to be tames."

"How do you do that so easily?"

"The *M* intersects with *commandeer* and the *S* intersects with *also-ran,*" Seth said.

"Yeah, but how can you know three down does that without looking?" It was a rhetorical question but Seth answered anyway.

"I did look, remember?"

Phil slapped the magazine closed. "Forget it. This one's too easy for you. You want me to wait for you at the cafeteria?"

"No, you go ahead, buddy."

Phil looked away, uncomfortable but grinning as if he held a secret. "I heard you told Baaron a few things."

"You heard that?"

"Yeah. True?"

"True."

Seth glanced over and saw that Phil was watching the dancers now. A pang of sympathy tightened his chest. If students would take the time to talk to Phil, they would find a very caring, endearing person behind his ungainly front. It made Phil an outsider, something Seth was all too familiar with. They weren't outsiders for the same reasons, of course. Phil was avoided, while Seth was simply shy around women and chose to do the avoiding. He'd long ago decided that women had an inexplicable effect on his mind, minimizing its ability to process thought in logical constructs. Never fail, females turned him into someone he really didn't think he was. Someone lost for clear thoughts and words.

Phil, on the other hand, would kill to sit alone on a bench with a girl. Any girl. He aggressively denied the desire, of course, but Seth could see past his claims.

Seth stood taller than the undergrad by a foot. He swung his arm around Phil's neck and pulled him into a playful headlock. "What do you say I set you up with Marisa?"

Phil grinned and turned red. "What are you talkin' about? No way, man."

Seth let him go. "Okay, your loss."

"So now you're Casanova? As if you could even do that."

Seth chuckled.

"Want to talk later?" Phil asked. "I have some ideas about the Strong Force you might like."

"Absolutely. I'll come to your room."

That got Phil smiling wide. He nodded. "See you."

"See you."

Phil broke to the left, hands deep in his pockets, head lowered. He glanced up at the dancers again but quickly looked ahead. Seth swallowed and crossed the parking lot for his appointment with Harland.

They had named the philosophy building Moses—ironic but appropriate considering its current occupant. Seth had always thought that the director of philosophy, Samuel Harland, Ph.D., was the spitting image of Charlton Heston, with his dirty blond hair and soft blue eyes. He was the only man in the place worthy of the building's name.

He knocked on the department head's office door, heard a muffled "Enter," and stepped in.

"Good day."

"Have a seat," the professor said.

Seth sat. "That bad, huh?"

"Unfortunately, yes. That bad. Baaron is seething."

Seth paused. If there was one person in his life he could confide in, it was this man. "You wouldn't expect the academic dean of an esteemed institution such as this to let a little folly get under his skin."

"You wouldn't," Harland said. "But for whatever reason, you most definitely do get under his skin."

"I engaged him in class using famous quotations—"

"I *know* what you did. If you had to quote from literature, you could have been a little more selective, don't you think?" Harland was trying to force his point, but he couldn't hide the glint of humor in his eyes.

"I know," Seth said. "It was stupid." He shook his head. "I don't know how I get myself in these crazy situations."

"You get into them by going over the top. Is that such a mystery?"

"No. And if it helps any, I've been kicking myself half to death. What is it with me and Baaron?"

Harland shrugged. "I think you know. You're a blatant challenge to his theories of order."

"On the other hand, I do think I spoke the truth," Seth said. "Isn't that what you've always told me? To doggedly pursue the truth?"

"Pursuing the truth and *presenting* it are two different disciplines. I think I've told you that as well. How do you suppose I would fare around here if I walked around blasting my peers into the next county? And with you this is becoming a habit."

"You're right."

Baaron was undeniably brilliant, deserving of his lofty status at the university. But put him in a room with Seth and half his chips seemed to go on the blink. He was an easy target, one that Seth couldn't resist taking advantage of now and then. It didn't help matters that Baaron reminded Seth of his father.

The tension had set in a year earlier, when Seth had written a paper on the Strong Force that questioned prevailing thought. The paper had been picked up by several scientific journals and published to some acclaim. It was hardly Seth's fault that the author of the prevailing theory, which his trashed, was authored by none other than Gregory Baaron, Ph.D. The world of physics was a small one.

"You're going to have to learn more tact. Yes? You have to learn how to blend in a little. Like I have."

Seth's attraction to Harland had been in large part a result of the man's genuine brilliance. If Seth had learned anything in his formal education, it was that intelligence had nothing to do with intellectual honesty. With being genuine. People who cherished both brilliance and bull-frank honesty were in short supply. The system applauded brilliance only so long as it lined up with the flavor of the day.

Samuel Harland, on the other hand, was anything but the flavor of the day. He had no interest in believing what the elitists believed so he could smoke his pipe in the Faculty Club with the rest of them. He simply and methodically took every thought to its logical conclusion and put his faith there, in what he saw at the end of the trail. For Harland, the end of the trail was a prophet named Jesus. He believed in God, and he believed that Jesus was God. More to the point, he was genuine about that belief. Misguided, obviously, but honest and consistent.

"Blend in, huh? Now you're going to become a plastic person too?" Seth asked.

"No. But I am interested in learning to live with plastic people. Maybe that's the difference between you and me, Seth. You're more interested in pushing them into the ocean."

The smile faded from Seth's face. "Well, you'll have to forgive me, but I'm not built for a system like this one. I can't seem to fit in."

Harland nodded. "I feel the same way half the time. Either way, we have to live in this system, and right now the system isn't looking too kindly at you. Baaron's got some of the faculty on his side—unbelievable but true. They're talking about official reprimands."

Seth looked out the window. "I'm thinking about dumping the program, Samuel. Heading back down south."

Harland raised an eyebrow. "You've said that before."

"Maybe I should have done it before. I talked to my mom last night. She lost her job."

Harland hesitated. "The best thing you can do for your mother is to finish your doctorate. What are you going to do—pump gas for a living?"

"You know as well as I do that I could walk out of here and get a job at any one of a dozen corporations that would pay well. No offense, but I'm feeling pretty heartless."

"I'm not sure you're the only one with real emotions here. Gregory Baaron bleeds as well as you do."

"But what color does he bleed?" Seth ran both hands through his disheveled mop. See, here he was again, dishing out the kind of response that never failed to land him on his head.

He glanced at the professor. "Sometimes I wonder if we've been invaded by the body snatchers and they've set up camp here, in the heart of doublespeak. Maybe we should file a motion with the city council to rename the city. We'll call it Doublespeak. That way we can all feel good, screaming about world poverty while we drive black Mercedes."

"Not a bad idea actually," Harland said with a shallow grin. "I drive a Pinto."

"That's why they tolerate you. They think your lime-green Pinto is really a piece of vegetation you've managed to hitch a ride on. 'The wacky philosophy professor may be intolerant with his beliefs about Jesus and all, but he's brought conservation to a whole new level, so we'll forgive him.'"

Harland began to chuckle. That got Seth smiling wide.

"Well, at least you haven't lost your humor," Harland said.

"The body snatchers despise humor. It's my Achilles heel. God knows reason doesn't work with these types—it's failed miserably. I can personally attest to this fact."

Harland just looked at him.

"Never engage in a battle of wits with an unarmed man," Seth said.

"Clever. Is that your own?"

"No. It's one of the gems I handed off to Baaron."

"No . . ."

Seth stared at the window and sighed. "I'm afraid so. Did you hear about the calculation I drew on the board?"

"I heard something about the Lagrangian field equation."

"That was part of it. But I solved an equation that limits possible futures to one." Seth smiled. "That should be music to your ears."

"How so?"

"It supports the existence of God."

Harland regarded him for a moment. "Do you really believe that God exists, or is he just a concept to you—a mathematical abstraction?"

"I'm not sure I see the difference, but yes, I do believe in God. We are living in a definite design. A design requires a designer. I see that like I see numbers—plain and simple. What I don't see is how man's attempts to know God through religion make any sense. The very existence of God contradicts the idea that we have free will or choice."

"I don't buy the conclusion," Harland said.

"What's there to buy?" Seth leaned forward and took a sheet of paper from Harland's desk. "May I?"

"Be my guest. This is the equation you wrote?"

"No. This is more of a hypothetical syllogism. In the vernacular." He spoke his argument as he drew it out longhand.

> (A) If an all-knowing God exists, then he knows precisely what THE future is. (He knows I'm going to cough in ten seconds.)
>
> (B) If God knows what THE future is, then that future WILL occur, unless God is mistaken. (I WILL cough in ten seconds.)
>
> (C) Because God cannot be mistaken, there is NO possibility that any other future, other than the one future which God knows, will happen. (There's NO possibility I won't cough in ten seconds.)

(D) THEREFORE, if God exists, there is only ONE future, which is THE future he knows. (I cough in ten seconds.)

Seth set the pencil down.

"If God exists, the probability of there being more than one possible future is zero. To believe God exists also requires you to believe that the future is unalterable. By definition. There is only *one* future, and no amount of willing or choosing or praying or churchgoing can change it. Religion has no purpose."

"Knowledge of fact doesn't necessarily prove singularity of future."

"You're only splitting hairs between knowledge of fact and probabilities."

Harland smiled. "For reasons of faith that won't make any sense to you now, I disagree. And I'm no idiot; I hope you'll give me at least that."

"Of course. But it seems to me that you're committing intellectual suicide to choose faith over logic."

Harland nodded slowly. They'd argued the subject on several occasions and he didn't seem eager to dive in again.

Seth looked out the window. "You should reconsider deism—"

A pigeon suddenly slammed into the window with a loud *thunk.*

Seth blinked. "Ouch. You'd think that would break the window."

"What would?"

Seth looked at him. "The force of the bird slamming into the window."

Harland looked at the window. "What bird?"

"What do you mean, what bird? You didn't just see that?"

"No."

Seth looked at the window. "You didn't hear a loud *thunk* just now?"

"No. I didn't hear—"

A pigeon suddenly slammed into the window with a loud *thunk.* It fell away in a flurry of feathers.

"Like that?" Harland asked.

Seth stared at the clear pane of glass. Yes, *exactly* like that.

"Huh, I could've sworn I just saw that ten seconds ago. Like a déjà vu." He shook his head.

"You okay?"

"Yeah." Odd. Very odd. "Maybe God's trying to get my attention with impossibilities."

"Impossible," Harland said. "He would have to interact with us mortals to take such action."

"You have a point."

"Since you feel so strongly about destiny, let me suggest that you're destined to shape the world, Seth. I doubt you'll do that from the beaches of San Diego. Another year here and you'll be out. Stay with it."

Seth sat back. It was like Harland to turn the tables on him. "Now you're sounding like Clive Masters with the NSA."

"Close enough. Anyone with half a brain would say you should finish."

Seth nodded absently. "So what are you suggesting?"

"That you play ball at the reception this Thursday. Smile, be nice. Try to keep your foot out of your mouth. Maybe even offer some kind of apology to Baaron—"

"Suck up."

"In the vernacular, yes."

"Become reasonable and do what's best for everybody?"

"Yes."

Seth stood and walked to the window. The pigeon was hobbling along the grass, still dazed from its fall.

"I wouldn't dream of anything else, Professor."

6

THE BRUISE ON HER FACE was hidden from Samir, but he had to know something terrible had happened by the tremble in her voice. The tragedy was too large in her mind to discuss at first—they rode in silence.

Miriam had awakened in the car and she wept for her friend, oblivious to Salman's demands for silence. She'd gone to her room and fallen asleep on a pillow soaked with tears. She'd heard of stonings and even drownings before, of course—they were an uncommon but real part of life in Saudi Arabia. But she'd never witnessed either. What would the world say if it realized that such atrocities were a part of life here in this far corner of the globe? It would rise up in horror and smash the mutawa. It would sweep militant Islam into the ocean and set the women free. It would put a gun to men like Salman's heads and pull the trigger.

She'd awakened at noon, feeling nauseated. The Sheik Al-Asamm wanted to see her. Her father. She'd washed away her tears and readied herself, clinging to the hope that he would bring sanity to her world once again.

Samir drove her through the modern streets of Riyadh, past new structures designed by Western architects. Nearly a quarter of Saudi Arabia's population was expatriate, imported labor and expertise to build the city and serve the House of Saud. The foreigners were effectively cut off from the lives of most Saudis, sequestered in compounds designed for them, but their touch could be seen everywhere. To many fundamental Muslims, the slow westernization of this, Islam's birthplace, was a blasphemous tragedy.

To Miriam it symbolized the hope of freedom.

They wound through the suburbs, sandstone brick and mortar construction. Square. Everything square. And then they were in the desert itself, stretching endlessly to Dhahran on the Persian Gulf. The Americans had used Dhahran as a base during the Gulf War; her biological father had lived near the city his whole life. Abu Ali al-Asamm. A great sheik; a great man.

"Sita was drowned by her father this morning for defying Hatam," she said.

"Wha—No!"

"Yes." She lifted her hand to her mouth, afraid she might begin crying again. The tires droned under them.

"The savage!" Samir said. "He is a pig!"

Miriam swallowed the lump rising in her throat.

Samir shook his head. "The mutawa have lost sight of reality."

"Abdallah was there."

"I'm so very sorry, Miriam. Some of the men in this country are beasts to their women." He looked out his window, jaws flexing in anger. "I could understand a beating, but drowning? It's a disgrace!"

"A beating?" she cried. "No man should have a right to even beat a woman! What gives a man that right?"

"The prophet Mohammed—"

"I don't care *what* the prophet did or said!" She spoke blasphemy, but in the wake of what she'd witnessed, she didn't care. "If he lived today, he would find another way to run a society. It's inhumane to drown your daughter, and it's inhumane to beat your wife!"

They were the strongest words she had ever spoken in Samir's hearing. He mumbled his agreement, but her words had obviously stung his ears. She sat next to him, as she frequently did when they were alone, for the rest of the trip. But today she sat dazed and numb and not caring.

Fifteen minutes after they left the city, Samir turned off onto a small sandy road that led to a large Bedouin tent, alone in the desert. Two Mercedes had replaced the traditional camels, each angled to form a kind of gate to the main canvas flap.

Samir stopped the car. Dust drifted by.

"He's waiting inside. We cannot stay long."

Miriam stepped out. A Bedouin woman, dressed in traditional black abaaya but without a full-face veil, exited the tent and watched her. The Bedouin veils rode on the bridge of the nose, allowing the eyes free access to the world.

Miriam reached the tent, removed her own veil completely, gazed into the smiling eyes of the strange woman, and stepped into the tent.

Abu Ali al-Asamm sat on a large silk pillow, the quintessential white-bearded holy man, talking in hushed tones to a woman on his right. A maroon carpet with gold weaving covered most of the floor, and on this carpet a single low table. Otherwise there was only a stand for tea and a large bowl of fruit—hardly the full makings of a typical tent. Obviously, they had come hurriedly with only what would fit into the cars outside.

"Miriam!" The sheik was on the heavy side, and getting to his feet was not as easy as it been even two years ago, when she'd first met him. He hurried over, grinning wide, eyes beaming his pleasure. "How is my daughter, hmm?" He took her hands and kissed them. "Such a beauty, my Miriam, just like your mother, may Allah give her rest. Come . . . come sit."

He waved to the table where the woman was already pouring tea. Her natural mother, Jawahara, had died during childbirth. This was Nadia, a new wife for Father. One of two.

"Thank you, Father." They sat. If only she could run away and live with her real father. Be freed from the suffocating veil in exchange for the Bedouin veil. Live by the sea in Dhahran, among the Shi'i.

Her father offered her fruit, and she took a large apple.

"So how is the house of Salman treating you these days?" the sheik asked. Wrinkles spread from his eyes, like crow's-feet, formed by a perpetual smile. Miriam felt a knot rise in her throat. She wanted nothing but to crawl into his lap and be held forever.

"Good," she said. Nothing could be further from the truth, but it was the correct answer.

Al-Asamm tilted his head and studied her face. "Really? Your eyes betray you, my dear. What is the matter?"

It was too much. She shifted her eyes. "I have a very good friend named Sita. She was fifteen and she was forced to marry an old man. She refused his advances, and this morning her father drowned her for shaming them. I . . . I was forced to watch."

"Oh, dear, dear, dear." The sheik clucked his tongue and shook his head. "It is an abomination. There are far more appropriate punishments than death. I am sorry, child. I am very sorry."

She nearly argued that *no* punishment was reasonable, as she had with Samir, but she rejected the notion. Her father might not condone the actions of Sita's father, but he was still a Saudi man steeped in tradition. The woman still had her place in his world, and it was far below the place of a man.

They talked for ten minutes—comforting conversation. Talk of the eastern province and Dhahran. About the Shi'i and the American involvement in the region. About Mother and how she had always wanted a daughter. Miriam had been her only child, but she had died happy. Yet Father had not brought her here to talk about Mother. The talk stalled and he took a deep breath.

"The world is changing, Miriam." He glanced at her carefully. "Perhaps after fifty years in opposition to this government, my day has come." He smiled and she smiled in return.

"How well do you know the hadith?" he asked, referring to the somewhat controversial Islamic writings.

"I don't know it well," she said.

"Then let me tell you that some would say I am still your father. That my blood rights supersede those of an adoptive father."

Miriam's pulse quickened. What was he saying? She was to go with him? "I would give everything to be your daughter, Father."

He chuckled. "And perhaps you shall. Perhaps you shall." He picked up his cup and sipped.

"But you are no longer a child, Miriam. As your father I would not be telling you stories or feeding you dinner. You are a beautiful woman, ready to be married. Ready to bear children."

"I'm not going to marry until . . ." She stopped there as a thought struck her. "I was to be given by Salman to a cousin," she said, pulse now pounding. "What are you saying?"

"I am saying that I'm going to exercise my rights as your natural father to give you in marriage."

She sat, stunned and unsure. The thought of marriage to anyone but Samir repulsed her. But maybe he knew of Samir and planned for her to marry *him!* The thought of escaping Salman's grip instantly appealed to her.

The sheik continued. "I will do it for the good of Saudi Arabia. For the sake of returning the country to the true teaching of Islam and for the sake of bringing my people, the Shi'i, into their rightful place within society." He paused. "King Fahd has ruled long enough."

"How? Whom will I marry?"

He smiled. "You are eager? I don't blame you, child, so am I. So am I." But he didn't tell her. Instead he told her about Khalid, the nephew of King Fahd. She listened intently as he laid down the details of a planned coup, not completely understanding until he revealed the last detail. They were going to overthrow the throne, and the plot depended on her marriage.

Then she understood. Her father had forged a new alliance. Once again she was the pawn.

"You will be married in three days' time."

"Three days!" She felt suffocated. "To whom?"

"To Khalid's son, of course. To Omar bin Khalid."

"Omar bin Khalid? That's impossible!" Miriam scrambled to her feet. "I don't even *know* him!"

The sheik stood. "And now you expect to *know* the one you marry?"

"I can't marry Omar," she snapped. "I love *Samir!*"

Silence, except for her ragged breathing. He stared, mouth agape.

For the first time, Sheik Abu Ali al-Asamm had met the true Miriam, and it had clearly sent a shock through his system.

"Samir?" he finally said. "That's . . . that's not possible."

She had made a terrible mistake. She saw that now and she knew that for Samir's sake she had to recover. She could not reveal the true depth of her love for him.

"No, you're right. It's not. But what if I did love Samir? You would still force me to marry a man I don't love? If Omar is the son of Khalid bin Mishal, then he's obviously a tyrant like his father. I don't know a single person who speaks well of his family. They are animals!"

"How dare you speak such things!" The sheik's nostrils flared. His anger surprised her. An image washed through her mind, a friend several years ago who'd argued about marrying and had been locked up until the day of the wedding as a result. Miriam suddenly felt desperate.

"I'm sorry, Father. But please, I beg you, don't do this to me!"

"Fathers have *always* given their daughters in marriage. Now you are telling me that you know better than I who is a good husband?"

She bit her tongue. He was tradition to the core.

"A *country* is at stake!" he boomed. "We have in our hands the power to save Islam from corruption, and you think only of your fantasies?"

Her father's wife stood near the corner, facing away. She would be no help, of course. But her posture told Miriam that the sheik's outburst was not a common thing. He had traded her once for peace, and he would do it again, this time for power.

She had to buy herself some time. *Three days!* A quiver ran through Miriam's bones.

"Father . . . forgive me. I was thinking irrationally. In one day my best friend has been killed and I learn that I have a wedding in three days. I'm losing myself."

He stared at her, composing himself. "Yes," he finally said. "I'm sorry."

"Forgive me."

He nodded, obviously relieved. "This will mean the world to me and to Islam." Sheik Abu Ali al-Asamm reached out and put a hand on her arm in a gesture of comfort.

"The wedding will be held in secrecy. Samir will bring you tomorrow and you will be pampered like a queen, I promise you. And when we are successful in taking the throne, your wedding will be celebrated in the open." He paused. "The groom has requested that the ceremonies of marriage be properly followed, including *halawa,*" he said, speaking of the traditional removal of all body hair below the neck prior to a wedding. The practice had been instituted by Mohammed in the 600s, when bathing was not common.

Miriam nodded, suppressing a sudden urge to vomit.

"Now go." He smiled reassuringly. "Before you are missed."

She dipped her head, replaced her veil, and left the tent without another word.

Samir dropped Miriam off at the Souq and agreed to pick her up in one hour. He'd tried in vain to find out what was bothering her from the visit with her father. He clearly didn't have a clue about the wedding. And to tell him would only crush him. She couldn't bring herself to do it, not yet.

The market was busy, as usual, with merchants bustling around their shops peddling their wares. The women floated around in black, dozens of Darth Vaders, lost behind their veils. Sultana came up and took her arm.

"The pigs!" she whispered harshly. "How could any sane man drown his daughter? If the outside world knew about this . . . They scream about the treatment of women in Afghanistan by the Taliban when it suits them, but when politics are at stake, they turn a blind eye."

So Sultana knew already. But the dread of Miriam's own troubles had blunted the horror of Sita's drowning.

"Poor Sita," Sultana said.

"I am being given in marriage," Miriam said.

Sultana stopped. They were abreast of a clothing store, and the merchant was staring their way. She grabbed Miriam's arm and pulled her to the end of the row. She kept her voice low, but urgent. "What are you talking about?"

"I met with my father this morning. He has given me in marriage."

"No! I thought he had to wait until you were twenty-one?"

"No. My *real* father. Sheik Abu Ali." Her voice trembled saying it.

Sultana looked at her as if she were mad. "The Shi'i sheik? What are you talking about?"

"He is my blood father, Sultana. I was adopted into King Fahd's family in exchange for loyalty. I was to be given in marriage by Salman when I turned twenty-one. I'm sorry; I wanted to tell you so many times. But I was under an oath."

Sultana stood unmoving, as if struck dead on her feet.

"Sultana, did you hear me? I am to be married—"

"To whom?"

"To the son of Khalid bin Mishal. Omar. The wedding is in three days."

"Omar bin Khalid!"

Miriam glanced around, self-conscious. "I'm scared, Sultana."

"Oh, dear! Oh dear, oh dear, this is terrible." Sultana hurried toward the brick wall that surrounded the market, stopped after four paces, and urgently swept her arm for Miriam to follow.

"Sultana? Sultana, please." Miriam felt hopeless. She was about to die the second death. "What should I do?"

Safe from bent ears, Sultana spun to her. "Do you know who Omar is? I know the man! He's my first cousin! I could tell you things about this man that would make you vomit." Sultana was shaking with fury. "I talked to Sita's mother. Do you know who pressured her father to drown her? I'll tell you. It was Omar bin Khalid."

"Omar! But how—"

"I don't know, but you *can't* marry him! I once saw him kick my niece in the head when she was three years old. For taking a toy from one of his nephews! She was in the hospital for a week. He's an animal!"

"I have to marry him. Don't you see? I'm my father's daughter, and I have to do what he says! Look at Sita!"

"And look who *killed* Sita!"

"And if I don't obey, then he kills me too! Is that what you want?"

"Stop it!" Sultana said. "Just stop for a minute."

They stood under the shade of a palm, breathing steadily in the afternoon heat.

"You're not thinking clearly," Sultana said. "Why does your father want to marry you to Omar bin Khalid?"

Miriam told her.

"This is enough to get us both killed. You're still not thinking clearly. Were all of our talks just that, the silly talk of stupid women?"

Miriam looked back at the shops. A woman draped in black faced them. Another prisoner. "You're right." She faced Sultana. "You're right."

"There's only one thing you can do," her friend said.

"What?"

"Run."

The word stunned Miriam into a momentary silence.

"You can't be serious."

"Yes, I am! You have to run. If you stay, you will either be beaten into submission or end up dead like Sita."

"Escape?" Miriam's heart began to pound. "Those were the plans of desperate women. They would never work."

"You *are* a desperate woman! And the plan will work. Does Salman still keep the same safe?"

"Yes. I think so."

A long silence stretched between them. Two years earlier, on a girlish whim, they had methodically drawn up plans for escape and convinced each other the idea would work. Not that they ever intended to use it.

"What if I get caught?"

"Then they'll force you to marry Omar anyway. That's why this is the right time to run. They need you, don't you see? They can't just kill you."

Her friend had a point. "They may not kill me, but there'd be a high price."

"The price of not trying could be higher."

Miriam stood still. Running sounded absurd. Most women she knew had a hard enough time getting out of the house, much less getting out of the country. Who was she to think she could run?

"What about Samir? I can't just leave him."

"Leave him? You're leaving him anyway. You think Omar will allow you to keep a convenient relationship with this secret love of yours? Don't be absurd! He'd kill you first!"

The image of Sita floating in her pool swept through Miriam's mind. She faced the wall. "How will I ever make it? When I went to America to study, I was under guard the whole time. I had *servants.* Now you expect me to just fly there and strike up a life on my own? Talking is one thing; actually doing it isn't like deciding to go on a shopping trip."

"No, of course it's not. But a shopping trip doesn't buy you freedom either. It's *freedom,* Miriam!"

"What if they come after me?"

"They will. But America's a big country. I'm telling you, Miriam, you have to run. Tomorrow."

"Tomorrow?" An involuntary shudder spread through Miriam's bones. The prospect of marrying Omar was sinking in, and it wasn't unlike swallowing acid. *Samir . . . dear Samir!*

"I'm not sure I can leave Samir."

Sultana grunted her frustration.

They had planned the escape down to the last detail: the permission to travel required of all women, the passport, the money, the destination—everything. And in a mad sort of way it made perfect sense. It would be like jumping off a cliff, but she was in a free fall already. Marrying Omar might be *worse* than death.

"Could you get me to Jiddah on one of your husband's Lear jets?"

"Of course. I travel there regularly—the pilot wouldn't suspect a thing. But why to Jiddah? I thought—"

"Being collected for a marriage wasn't part of our plans. My father told me they will come for me tomorrow, but if I convinced Samir that I had to go to Jiddah for an urgent shopping trip, they would be forced to wait until my return. It will buy us time. And send them in the wrong direction."

"Samir knows about the wedding?" They were talking quickly, in hushed tones now.

"No."

The wedding—it sounded strange. Horrible. "I would double back to Riyadh for a flight to Paris and then on. If I'm doing this, I have to do it right."

Miriam saw the faint outlines of a smile through Sultana's veil. "That's the Miriam I know."

They talked for another twenty minutes, reviewing the plan with care. Sultana finally took her arm and steered her back toward the shops. "We have to be careful. Is Salman due back tomorrow?"

"Not for three days."

"Then bring all the documents with the money and meet me at the airport tomorrow morning at nine o'clock. I'll tell Samir I am expecting you."

They entered the market and walked silently for a few minutes. It was sudden—impossibly sudden. But that was the only way it would work.

"Can you get a flight schedule for Paris?" Miriam asked.

"Of course. If you have any problem, call me tonight. I'll do the same."

Miriam took a deep breath. She was going on the run.

7

THE DANCE SQUAD WAS IN HEARST FIELD, next to the gym, when Seth entered the field. Some called them cheerleaders, but these girls were hardly the kind Seth had seen in high school. They were the kind who competed on ESPN2 at the national championship level and eventually went on to dance on cruise ships or, in some cases, Broadway.

The squad leader was a blonde named Marisa, a bright physics undergraduate who'd approached Seth for help on several papers. He'd never quite figured out what she needed help with, but he spent an hour in the park with her once, discussing the distinctions between nuclear physics and high-energy physics.

Marisa was a walking oxymoron—an intelligent student who seemed determined to hide behind a Hollywood persona. She'd smiled and asked him why he didn't have a girlfriend. And when he blushed, she had drawn her finger down his arm and said she thought he was a mysterious man. She suggested they get to know each other.

Two evenings later, Seth had found himself on his first date in three years. Everything progressed surprisingly well at first. She, the perfect twenty-one-year-old babe with enough beauty to boil the blood of most men, and he, the *mysterious* wonder-brain with enough brains to send most women, not to mention men, into the deep freeze.

They'd gone to the Crab Shack for dinner, and with each crab leg, her flaws increasingly annoyed him. Her blind acceptance of a news anchor's point of view, as if being housed in a television made one God himself; her wisecracks about Professor Harland and his silly right-wing bent, followed immediately by her audacious use of the word "tolerant"; her affectionate comment about the Clinton legacy. By the time they got to the main dish, even her white teeth looked plastic to him. How could such a bright student be so easily swept into this pap?

He'd become so distracted, in fact, that he took a sip of the hot butter, mistaking it for his iced tea. She'd laughed, of course, a high-pitched young laugh. Now her youth glared at him. He was twenty-six; she was twenty-one. A mere pup, flashing her plastic teeth and raving on about a world she saw through distorted glasses.

To Seth's amazement, she had asked him out for a second date the next day. He'd politely declined. It was the last time they'd talked.

Seth was just thinking he'd give the squad a wide berth when a slouched figure just turning from one of the girls caught his eye—a form Seth could swear was . . .

It was Phil. Phil had actually overcome his fears enough to talk to one of the girls. By the looks of his sagging shoulders, his fears had been entirely justified. He looked as dejected as a wet breadstick.

Seth broke for the squad, watching Phil slink away. He wasn't sure what he could possibly do about his friend's failure—as Phil had said, he wasn't exactly Casanova himself. But rejection at the hand of such stunning creatures was tantamount to death for a young man like Phil. There was no way Seth could just stand and watch.

He didn't recognize Marisa until she had seen him, and by then he was committed. He nodded and smiled. She must have mistaken the gesture as encouragement because she immediately whispered something to the others and then broke into a punchy cheer that made as much use of her hips as it did her mouth.

Why did she do that? She had the brains to be a doctor or a psychotherapist, and here she was playing *Animal House.* It was as if she had a split personality. Not unlike him in some ways.

Seth covered his embarrassment by clapping and saying, "All right, way to go," or something similar; he wasn't positive because his mind was shouting him down with objections.

All six faced him, wearing slight grins. He wondered what Marisa had told them. All thoughts of stepping in like a hero to defend his friend left him. He almost veered right, toward the gym. That would look natural enough. Just Seth going to the gym for his daily buff-up workout. On the other hand, Seth going to the gym wasn't exactly common, was it?

"Hello, girls."

"Hi, Seth."

He stopped and shoved his hands into his pockets. "What are you guys doing?"

Practicing their dance, you idiot.

"Working on our backflips," Marisa said.

"Cool."

Silence.

"Can we help you?" one of the others said—a brunette who looked like she'd borrowed her legs from a horse. Seth avoided her eyes and looked at Marisa.

"No, I was just going—"

"I heard about your fun with Baaron yesterday," Marisa said.

"You did? Yeah, that was pretty bad."

"For him maybe. I heard you came out pretty good."

Seth grinned, nervous. "That depends on how you look at it."

"I think the student body understands exactly what happened."

Seth wasn't sure what she meant. "The irony is that Baaron's holding a reception in my honor tomorrow night at the Faculty Club."

A redhead with hands on hips blew a round pink bubble and then popped it loudly. "What kind of reception?" she asked.

Seth felt inordinately awkward. "Well, there's this award called the Dannie Heinman Prize. Mathematical physics. It's a pretty big deal to the faculty."

"Who'll be there?" the redhead asked.

"It's a faculty reception," Seth said. "Two hundred or so faculty."

She blinked. "Two hundred? Who are you, the president?"

"No." Seth smiled, embarrassed. "Like I said, it's pretty important to some people."

"What's the dress code at this thing?" Marisa asked. She was grinning mischievously, and Seth wondered what she was thinking.

"It's a black-tie affair. Not exactly my first choice."

"But the party's in your honor, right?"

"I guess you could say that."

"How would you like to spice it up a bit?"

"What do you mean?"

"We could dance," Marisa said, beaming.

"Oh, please!" the brunette said.

Marisa turned to her. "Why not, Maggie? What's wrong with a little routine to liven up the party?"

"Not exactly the kind of party—"

"Exactly! It's not exactly *Seth's* kind of party, so we add a little flavor."

The idea suddenly started to take root in Seth's mind. In some ways it was an irresistible idea. Harmless.

"Will Brad Baxter be there?" the redhead asked. Brad was the director of physical education.

"Could be," Seth said. "Do you want him to be there?"

"You can do that?"

"Sure," Seth said.

They were looking at each other, not objecting. Except for Maggie. "What do you want us to do?" she asked. "Backflips on Baaron's table? I'm not sure I like this."

"It's harmless, nothing they can actually do anything about," Marisa said.

"What? Backflips?" Maggie asked.

"Actually, I had something else in mind. Something more MTV than ESPN."

Maggie looked away. "See? I was right."

"Lighten up," Marisa said. Then to Seth, "What do you think?"

"Actually it could be kind of fun," he said, grinning.

"Do we look like strippers to you?" Maggie said.

"No." Seth felt his face go red. "That's not—"

"Maggie! Give it a rest!" Marisa said. "This will be fun." She turned to Seth. "So you want us to come in and do a sexy dance, maybe heat Baaron up a little. I don't see the harm in that. This isn't exactly a parochial school, right? How do you want to work this?"

Suddenly the idea had become his. Marisa was a smooth operator; he would give her that much. He could see her running for Congress one day.

"Well. When I stand up to give my speech—they always want the guest of honor to tell them how indebted they are to Berkeley—and when I get to a certain point, you could come in from the sides and do your . . . routine."

The others were beaming. The idea had taken root. "So that's it?"

"Maybe table dances would be a good idea. All the department heads and a grand finale with Baaron." What was he thinking?

"I don't know," Maggie said.

"I love it!" Marisa said. "When was the last time the faculty gave us our due? Just think about that, Maggie. This will loosen them up a bit. Talk about making a splash."

"You're sure there's nothing they could do?"

"Please, it's only a dance! We're not going in there with picket signs and beating them over the heads. This is Berkeley!"

"She's right," Seth said. "If there is any heat, I'm sure it'll come down on me anyway. I seem to have a propensity for heat."

Red flag, Seth.

Lighten up, it's harmless!

Marisa looked at the others for a quick approval. A string of "I'm in's" and a halfhearted shrug from Maggie settled the issue.

She turned back. "Okay, we're on. Any other surprises?"

"Only one." Seth faced the petite blonde that Phil had been talking to. "I have a friend who needs a date. He was here a minute ago. The handsome guy with the pocket protector. Trust me, he's very charming once you get to know him."

"You . . . you want me to go out with that guy?"

Seth nodded. "Just ask him out to dinner. Maybe a movie."

"No problem," Marisa said. "Right, Suzi? He's charming."

"Okay."

"You'll do it?" Seth asked.

"Sure. Kind of felt sorry for him anyway."

Seth nodded. "Okay. Good."

Maggie crossed her arms and turned to leave. Her foot caught on Marisa's shoe and she tripped. With a surprised gasp she sprawled on the ground.

Seth instinctively jumped forward to help her up. It was something he'd learned from childhood, in a house where his mother often ended up on the ground. You always help the helpless. Always.

But suddenly Maggie was standing, not lying on the grass.

Seth jerked back and blinked.

Maggie crossed her arms and turned to leave.

He'd seen this!

Her foot caught on Marisa's shoe.

He'd seen exactly this, just one second ago!

This time Seth leapt forward just as Maggie began to fall. He caught her on the elbow and pulled her back.

"Whoa!" she exclaimed. "Watch your feet, Marisa." Then she walked off.

"Don't worry about her," Marisa said. "That was pretty quick."

Seth stared at the ground, stunned by what had just happened.

"Seth? You okay?"

"Huh? Yeah." He took a step back, looked up at them, and started to turn.

"I'll call you for details?"

"Sure. Call me."

8

SAMIR DROVE MIRIAM FROM THE MARKET where they'd left Sultana. Miriam watched suburban Riyadh drift by like a dream made of mud and brick, her stomach tied in knots. Her voice came tight and strained, that much she couldn't control, but she managed to pass it off on Sita's death.

Of course, she couldn't let Samir know the truth: She was actually considering—no, planning. She was actually *planning* to flee the country, Allah forgive her. She didn't dare tell him. Not only because he had a direct line to her father, the sheik, and so by default to Omar, but because telling Samir would put *him* in terrible danger. When Omar discovered her missing, he would naturally suspect Samir's involvement and question him thoroughly. The less he knew the better.

The knowledge that in the morning she would betray him made her ill. She repeatedly swallowed the lumps that choked her throat. She couldn't even tell him good-bye! She did slip a hand over to him and squeeze his hand. He simply blushed and drove on. One way or another, she knew they would end up together—they'd been born for each other. She would leave a letter for him with Sultana, telling him of her undying love and begging him to come for her. A tear slipped from her eye. *Get ahold of yourself, Miriam!*

Miriam explained Sultana's insistence that she must accompany her on a private shopping trip to Jiddah the following day. It was a private getaway, only for part of the day, she explained, so please don't tell any of the others. Samir agreed with a knowing smile and a wink.

If only he *did* know!

She left Samir in the garage, hurried into the house, and walked straight for her room without removing her veil. Nothing must appear out of the ordinary. The last thing she needed was for Haya or Faisal to see her with a tear-stained face. Fortunately, neither of them was around. Miriam locked the door to her room, walked to the bed, and sank to it slowly. Alone for the first time, she lowered her head into her hands and wept.

An hour slipped by before she wiped her eyes for the last time and stood up. A full-length mirror showed her standing, still dressed in her black abaaya. The princess. She walked up to the mirror and studied her face. Her eyes were red and swollen, but the dark tones of her skin hid most of her crying well. She sniffed and ran her hands back through her shiny black hair. A very small black freckle spotted her right cheek. When she was thirteen, she'd wanted it removed. But then she'd looked through a copy of *Cosmopolitan* magazine that Sultana had smuggled into the country, and she'd seen a stunning model with a similar mark on her cheek. She agreed with Sultana that men must be attracted to it, or the makers of the magazine would have covered it up.

That had been six years ago, and, other than family, the only man who'd seen her face was Samir. Her life had been divided between heaven and hell, she thought. A princess in a prison. And under Omar . . .

She turned from the mirror, set her jaw, and pulled off her abaaya. Then it was time to get on with it!

Salman owned a large oak desk he'd flown in from Spain. Actually, he owned four identical desks, one for each of his villas. Miriam assumed they all had fire safes under them, like the one in his study. It had taken her nearly a month to find the combination two years earlier—part of the escape they'd planned. Haya knew the combination, of course. Someone besides Salman had to know how to access the valuables. He had entrusted his young bride with the code, knowing the young girl would never dream of abusing his trust. And in her youth, Haya certainly did not suspect that she *was* violating that trust by bragging about the combination to Miriam late one night. Coaxing the numbers from Haya had not been an easy task, but when Miriam slipped into the office later that same night and opened the safe, she knew it had been worth it.

After washing her face and applying some color around her eyes, Miriam went out to find Haya. She was in the piano room, plunking away some awful tune that had no business being played beyond sealed doors. She stopped and stood as Miriam walked in.

"Have you seen Faisal?" Miriam asked.

Haya stared unblinking and for a moment Miriam imagined she knew of her plans. Haya turned sad eyes toward the French doors that led to the gardens. "No."

"Sita was a very good friend," Miriam said.

"Her father is a barbarian."

"And so is Salman."

Haya hesitated. "Yes. He is."

"I hope he doesn't take my insubordination out on you."

"Salman will get over it," Haya said, turning. "Did you buy anything?"

"No."

"Hmm. What were you shopping for?"

Miriam took a breath. She walked over to the piano and traced the polished black wood with her finger. "I won't be single forever, Haya. You know that."

Haya faced her. "Of course. Although you are becoming an old maid. What man would want an old maid?" A teasing glint shone in her eyes.

"If I'm lucky, *no* man will want an old maid." The corner of her mouth lifted in a half-smile, then fell again. "But I don't think I'll be so lucky. I turn twenty-one in three months."

Haya nodded. She knew about the age restriction, but no more.

"I've decided to start a new wardrobe," Miriam said. "I won't have long to spend Salman's money, so I should make the most of these last few months."

Haya nodded.

"I've also decided, after today, that the shops in Riyadh are too conservative for my tastes. Sultana is taking me to Jiddah in the morning. Just for the day. And if Jiddah doesn't have what I want, I'll just have to go to Spain, won't I?"

Haya smiled. "Maybe I should come with you."

"Wonderful idea. Although I'm not sure Salman would approve." Haya would not be allowed to leave town after this morning's outburst. Not until Salman had flushed the anger from his blood. A shadow crossed the younger girl's eyes.

Miriam pushed, encouraged by her progress. "But you won't tell him that I've gone, will you? We're flying in one of Sultana's husband's jets in the morning and will be back in the afternoon."

Haya's eyes went blank. She walked to the piano and sat. "Don't worry, your secret is safe with me," she said. "Maybe I'll join you for the trip to Spain, but you're right about Salman."

Miriam walked over and kissed Haya on the cheek. "Thank you, Haya." She turned and left the room. It was a good-bye kiss—after this evening she might never see Haya again. The thought held some sadness.

Miriam went carefully through her possessions, deciding what she could take that would fit in a single carry-on suitcase and a vanity. In the end, she settled for what Sultana and she had agreed on in their initial planning: two changes of Western clothes—jeans and blouses that would allow her to blend into California; basic toiletries; the Qur'an; one jewelry box filled with her most expensive jewels—well over a million dollars' worth; and a CD Walkman. The rest of the space would go for the money. With money she could buy whatever she needed in the United States.

She had talked scandalously with Sita and Sultana about embracing Western ways one day, and now that day was here. Jeans might not be acceptable in Saudi Arabia, but Miriam could hardly wait to don them at the earliest possible opportunity. She felt desperate to distance herself from the abaaya and smother herself in the symbols of freedom.

In the United States she would be anything but Saudi. She would eat and walk and talk like an American. She'd done it before for a summer in California, and she would do it again—this time permanently. Her accent might be English, but her heart would be American.

The evening crept by like a slug making its way across a pincushion. Faisal came home, his normal obnoxious self, wearing an air of superiority. He wouldn't tell them what Salman intended to do about the morning's events, but the glint in his eyes said that some form of punishment was forthcoming. Haya's dread was enough to turn the house into a mausoleum for the night.

It was 1 A.M. before Miriam slipped through the darkened villa and entered Salman's office carrying her small suitcase. Except for her own breathing, the house was dead silent. She walked lightly on the thick carpet across to his desk, trying in vain to still her heart. She had to kneel to reach the safe under the desk. Using a flashlight she dialed the numbers in the order she'd burned in her mind. But her fingers trembled and she overshot on the first try. The second produced a soft click and she pulled the door open.

She played the flashlight's beam over the contents, positioned exactly as they had been two years earlier: the passports and traveling certificates on a small shelf and wads of cash on the safe floor. Like most Saudi men in his position, Salman kept a healthy stash of money in the event that a political emergency might force him on the run. There were several stacks—euros, francs, and American dollars. Miriam was interested only in the dollars.

She paused long enough to satisfy herself that the house was still asleep. Working quickly, she shuffled through the documents and withdrew her own passport and a blank traveling document. She would have time to execute the document giving her permission to travel to the United States and sign it with Salman's signature tomorrow. They had all practiced the appropriate forgeries—Miriam only hoped hers would stand up to scrutiny.

She pulled out twenty bundles of hundred-dollar bills, each an inch thick, and placed them in the suitcase. They'd guessed it was roughly $500,000. A small amount of cash in royal Saudi terms, but enough for a start in America, surely. If not she could always fall back on the jewels.

Miriam closed the safe, spun the dial, and left the room with a new tremor in her bones. She had just committed an unforgivable crime and had no doubt Salman would insist on amputation if she were caught. The traditional punishment for stealing was one he would be only too glad to enforce, especially on a daughter he resented.

It took her an hour to pack and repack the case, hiding the money beneath the clothes. The airport authorities rarely checked the bags of royalty, but there was always the possibility. Unless they rummaged through her clothes, they would find nothing. Of course, if they did open the suitcase, they would rummage, wouldn't they?

She finally locked the case and forced herself to bed again.

The morning came slowly and without a wink of sleep. The two hours of light leading up to her departure with Samir went even more slowly. Miriam walked downstairs at eight-thirty and saw with no small relief that the house was still quiet. She donned her veil one last time and walked to the garage, carrying the suitcase in one hand and her vanity case in the other.

Samir helped her with the bags. If he noticed the weight, he didn't show it. Once again she was thankful for the abaaya that hid her skin—the adrenaline racing through her blood had surely flushed it red. Or drained it white. She only hoped he wouldn't notice the tremble that had set into her limbs.

What if Salman came to withdraw something from his safe before Miriam got to the airport? What if Samir dropped the suitcase, spilling its contents on the ground? What if . . . There were too many what ifs! *This is a mistake, Miriam! You should run back to the house. You could tell Samir that your cycle came early.*

They pulled away from the villa. Traffic bustled with expatriates headed to work and Saudis headed to oversee them.

"What do you suppose the weather in Jiddah will be like today?" Miriam asked.

"Beautiful," Samir said. He cast her a side glance. "As beautiful as you."

She forced a smile under the veil. "And how do you know that I haven't grown warts under this sheet?"

"Warts or no warts, I would love you, as Allah is my witness."

"Before you saw me unveiled, I was just a walking sheet. And then you saw me and I am your undying love. What if I'd been ugly?" They teased each other often in the car's privacy, but now the talk felt distant. Fleeting.

"Okay. I admit that I'm a man. And like most men, the beauty of a woman does strange things to my mind." He gave her a coy smile. "Your beauty nearly stops my heart. I honestly don't know what I would do, seeing you walk around the house unveiled. It might kill me."

They passed Riyadh's water tower, a structure that made Miriam think of a champagne glass every time she saw it.

"You would have to marry me first." She turned to him. "We can't pretend forever, Samir. You know as well as I that I will be married within the royal family. I have to produce a son of royal blood, remember? That's the whole point of this agreement my father made."

Samir cleared his throat and stared ahead.

"As long as we're in this country, we'll never be allowed to marry," she said.

"Then we'll have to leave this country," he said.

It was the first time he'd said it. Miriam's heart skipped a beat. But no, she couldn't say anything now.

"We will?"

He looked at her and then returned his gaze forward. "You think I don't realize how impossible our situation is? I've thought of nothing else for the last year. We have only two options. Either we accept the fact that we can never love each other as a man and woman are meant to love, or we leave the country. Leaving would be . . . dangerous. But I think . . . I really think I would die without you." He paused and took a breath. "I am a good Muslim, and I will always be a good Muslim. I love this country. But if it makes no difference to Allah, I think I will take you as my wife."

Miriam felt her heart swell. Everything in her wanted to tell him why she was really going to Jiddah.

She reached a hand over and rested it on his arm. "Samir . . . I would leave Saudi Arabia to be with you even if all the king's guards were after me." A tear broke from her eye and she fought to control her emotions. "I want you to make me a promise."

"I would promise you my life," he said.

"Then promise me that you *will* marry me. No matter what happens, you will marry me."

"As there is no God but Allah, I swear it," he said.

She wanted to lift her veil and lean over and kiss him. She glanced around, saw that the closest car was nearly fifty meters back, and did just that. She kissed him quickly on the cheek and her lips felt on fire at the touch.

He blushed and glanced in the rearview mirror. His eyes suddenly grew misty and he swallowed. "If I had been born a prince," he said, "then I wouldn't bring any danger—"

"You *are* a prince! You will always be a prince. The only real danger I face is being separated from you," she said.

They drove toward the airport in a heavy silence of mutual admiration and desire, and Miriam thought her heart would burst with love.

9

SULTANA WAS WAITING by her husband's black Mercedes. A white Lear jet waited on the tarmac, door open and engines already running. Princes typically owned several jets—Sultana's husband owned six. The pilot, an American with whom Miriam had flown before, walked out to greet them, grinning wide. Then they were aboard and the door shut and Samir was gone.

Ten minutes later they were airborne.

Less than an hour later they landed at Jiddah International Airport, on the coast of the Red Sea. Shut off from the pilot, they had talked freely and completed the paperwork that gave Salman's permission for Miriam to travel alone and out of the country. Sultana's confidence fed Miriam's, which was growing with each step. The main terminal was filled with white and black, men and women. Mostly white. The ticket counters for Saudi Arabian Airlines stood to Miriam's right. She stood with Sultana in this sea of wandering men, cloaked in her abaaya, and a wave of doubt swept over her.

"What if Hillary doesn't remember me?" she asked. "Just because she taught Middle Eastern studies doesn't mean she'll be friendly—"

"Stop it before you talk your way out of this!" Sultana said. "There's a plane leaving in forty minutes. If you hurry, you can catch it."

Miriam looked around again. Her friend's hand rested on her arm. "Go with God. And tell them about us in America. Tell them the truth."

"What if my father has already discovered me missing—"

"If you don't go right now, I'm going to start screaming. Do you want that? Every policeman in the terminal will come running."

Miriam forced an anemic grin. "Okay, I'm going."

"Take care of yourself."

Miriam walked awkwardly to the counter, the small suitcase in her right hand and the vanity in her left. She stood in line and yet again was grateful for the veil. The very prison they forced her to wear was now her means of escape.

"May I help you?"

She stepped up to the counter. "Yes, one ticket to Riyadh, please."

The man eyed her curiously. "Papers."

She handed over the forged documents. It was highly unusual for a woman to travel alone, but the papers explained the emergency nature of her trip, expressly authorized by Salman bin Fahd. A cousin had taken ill in Paris and there was no male companion to accompany Miriam. Whatever the man behind the counter thought, he was in no position to question the son of the king.

Miriam declared no luggage, took her ticket, waited to board, and then entered the plane with the others. An hour later the plane landed in Riyadh, and Miriam thought again about aborting. She could still call Samir to pick her up, hurry back to the villa, and return the cash. Or she could catch another flight back to Jiddah and fly back with Sultana. And then what?

Then she would be forced to marry Omar.

Her feet carried her out to the main terminal. The ticket counters ran along the far wall, and for a moment she wasn't sure if they were the gates to heaven or to hell. She turned and walked toward them. *Just one foot in front of the other,* she thought. *Just carry through. You've gone too far to go back. If they refuse to sell you a ticket to Paris, you will fly back to Jiddah.*

But they didn't refuse to sell her a ticket.

Once again she climbed on board, muscles strung like wires under her abaaya. The large DC-10 lifted off and slowly turned to the northwest. Every time a steward walked down the cabin, she half expected him to approach her with the news. "I'm sorry, ma'am, but your foolish plan to run from your marriage to Omar has been found out. We are under orders to turn the plane around and return you to Riyadh, where a group of a hundred mutawa are waiting at the airport to beat you."

But again her fears failed to materialize. The plane landed. The passengers deplaned.

Miriam walked cautiously down the gangway, half expecting to see authorities there, armed and waiting. She paused ten feet from the terminal entrance, struggling to still her breathing. A young man stepped around her, staring. In her fear, she'd almost forgotten that she was wearing the abaaya. Now the fact smothered her like a black fog. She was dressed like an apparition.

She reached up, pulled off her veil, stuffed it up her sleeve, and forced herself forward, into the terminal.

Hundreds of colorfully dressed people strutted or milled about, and she was sure that most of them were looking in her direction.

Why's that person dressed like a ghost, Mommy?

Miriam scanned the crowd quickly, breath frozen. No religious police! Or were they hiding to avoid a scene? She located a bathroom sign up the hall and struck out for it with a new urgency, avoiding any eye contact with curious onlookers.

Is that Darth Vader, Mommy?

She had to relieve herself. Not her bladder, but her body. She had to shed this black cloak. A wedge of black caught her attention and she glanced up to see another woman dressed in an abaaya, fifty meters ahead. She still wore her veil and trailed her husband by several meters. A pang of empathy surged through Miriam's chest. She wanted to run up there and rip the veil from the woman's head.

Run! Run, woman! You can be free!

The sight emboldened her. Miriam barged into the bathroom and entered the handicapped stall. She threw off her abaaya in a frenzy, set the suitcase on the toilet, unlocked the latch, and flipped it open. One of the hundred-dollar stacks fell to the floor in her haste to pull out her jeans. She stared at it, suddenly horrified.

The rest room door opened and someone entered. Miriam bent

for the money, shoved it back under her clothes, and quietly closed the case. But she was afraid to engage the latch for the noise it would make.

Her fear wasn't reasonable, of course. No one was going to bust in here and grab her because they'd heard two latches clicking closed. What was she thinking?

The door opened and closed again. She was alone again.

She dressed as quickly as her trembling hands would allow. She'd thought to discard her abaaya in the waste bin by the sinks, but now she wondered if it might be better to flush it down the toilet.

But that would be impossible. The toilet would only flood!

Miriam scooped up the garment, grabbed her bags, and left the stall. She crossed to a large waste can, set her cases down, and summarily shoved her abaaya through the opening. She faced the mirror.

Her image stared back, face ashen, arms and neck bare. What was she doing?

She lifted her hand to the collar of her canary blouse. It froze there. She was naked! Oh dear, what did she think she was doing? She couldn't walk out there like this, baring her skin to the world! She should at least keep the abaaya as a backup.

Panicked, she reached into the trash, closed her hand around the robe, and pulled it out. Now she stood facing the mirror with a wadded black garment in her left hand, looking like a fool.

Miriam grunted and pushed the cloak back into the garbage bin. She covered her face with her hands. *Calm down, Miriam! You're acting like a child!*

The door opened. Her eyes sprang open. Light seeped through her fingers but she did not remove her hands. She'd frozen.

The woman walked past her and then stopped. "You okay?" she asked in French.

Miriam lowered her arms. "Yes," she said. *"Oui."*

The woman smiled and stepped into a stall.

Miriam turned back to the mirror. That was it. Just "You okay?" and "Yes." The woman was only concerned, not horrified. And Miriam had responded perfectly! She had frozen for a moment, true, but she had recovered quickly. *You okay? Yes!*

Yes, yes! I am okay.

It was then, standing in front of the mirror alone once again, that Miriam felt the first jolts of true freedom race through her blood. Jiddah had been Saudi Arabia. Riyadh had been . . . well, Riyadh was the *capital* of Saudi Arabia. And the DC-10 had been an extension of the Arabian Peninsula. Another prison, only in the sky.

But now she had shed her prison and pulled on blue jeans. Now she was a woman among a thousand other women who walked the terminal in complete anonymity and freedom. She stood transfixed by the thought. Only several hours earlier she'd walked the terminal in Riyadh like a shadow. Now she was in Paris, free! She wondered why more Saudi women didn't flee.

Maybe, Miriam, because they, like all people who possess a thimbleful of common sense, know that in the end they will be dragged back. Kicking and screaming, or beaten into submission, but back either way.

Miriam picked up her two bags, turned for the door, and walked out. The terminal bustled with activity, but none of it was focused on her, was it? None at all. She was just another woman. She'd been out of the country to Cairo, to Madrid, and to San Francisco, but never alone. There had always been a man along to tell her what to do. But now she was *just* a woman. Alone, without a master.

Miriam cleared immigration in ten minutes and immediately purchased a ticket to Chicago. Her destination was San Francisco, but as planned, she bought her tickets in single legs to slow any pursuit.

She spent an hour just walking the terminal, browsing the shops, feeling more alive than she could ever remember. She bought a mug with *Paris* etched in gold and she had no idea how much it cost—less than the hundred-dollar bill she handed the clerk. Didn't matter; she wanted a memento of her first truly free day.

The transatlantic flight to Chicago on United Airlines was a joy.

She flew first class, because the royal family always flew first class, and an escapee deserved nothing less. She watched an in-flight movie titled *Lord of the Rings,* full of magic and strange creatures that made her laugh. A bit scary in parts, but magical. Several passengers kept looking her way, and she finally apologized for her outbursts, unable to hide her grin. She wanted to tell them more. That she was escaping from Saudi Arabia and a horrible man named Omar who would have beaten her until she bled if he wanted to. So really they should be glad that she was sitting here laughing at trolls and goblins and strange creatures instead of marrying one. She wanted to say that, but she didn't.

She wasn't sure if it was the wine or the growing contentment, but she finally fell asleep.

A friend of Sultana's who lived in Spain had modified Miriam's student visa two years ago, insisting that it was good for four more years. For a few horrible minutes in the immigration line at O'Hare, Miriam began to have her doubts. But then she was smiling politely at an officer and walking past, stamped passport in hand.

She was in the United States. Wearing jeans and a canary blouse. Free to go where she liked. Carrying $500,000 in her bag. She nearly screamed out her thanks to Allah right then, fifty feet beyond the immigration line, but she settled for a muttered word of gratitude.

But by now, the wheels would be turning in Saudi Arabia. Sultana would be screaming her denials; Samir would be vowing ignorance and dying of worry . . . dear Samir. Salman would be pacing in rage, and the sheik would be wringing his hands. And Omar . . .

Omar had just learned that women weren't dogs after all. Women could do more than make babies and cook and please their masters. They could refuse men, for one thing.

A group of young men that she recognized from the flight passed her. On the plane the four talking heads had laughed too loudly and sworn regularly. Now she saw they wore baggy jeans that looked like they might fall around their ankles if they stood still. She'd never seen the like! The sight made her feel oddly vulnerable and alone here in this sea of humanity. She had been set free, yes, but into what kind of sea?

Miriam purchased another ticket, to San Francisco, and spent two anxious hours waiting for its departure, vacillating between the thrill of her accomplishment at getting this far and worry that she had escaped only to become lost and eventually dragged back to Saudi Arabia. What if Omar had somehow beaten the truth out of Sultana and was even now waiting for her in San Francisco?

Her flight landed in San Francisco at three o'clock in the afternoon, and Omar wasn't there. Then she truly was free, wasn't she? Jiddah, Riyadh, Paris, Chicago, and now San Francisco. She had really done it.

Miriam hailed a taxi at 3:30.

"Where to?" The driver looked Indian or Pakistani. She wondered if that made him Muslim or Hindu.

"Do you know where Berkeley is?" she asked.

"University of California at Berkeley? Yes, of course." His accent was British Indian and she loved it. She loved everything.

"Yes. There is a house on a street near the university. Could you take me there?"

"To where? Do you have the address?"

"No."

"Then I can't take you there, can I?"

"But you can take me to the university. I think I will remember from there, although the last time I had a driver who knew where to take me."

"But I've never been there, have I? So how can I take you where I've never been?"

He looked her over, smiled politely, then pulled into traffic. His name was Stan, he informed her, although she doubted it. Good enough, let him be American if he wanted to be. She was doing the same. Stan drove her north on 101 and then over the Oakland Bay Bridge—a bridge he clearly resented by the way he hurled words of frustration at the "fool drivers" who hindered his progress. She laughed, which got him laughing too, and by the time they exited University Avenue for a small side street she recognized, Stan was very friendly. Practically in love with her. She knew because his eyes said so. They were watching her and speaking in the same way Samir's eyes spoke to her the few times she hadn't worn her veil.

She decided then, riding in the yellow cab with Stan from India, that she would never again place a black sack over her head, as long as she lived. Allah had given her a beautiful face to be *looked* at like a flower, not hidden like a slab of moss.

Ten minutes later they found Hillary's house, three streets off University Avenue, as it turned out. Miriam paid Stan his fee and gave him an extra hundred dollars for his kindness. For affirming her.

Professor of Middle Eastern Studies Hillary Brackenshire (or Brokenshire, Miriam could not remember which) was a tall skinny woman with skin three times her age and gray, wiry hair that she hardly bothered to brush. She reminded Miriam of a walking thistle, the kind of woman impossible to forget. The professor had been fascinated with Miriam during Miriam's summer months at Berkeley, a natural reaction considering her field of study and her infatuation with Islam. She'd always considered Miriam's dissatisfaction with the Saudis' treatment of women naive, and said so. Otherwise they'd had many long and cordial conversations about Saudi culture.

Miriam had hidden her relationship with Hillary as a small act of rebellion even then. As far as she knew, only Sultana knew of it. Miriam desperately hoped the woman would be glad to see her. If not, she would go to Plan B, which was hardly more than starting out in a hotel on her own. She set her cases down, glanced around nervously, and knocked on the door.

Within ten seconds the knob rattled, and then the door swung in. Hillary stood there, dressed in a house robe, despite it being only five in the afternoon, looking as much the wrinkled porcupine as Miriam remembered.

"Yes? May I help you?"

Miriam hesitated. "Do you remember me?" Obviously not. "Miriam. I studied at Berkeley two summers ago."

Hillary's eyes widened. "Miriam? The princess?"

Miriam smiled. "Yes, the princess. Although I'm not sure that I'm a princess any longer."

"Come in! Come in." Hillary waved her in with a flapping hand. "My dear, it isn't every day a princess comes to my door." She saw the suitcase and glanced up at Miriam and then past her to the street. "Where's your ride?"

"I came in a taxi."

"Let me help you."

"Thank you."

Miriam entered and looked around at the rather humble setting. An ungainly papier-mâché bell sat on the mantel. Dried leaves glued together to form picture frames hung over a well-worn brown couch. The lampshades looked like they were made of pillowcases—the same yellow ones Miriam remembered from her last visit. Hillary, a self-proclaimed naturalist, did no better with her living room than she did with her hair, Miriam thought.

"What do you mean, you're not a princess?" Hillary asked, turning mid-room.

"What do I mean?" Miriam set her vanity case on the floor. "I mean that I've run from the House of Saud."

Hillary blinked. "You've . . . you've run? You can't *run* from the House of Saud! You *are* the House of Saud."

Miriam laughed lightly. "Yes, I suppose I am. But actually"—she looked around, strangely intoxicated by the simple freedom found in Hillary's mess—"actually, I've fled. Imagine that. I left Saudi Arabia and I've come to the United States. And I was wondering if you might help me for a few days."

She wanted Hillary to run and hug her, delighted with her courage. Instead, the professor just stared, unbelieving.

"That's impossible," Hillary finally said.

"Exactly! But I've done it!" Miriam felt her face broaden into a smile.

"No . . . I mean you can't run from who you *are!* You're a *princess,* for heaven's sake!"

It occurred to Miriam that Hillary really had no clue, professor of Middle Eastern studies or not. She should have been discouraged, but the joy of her success would have none of it.

"May I stay with you for a day or two?"

"Well . . . sure. What about the Hilton? Last time you had the whole top floor and now you want to stay with me?"

"Yes."

"Why on earth—"

"Last time I was a princess. Now I'm just a woman." She forced a quick grin and twirled as if she wore a dress. "See, a woman. I'll be out of your way tomorrow. The next day at the latest."

"Sure. Does the embassy know you're here?"

"I told you, I'm running. That includes the embassy."

"So then, you're a fugitive?"

Hillary's tone stopped Miriam. "Yes. Do you have a problem with that?"

"No. No, of course not. Your secret's safe with me. You're welcome to stay as long as you like." Hillary smiled wide. "As long as you promise to tell me all about it."

"I will."

"Good. Now, a princess must have tea. I have a wonderful herbal blend. China Moon. Yes?"

"Yes."

"Be right back. Have a seat." Hillary slid into the kitchen.

Miriam stood still, breathing deeply. Gratitude as she had never felt it rose through her chest until she didn't think she could hold it in. She kicked her shoes off, lifted both arms to the ceiling, and twirled around on the worn carpet, grinning from ear to ear. She hardly knew she was going to yelp before she did so—a full-blooded Arabian yelp with an ululating tongue.

From the kitchen, porcelain rattled and then crashed. Hillary had dropped the teacups. But Miriam didn't care. She only twirled and then bounced back into the soft sofa, laughing.

She was free.

10

OMAR BIN KHALID watched the great white hall through the study's cracked door. Greek columns supported an elegantly carved ceiling forty feet above the glassy marble floor. His father had paid a famous artist two million dollars to paint huge portraits of each Saudi king, five of them including the one he now planned to kill, Fahd. The canvases peered over the hall from the far wall like sentinels craning for a view of history's next chapter.

Clacking feet echoed through the towering chamber, but he couldn't actually see to whom they belonged yet. He'd called his father from a high-level meeting with the news less than five minutes ago, and now the sparks were going to fly. As well they should.

The woman had fled.

Khalid bin Mishal bin Abd al-Aziz turned the corner and swept into view, his arms swinging with each long step, his thobe swirling around his ankles. Omar eased the door closed, crossed the office suite, sat on the black leather sofa, and crossed his legs casually. The office was a study in the trappings of immense wealth. Not a single item, from the immense gold-layered desk to the quill pens in the drawers, could be bought on the open market. It was all custom-made. Even the thick white carpet had been woven of camel's hair for this room and this room alone.

The door slammed open and his father walked in. "What is the meaning of this?"

Omar stood and dipped his head in respect. Many sons in Saudi Arabia refused to show even their backs to their fathers out of respect. Rather limiting in Omar's mind and therefore unnecessary. He did respect his father, of course, although in fits and starts. Now was a good time for a start, he thought. Not only was his father likely to be the next king, but Omar knew that what he was going to ask of his father would not be easily granted.

"She left the country yesterday for Paris."

"Paris!" Khalid walked to the center of the room. "She left with whom?"

What Miriam had done still made no sense to Omar. She had actually fled his marriage. Why? A woman could hand a man no greater insult.

"On her own. She presented the airport authorities with forged travel documents. She was on a trip to Jiddah, took a flight to Riyadh, and then on to Paris."

"So then she is in Paris now?"

"No, we know from our sources that she's in the United States. California, where she attended school for a summer."

Khalid stared cold. "And her father? Salman?"

"Furious."

"So King Fahd knows," Khalid said, turning. "And if the king knows his precious daughter has fled, he will want to know why."

"That's hardly the point here," Omar said. "He will never find out the truth. I, on the other hand, have just been spit upon by a woman. My bride has—"

"She was not your bride, you fool! She was the means to the throne and nothing more. Without her, there *is* no throne."

"Without her marriage to me, you mean."

His father looked at him with contempt. "This is about Saudi Arabia and Islam, not your—" He made a spitting sound in disgust. "Where is the sheik?" he asked, sitting behind the large desk.

"I've talked to his people already. There is no deal without the marriage. Miriam's adoption binds him to King Fahd. Only a marriage would supersede that."

His father cursed. "We fight to return the country to principle, and now principle stands in our way. Living with the Shi'i will be like sleeping with the devil. We should kill the lot of them."

"Then kill them. But you are right: Without the wedding there is no throne."

"The woman has fled." Khalid shook his head and closed his eyes. "Of all the insolent . . ." His eyes opened, blazing. "Everything! We thought of every possibility. But this? Who could have thought a woman would have the spine, much less the brains, to flee? What kind of daughter has Salman raised? You see, this alone is why we must overthrow the throne! The king's own adopted daughter is asked *one* thing—to marry a prince—and she runs like a coward! Don't women know their place any longer?" His jaw muscles ground with fury.

"Apparently not. Which is my point," Omar said.

Khalid ignored him. "And what if King Fahd learns of our plan? What do you suppose then?"

"He would never have the proof."

"You're right. But if he even *suspected*."

Omar paused. "If I were him, I might kill the woman, prevent the marriage."

"But if the king killed the woman, his bond with the sheik would also be broken. The sheik would be furious." Khalid paused with a thought. "It might open him up to aligning himself with me without a marriage."

"Then kill the woman and blame it on the king," Omar said, thinking the end would be fitting.

"It might come to that. But the king would deny it as quickly as we would. We have no guarantees that the sheik would react to his daughter's death by taking sides with me. And I can't very well ask him, can I? If he even suspected my hand in her death, it would seal the matter in the king's favor."

Khalid pushed his chair back and walked to a window that overlooked a pond spotted with a dozen geese.

"So the woman is still our only option," he said. "She won't escape as easily as she might think."

"Then let me bring her back," Omar said.

"You?"

"Yes, me. You're right, this is about the throne. But I've been insulted as well. The least I can do is retrieve her and teach her manners."

"So now there is to be a marriage and *both* parties will be gone?" He turned back, hands clasped behind his back. "We'll send Assir and Sa'id."

"You don't trust me? I *trained* Assir and Sa'id. This woman has offended *me,* not Assir!"

"Then collect your dues when they drag her back. We can't risk your involvement. Not yet."

"And what if they don't bring her back?"

"She is a woman. They will."

"But if they don't. Then I will go."

Khalid walked for the door, jaw set. He spoke without turning. "Don't worry, Omar. One way or another, you will have your woman."

Hilal was a thin man with sharp features, the kind of man who might be nicknamed Knife or Edge for the way his bones pressed against his skin at his elbows and cheeks and nose. He was also the head of King Fahd's personal security and arguably as deadly as he looked. Hilal sat to the right of King Fahd, and Salman faced them both, feeling rather insignificant, despite the fact that he was the son of the king. He resented the fact.

"You tie my hands with all these restrictions for years, and now you wonder how I could have raised such a rebel? Please, Father."

The king frowned. "I told you to keep her in good health and to keep her from marrying until she was twenty-one. It was too much to ask?"

"She was a favored child," Salman protested. "You see, you spoil a child and this is what happens. Bring her back and I promise you, she will think twice about defaming our name again."

"We're beyond that. When she comes back, you will find her an appropriate husband and be done with her. She's nearly twenty-one."

Hilal lifted thin fingers to his beard and ran them gently through the black strands. The king looked at him with a raised brow. "Yes?"

"It's the question of why that bothers me, Your Highness. *Why* did she run?"

"Yes, I was going to ask that. Why did she run, Salman?"

Salman glared at his father. "You're accusing me?"

"No. Believe me, if you had done anything I disapproved of, I would know about it. I'm not blind, not even in your house."

The revelation gave Salman pause. He immediately wondered which of the servants was spying for his father. "Then your guess is as good as mine. She was a rebel from birth. What do you expect from Shi'i blood?"

Hilal cleared his throat. "She may have been a rebel, but she took great risks in leaving. According to the Berkeley professor who contacted the State Department, Miriam is persuaded that she barely escaped with her life. In my opinion she believed she was in grave danger, if not for her life, then for her freedom."

Salman made the connection immediately. "Marriage? She's not betrothed."

"No."

For a moment they were silent.

"Either way, I don't like it," Hilal said. "You know how important she is to our concerns. I would request to collect her myself, Your Highness. We must find out why she fled."

"She's only a woman who's run off to find her fantasies," Salman said. "You're overreacting."

"Am I? You should stick your head out of your palace now and then, my friend. Our kingdom isn't as stable as it once was. The public is growing restless—Al-Mas'ari and Bin Laden were not without influence."

"And what does Bin Laden have to do with my daughter? Please."

"There are others. The Shi'i minority, for example. Abu Ali al-Asamm is no longer a small man. His popularity has been fed by men like Al-Mas'ari and Bin Laden. By name he may represent only the Shi'i minority, but ideologically he represents a groundswell that has revolution in their minds. Miriam is our connection to Sheik Al-Asamm. Or had you forgotten?"

Salman felt small in the cutthroat's presence. Why did his father allow Hilal to speak like this to his own son?

"In many ways," Hilal continued, "the future of Saudi Arabia rests in the hands of Miriam. If the militants were to learn of her adoption, we would find ourselves looking at more trouble than we are ready for."

"Then you should kill her," Salman said.

"Please," the king said. "She is our link to Al-Asamm's loyalty. Are you listening? Killing her would undo what I set out to do by adopting her in the first place."

"Yes, but you don't know Miriam as I do. She is a wild one. What will you do if she marries an American?"

"You think American men marry the first woman who walks in front of them?" the king said. "Where do Saudis get this notion that America is one large brothel? I believe my own father was more interested in brothels than the Americans. The West is not our enemy; our own *subjects* are our enemy." He looked away, disgusted. "We will have her back in the time it takes to fly over and collect her."

"I wouldn't underestimate her spirit of rebellion," Salman said. "It took some thinking to break into my safe, and it took even more courage to steal the money. She was always the aggressive kind. I've never trusted her. And if you ask me, Samir was involved in her escape—I always thought she had him bewitched."

Hilal looked up sharply. "Samir? We questioned him thoroughly. He knew nothing. What do you mean, bewitched?"

Salman hesitated, remembering the occasional glances he'd seen the driver give Miriam. "I mean that they spent time together. Alone. In the car, of course, but if you hadn't insisted I keep him, I would have let him go years ago."

"You never spoke of a relationship between them," Hilal said.

"Why should I? He's only a driver."

"He's Al-Asamm's man, you idiot!"

"Watch your tone, Hilal," the king cautioned.

Salman stood. "The sheik's man? You've allowed a *Shi'i* into my house?"

"Miriam is the *daughter* of a Shi'i," the king said.

"And I've never liked her. What if Sheik Al-Asamm has something up *his* sleeve? Have you thought about that? What if your precious Miriam is part of *his* schemes?"

"Then Miriam will die," Hilal said immediately.

They looked at each other in silence.

"We've always known that the sheik is not without his options," the king said. "He may try to undermine us, but he had that option before our agreement as well. In fact, he was pursuing it. If he uses his daughter as a pawn to do so again, we will be forced to kill her."

"So you *are* willing to cut your bond of loyalty with him," Salman said.

"If his daughter is part of a plot to bring me down, my boy, his loyalties are gone already," the king said.

They sat in silence for another brief moment. "So," Hilal said, "I will contact the Americans and leave immediately."

"The Americans will help you?"

"We don't need them; we know where she is. We've already arranged to pick her up. But if we did need them, I'm confident they would help us. Whatever you may say about the Americans, you can't say that they're idiots. They know what would happen to the Middle East if the balance of power were to shift in Saudi Arabia. They will bend over backward to keep the House of Saud in power. The fate of one woman is nothing in the large picture."

For the first time since entering this room, Salman began to see. A soft smile crossed his face. Miriam really had no clue, did she?

11

THE FACULTY CLUB may have been one of Berkeley's oldest buildings, but it was also one of its most stately. A good enough reason for the faculty to claim it for their club, Seth thought. Tonight they had come out in droves, and it had more to do with the food and the fact that APS had flown in last year's recipient of the same award, Dr. Galvastan from Harvard, than his own appearance. Black gowns and jackets filled the hall, and Seth had followed suit. He'd rented a tuxedo and combed his hair, and on a night such as this, it felt good to blend a little.

Problem was, as soon as any of the faculty recognized him, they sidled over to offer their two bits.

"Seth! There you are. Lovely to see you." Grin. "Here's the official schedule for this evening."

"Well done, Mr. Border. You've made Berkeley proud."

"Congratulations, young man. We're so proud of you."

"You'll make a good professor yet. Good job, man."

These were invariably followed by a look at his attire and a pointed smile that spoke a self-righteous satisfaction. *About time, boy.* It took him fifteen minutes to work his way past enough of them to find breathing space in the Great Hall.

He paused next to the Kerr Dining Room, poked his head in, and scanned the room. Round tables covered in white linens dotted the floor, each one candlelit and impeccably set with antique silverware. The room boiled with a gentle hubbub, two hundred heads of hot air expanding the significance of their small worlds. It was a wonder there was any oxygen left in the place.

Seth slipped in through the side entrance and headed for the long table they'd set up at one end for the guest of honor and other notables.

"Seth."

He turned to the low voice. It was Dr. Harland, holding a drink.

"Glad you could make it," Harland said with a twinkle in his eyes.

"Evening, Professor."

"They've come in force for you, haven't they? You okay?"

"Never better," Seth said.

A faculty member he didn't recognize walked by, stuck out her hand, and offered her congratulations. Seth took the hand and nodded.

Harland took a sip from his glass. "I see you dressed the part."

"I'm here to make an impression, right?"

Someone slid past his back, and he turned to see a woman with hair going every which way but down. Professor of Middle Eastern Studies Hillary Brackenshire. He knew her because of his interest in the region and the single class he'd suffered through under her instruction. She turned to see whom she'd brushed, and her face reddened.

"Seth! Congratulations. You must be *very* proud!"

"Hello, Dr. Brackenshire. Thank you."

She opened her mouth as if to say more, but then thought better of it and just smiled. It wasn't until she turned to leave that Seth saw the young woman standing several feet to her right. Her round haunting eyes peered into his for a moment, and then she turned with Hillary and walked away. She wore a white dress fitted to a slender frame. Her hair hung below her shoulders, jet black and shiny. Arabic, if he were to guess. Mideastern at least.

"I haven't seen her before," Harland said, following Seth's gaze.

"I haven't seen half these people before."

Harland nodded and sipped his drink. "Please tell me you've given some thought to our little discussion."

"You know me, Professor. I always give whatever you say a little thought. In this case much thought."

"And?"

"And"—he nodded at a passing professor—"I think you're right. I should finish my formal education."

"They've brought the big guns in; I would tread carefully."

Seth ignored the comment. He'd thought about telling Marisa to can the dance—had actually picked up the phone an hour ago to put an end to it.

But he hadn't. "Remember the pigeon that hit your office window?" he asked.

"What about it?"

"I thought I saw it before it hit."

A waiter passed by and Harland set his empty glass on the tray. "The mind's a curious thing," he said.

"It happened again."

"You saw another pigeon hit my window?"

"No. I saw a girl fall before she fell."

"Interesting. It happens."

"Yeah. Well, it happened all right. In living color."

"Hmm." Harland obviously thought nothing of it. He was right, it did happen. People saw things they'd swear they'd seen before, despite knowing they hadn't.

They walked toward the podium. Baaron was up there already, and his glance met Seth's.

"Just in case things do go badly tonight, I want you to know something," Seth said. "When I think of a man I would like to call my father, your face comes to mind. You're the kind of person who builds my faith in a benevolent God despite our differences on the matter. I owe you my gratitude and I never take your advice lightly."

"I would gladly accept the position were it not filled."

"It isn't filled. I once knew a man, a sperm donor who brought me into this world and then made sure I regretted it. I don't know anyone I would call a father."

"Then as your newly adopted father let me reiterate my advice. Be nice tonight, Seth."

Seth stopped by the end table. Baaron was dinging his fork against a crystal wineglass by the podium. The heads began to turn his way.

"Have I ever *not* been nice, Father?"

Seth stepped up on the platform. A spontaneous clap spattered and then swelled across the dining room. Seth gave them a quick bow and walked for his seat. The guests took their seats and Baaron began his spiel.

Dr. Galvastan stood from his chair next to Seth's and spoke quietly. "Well done, Mr. Border. Well done. It's genuinely an honor to finally meet you. I've heard your name floating around Harvard for a couple of years now."

Seth took his hand. "Thank you. Probably the source of all those UFO reports in the region." He winked. "Floating names are often mistaken as alien ships."

"Yes. Yes, of course." Galvastan blinked.

Seth took his seat and waited while Baaron droned on. They looked like a convention of penguins, he thought—seated in nice round circles and dressed in black and white. Maybe he was too hard on them. The two hundred or so minds gathered here represented more academic achievement than some entire countries. That said something. It wasn't their fault that they were stuck in their narrow ruts. And who was to say that his mind really saw things any more clearly than theirs? Sure, he saw things by rote that most of them were incapable of seeing at all. The relationship between simple facts, for example. How numbers worked and how logical constructs formed on the most fundamental levels. But did that make him better than these penguins smiling up at him?

It occurred to him that what he was about to do represented its own kind of narrowness. A cold sweat broke out on his neck and he took a sip of water. Maybe he should call off Marisa after all. It wasn't too late—he could skip their entrance cue.

"So, without further boring you with the details of our institution's educational prowess, I present to you the man we've all gathered to honor." Baaron turned his way. "Seth Border."

Applause filled the room and Seth stood to his feet. *Here we go.* The applause died and complete silence settled for the first time.

The girls were to come out when he said *Baaron.* It would be in the middle of his speech, he'd told Marisa, and he would say it with great hoopla. Like an introduction.

Seth stepped behind the podium and looked out at the eager faces. The Middle Eastern studies professor, Hillary, stood near the back and slipped into the hall with the Arabic woman. Odd time for a bathroom break, he thought.

The words of his speech sat in his mind like crows on a telephone line. "Thank you for those kind comments," Seth said into the microphone. His voice echoed loudly. "There's no one I would be more delighted to be introduced by than Dr. Gregory Baaron."

A door banged open to his right.

"Give me a *B!*"

Seth jerked. It was Marisa and she stood with one fist over her head, scantily clad in black. She looked at him and winked.

"B!" a chorus of voices rang from his left. He turned. Five girls swirled from three doorways, dressed in a cross between cheerleaders and burlesque dancers. Seth had suggested racy; they were indeed racy. A few nervous chuckles rolled through the auditorium. A few stunned gasps.

They were also early.

"Give me an *A!*"

"A!"

They swung their hips and flashed coy smiles and honed in on the table to Seth's right where Baaron sat, tomato-red already.

The chant continued, but Seth shut it out. For the first time in a long while he was at a total loss. He should do something—encourage them, discourage them, swing his hips with them, stop them in outrage. Anything. But he couldn't. He looked over at Samuel Harland's table and saw the man shaking his head. The girls had formed a line in front of Baaron and were definitely looking more Las Vegas than Lawrence Welk. The place fell silent except for the girls' chant. He should do something. He should definitely do something.

But he couldn't. His mind had gone blank.

The image hit him then, like a Polaroid shoved in front of his eyes. Like the pigeon in Harland's office.

A gun. A browned hand with white knuckles. A face twisted in rage. Another face screaming in pain, with viselike fingers squeezing its cheeks together.

Seth gasped.

He was aware that some of the faculty were staring at him, but what was happening here, in this room, felt distant to him. Why was he seeing this other—

His field of vision broadened crazily, and he saw that the face belonged to a woman. To the Arabic woman he'd seen with Hillary. She was in the women's bathroom—he knew that because of the stick figure on the door. She was in the women's bathroom, and a man clenched her face with one hand and waved a gun at it with the other.

And then the image was gone.

A dancer was climbing onto Baaron's table in a way that might have turned Seth himself red a few seconds ago, but the moment played like a sideshow. His heart was hammering, but it was from the images that had just played through his mind, not the brunette's sultry approach to Baaron.

For one lost moment Seth stood dumb. Was it possible that the Arabic woman really was in the bathroom with a man who held a gun? That the other two incidents hadn't been strange tricks played by his mind but actual precognition?

The images suddenly crashed through his mind again. This time the man's hand hit the woman's face.

It struck him then that he'd been able to keep Maggie from falling when he'd seen her trip before she'd tripped. What if . . .

Seth whirled from the podium, took two long steps to his right, vaulted the head table, and ran for the hall, leaving the penguins gawking. Let them. He had not only lost his stomach for the dancers, but he had to understand what was happening to his mind. And if what he was seeing was real . . .

Seth sprinted for the women's bathroom, slid to a stop in front of the door with the skirted stick figure, paused for one last moment, and then slammed through.

"Hey!" he shouted.

His voice echoed back at him. A long mirror showed a man dressed in black and white with blond hair, hands spread like a gunslinger. That would be him. He glanced around. No urinals—stalls only. The bathroom was empty. The swinging door hissed shut behind him.

"May I help you?"

Seth spun to his right. The Arabic woman stood in the doorway of the last stall, eyes wide.

Seth just stared at her, confused.

"This is the ladies' toilet," the woman said.

He looked to his left and slowly relaxed.

"Hillary?" the woman yelled. She was calling for the professor.

Seth looked at her again. "No one's here."

The woman stepped out of the stall tentatively. "Hillary!"

"I told you, no one's here."

"Where is Hillary? What have you done?"

"Nothing." Something was gnawing at the back of Seth's mind. "I . . . I thought something was wrong, that's all." He looked around one last time. "I guess I was wrong."

"Hillary was just here."

He heard the light sound of feet, and it occurred to him that Hillary's absence might be a problem. He spun around and pulled the bathroom door open a crack.

He saw two things at once. The first was Hillary, disappearing around the corner at the far end of the hall. The second was a dark-skinned man walking for the bathroom, head down, now just twenty feet away.

He knew in that moment that this man was going to beat the snot out of this woman behind him. That's what he'd seen!

Seth didn't have time to analyze what had happened.

He simply moved with an instinct bred through a decade of beatings at home.

He released the door, leapt for the woman, grabbed her arm, and pulled her toward one of the stalls. It never occurred to him that she might not want to go with him.

She screamed, and he ducked, startled. Panicked, he threw his free hand over her mouth. "Please! I'm helping you here! Shut up or you'll get us *both* hurt!"

Not exactly the most comforting words in the middle of a mugging. She tried to scream again, through his fingers, but he managed to muffle her voice. Time was running out. He tried to drag her, but she was having none of it.

"Stop it!" he whispered frantically. "Someone's coming for you!" He glanced at the door. A brief question skipped through her eyes. Seth lifted her from her feet and crashed through the stall door. The toilet lid was open. He hefted the woman up on top of the toilet bowl and let her go—all but her mouth.

She teetered, struggling for balance on the narrow ceramic ring.

He snatched a finger to his lips. "Shhh! Please, you have to trust me," he whispered. "There's someone coming . . ."

The door to the bathroom opened.

It occurred to Seth that he had accomplished nothing by dragging her in here. They were sitting ducks, for heaven's sake! One look under the doors and the gunman would see his feet!

His heart pounding like a hammer, Seth let her mouth go, grabbed the toilet-paper holder for balance, and eased up onto the seat, pushing her back in the process. Now they both stood on the toilet with a bowl of blue water between their feet. She must have understood his concern, because she kept her mouth shut.

Still, only a deaf person could have missed the thumping that had come from the fourth booth. This fact was not lost on Seth.

He pressed against the woman, mind scrambling. Solving mind-boggling mathematical equations was one thing; being stuck with a strange woman on a toilet seat was another thing altogether.

Her hair was in his mouth; the booth smelled like perfume; she was breathing hard and her breath was hitting his neck. These abstract distractions skipped through his mind in the space of a single heartbeat. He had to get her out of here. Thinking that the man would simply pass by the noisy booth because there were no feet on the floor was absurd.

Seth's back was to the door. He shifted his feet to turn around. The woman suddenly teetered to her left. She threw her left hand out and it thumped loudly on the stall wall. A loud *plop* sounded in the toilet water.

Seth froze and then looked down. A white shoe bobbed in the blue water. Her white shoe. He'd knocked her foot off its perch, and her shoe had fallen into the water.

But it was the sound, not the shoe, that raced through his head. He looked into her eyes, wide and wrinkled. Somewhere between horror and fury.

That was it. They had to get out of this deathtrap now.

Seth spun and jumped to the floor. The stall door was much closer than he remembered, and he slammed into it. The whole thing shook with his weight. The woman landed behind him, but as he straightened, she fell backward, the toilet at her knees. She instinctively grabbed his waist and together they toppled onto the bowl. Into the bowl.

It was time to abandon secrecy. "Let go!" Seth said.

"Get off me! What are you doing?"

"I'm trying to . . ."

He shoved himself up and was rewarded with a grunt from her in the process. "Sorry."

He pulled her up. The shoe floated in the blue water like a sailboat. Without thinking, he shoved his hand into the bowl and snatched the shoe up. Clutching the dripping shoe, he jerked the stall door open and stumbled out.

They spilled into the bathroom and pulled up three feet from an Arabic man, who stared at them in disbelief. Seth knew beyond a doubt now—this was the man he'd seen in that flash he'd had. And if this man was indeed real, then his intention to hurt the girl must also be real. *Make no mistake about it, Seth boy. This is a bad dude.*

The woman uttered a cry of horror. The man's attention shifted to her, and Seth saw the change in his eyes immediately.

Seth did the only thing that made any sense. He tossed the toilet-watered shoe at the man, grabbed the woman's hand, and ran for the door. The man cursed in Arabic behind them.

Seth shoved the door open. It thudded into flesh and bone, and someone yelped. Seth yanked the girl through the door and sprinted down the hall toward the back exit. At the corner he glanced back and saw another Arabic man climbing to his feet.

"Hurry!" Seth said, the woman's hand tightly in his own. Back around the corner the sound of running feet pounded on the carpet.

Seth leaned into the exit bar. Then they were out the back, breathing hard and facing the cool night.

"This way," he said, cutting to his right. She seemed eager enough to follow now. Something about seeing the men back there had done wonders to her attitude. She pulled him to a stop, reached for her foot, and yanked off the remaining shoe.

He released her hand and they ran full tilt, past Wurster, past the Hearst Museum, across Bancroft Way, and onto College Avenue.

"Stop!"

It was the woman, just behind him. He slowed to a side skip and then to a halt. She was heaving, hands on knees. Seth looked past her to the street they'd crossed. Nothing.

"Where are you taking me?" she panted.

Good question. The sounds of a commotion drifted from the direction of the Faculty Club. He thought it was more likely Marisa and company than the two Arabic men. Either way, he felt exposed out here on the street.

"We have to get off the street. My car's over here."

She stood and walked up to him. Her white dress was torn along one thigh. Now that he thought about it, he had heard the sound of ripping cloth on their exit.

"Your car?" She glanced back. "Please, I have a friend who I have to find. We have to—"

"Hillary? Trust me, Hillary is not your friend."

The woman faced him, eyes round in the streetlight. "Why?"

"I think she led those men to you."

"How do you know this?"

"I just do. I also know that those two men weren't planning on dancing with you." He looked past her again. Still nothing. "We got lucky back there, but if they find us debating here in the street, I doubt it will go so smoothly."

"And I suppose you think dragging me through a bathroom *is* smooth?"

He glanced over her shoulder. Still clear. "Please, let's get off the street." He started for the parking lot and she followed, glancing back.

They cut across the parking lot and came to a brown '83 Cougar, rust conveniently hidden by the shadows. His hands shook as he twisted the key for his door. He looked at the parking lot entrance one last time. Still no sign of pursuit. He opened the door and slid in.

What are you doing, Seth? You have absolutely no idea what you're doing. He gripped the wheel and shook his head. The passenger door wasn't opening. He looked out the windshield and saw the woman standing by the hood, arms crossed, chewing on a nail. He cranked his window down and stuck his head out.

"Get in."

He pulled his head back in and rolled the window up.

She wasn't moving.

Please, dear lady, I'm not your enemy here.

This time he climbed out. "Look, I'm just trying to help here. You think *I* understand this?"

"No, I *don't* think you understand this. And you'll forgive me if it gives me some concern. A man who has shoved me into the toilet and then dragged me down the street is now asking me into his car. I might have taken my chances with the mutawa. How do you know about Hillary?"

"Those were mutawa?"

She just looked at him.

"You're from Saudi Arabia?"

She hesitated. "How did you know?"

"You speak perfect English with an English accent. The Saudi religious police are after you. Simple deduction."

She closed her eyes and breathed deeply through her nose.

"You're on the run," he said. "You've fled Saudi Arabia and now someone in your country wants you back." Her eyes flashed open. "Which means you're someone important. And since no woman is important in Saudi Arabia, you must be royalty. A princess on the run. I'm surprised you made it out of the country."

"How could you know so much about Saudi Arabia?"

He shrugged. "I know about Islam. Anyone who knows Islam knows about Saudi Arabia. Either way I know enough to know that if I'm right, you're in a world of hurt. These guys didn't fly halfway around the world to give up."

"A world of hurt? If you would speak proper English, it would be better for me."

Her demand took him off guard. "Sorry. It's slang, and it means your world must hurt. Or something similar. Not exactly your *world—*"

"I'm not an imbecile," she said. "I get the picture."

"Get the picture?" he said with a grin. "Where did you learn that?"

"You think I've never been to America?"

"So. A Saudi princess who has fled her country, speaks perfect English, understands a few colloquialisms, and is in a world of hurt."

She looked at him for a moment. "Yes. I am a princess and I have fled my country. My name is Miriam."

"Miriam." There was something appealing about her, Seth thought. She was . . . different. "Will you please get in the car, Miriam?" He looked around. The lot was empty.

"What is your name?"

"Seth. I'm sorry—"

Seth's horizon blurred and he froze. He could still see the parking lot, but his mind clouded on the edges. And then he saw two Mercedes driving down two parallel streets. And he saw that the two streets covered the only two exits of this parking lot.

He blinked and his mind returned to normal.

Seth fought a sudden relapse into panic. He jerked his head to the right exit and then the left. Nothing. He took two steps around the hood for Miriam, but he immediately turned back for his own door. What was he going to do, drag her in like he had back at the stall?

"Get in the car! Quick, get in the car!"

She still didn't move. If he couldn't get her to move now . . .

He slammed his fists on the hood and yelled each word distinctly. "Get—in—the—car!"

She scrambled for the door and tugged. It was locked.

Seth dove in, unlocked her door, and twisted the ignition key. The motor growled to life. Their doors pounded shut.

"What is it? Why are you yelling at me?"

"They're coming! I'm sorry, I didn't mean to yell, but they're just—" He craned for a view of the exit and saw that the coast was clear. *Okay, baby, just sneak on out. Maybe this time you're wrong. Intuition can only be so good, right?*

He grabbed the stick shift with a trembling hand and nudged it into drive. The car eased out into the lane, lights still off.

"How do you know all this?" she asked. "Where are we going?"

"Shhh. Please."

Come on, baby . . .

The tires crunched over the asphalt, loud in the night. His hands pressed into the wheel, white in the knuckles. How *do* you know all this, Seth? The Cougar rolled toward the exit.

Yeah, baby. Yeah, we got it. We—

Lights glared in the mirror. He glanced up. Twin lamps blazed toward them from the back entrance. Seth slammed the pedal to the floor. The Cougar surged forward, roared past the last three cars in the lot, and shot out into the street.

Another set of lights, the ones from the second Mercedes he'd seen in his mind's eye, glared through Miriam's window on a collision course. They would have collided too—broadside at thirty miles an hour—if Seth had kept his cool and yanked the wheel around to escape the Mercedes. The sudden change in direction would have slowed the Cougar enough for the onrushing car to end things right there. But Seth didn't turn the wheel—he froze like a stone behind the wheel, unable to turn as he should have.

The Cougar flew across the street in a fly of sparks, missed a parked car on the passenger's side by inches, pounded over the curb with enough force to bend both rims, and roared over the lawn of the U.C. Berkeley Art Museum.

"Turn! Turn, turn!" Miriam yelled.

They were zeroing in on a thick maple. Seth wrested control of the beast back and spun the wheel. The Cougar laid a broad swipe of the lawn bare and shot onto Durant Avenue, where Seth managed to swing the car into the right lane.

But now the Mercedes was on Durant as well, back on his tail.

"Hold on, baby! Ha!"

Seth floored the Cougar, and the 454 muscled them down the street with enough acceleration to snap their heads back into the seats. Strange—he was terrified, the cold sweat on his neck said so clearly enough. But he was also alive, wasn't he? Really alive. Like being airborne in a twenty-foot wave with foam roaring two feet overhead. He'd almost forgotten why he loved surfing. Clive Masters might have been onto something after all.

Miriam was making a small whimpering sound. She twisted in her seat, saw the pursuit, and became a different woman in the flip of a switch.

"Faster!"

"We have a red light—"

"Drive faster! Faster."

"Faster," he repeated and nailed the throttle. They split the intersection of Durant and Bowditch at a good sixty miles an hour. The Mercedes slowed for the light, and then crept through.

"Fast enough?"

She didn't respond.

By the time they reached Shattuck, the Mercedes's lights were weaving in and out of view. By the time they hit Interstate 80, the lights were gone.

They headed south, and Seth had no idea where they were going. They just headed south.

"They're gone," Seth said.

She looked back. "Yes."

"Now what?"

She looked over at him, face white with strain. "Maybe they will come again."

"Maybe you should tell me what's really going on," he said.

"Maybe you should tell me how you knew," she said.

How he knew. He didn't have the faintest. But that didn't matter. What did matter was that he *had* known. He couldn't shake the thought that he was meant to be here, riding down the freeway with a woman named Miriam from Saudi Arabia.

And even if he wasn't necessarily *meant* to be here, in some strange way he *wanted* to be. Because she needed him; because he had just felt his blood flowing, really flowing, for the first time in years; because his mind had pulled a couple of very cool tricks back there, and it had been the third time in three days.

And then there was the fiasco back at the Faculty Club.

Yes, he belonged here. At least for the moment.

"You first," he said.

12

HILAL STARED OUT THE FLOOR-TO-CEILING windows of the Regency's twenty-third floor, overlooking the millions of lights along the San Francisco Bay. A strange blend of emotions crowded his chest—the same as every time he visited the United States—a mixture of hatred and sadness that left him empty and sick. Somehow Europe and Asia were different. He'd seen plenty of large cities full of excess, beginning with Riyadh, which in many ways bled more excess than the rest put together. If the princes were known for anything, it was spending money. No, it wasn't the wealth rising from San Francisco's coastline that bothered Hilal.

It was the unlimited freedom of every citizen to bask in this wealth that bothered him. Nowhere else in the world did as many people have as much as in America. Perhaps Singapore was an exception. But the citizens of Singapore paid the price of personal freedom with rules. Rules for every imaginable conduct, from chewing gum to smoking, not unlike the rules found in the traditions that governed his own country.

But here in America, the people enjoyed both immense wealth and unparalleled freedom, and the injustice of it disgusted him. The combination was what made America great. The mutawa would accuse him of straying from the edicts of the prophet and coddling to the infidels for such a statement, and in some ways they would be right. But even Mohammed had understood that certain rules must be bent for the sake of political gain. How many times had he changed his own rules for political gain?

Unfortunately, only a few truly understood that Saudi Arabia faced political extinction if she did not adapt to the changing world. Fortunately, King Fahd was one of those. He understood that marching through the desert cutting off the heads of those who refused to profess allegiance to Mohammed was no longer acceptable in this modern world. Never mind that his Islam had always swung the sword to broaden its borders. Never mind that Fahd's own father, Aziz, had spent his days swinging the sword to establish the kingdom. Never mind that the Qur'an itself called for the destruction of the infidels. Things had changed. Those *infidels* were now the strongest power on earth, and they showed no signs of weakening. Mohammed's sword may have given birth to Islam, but today the prophet would surely put away the drums of war and take up a song of peace for the sake of preserving Islam. An advisable tactic when facing such an immense enemy. In fact, Mohammed himself had once called the Christians and Jews his friends—until he grew an army large enough to bend their wills. So now it was time to reverse the course and return to the peace the prophet first taught.

The militants needed to put more emphasis on Mohammed's example and less on his words. If they refused, they would be the end of Islam.

Hilal turned from the window and poured himself a scotch. It felt good to be in a country where he didn't have to break the law to do what he did normally. He threw the drink back and swallowed.

A black nine-millimeter Browning lay beside the briefcase on the bed. His contact had delivered the weapon to him an hour earlier with a few other items he'd requested. Another benefit of freedom.

Six hours earlier he arrived and learned that the woman had fled Berkeley. Sorting out the details of what transpired at the university had not been easy. Evidently, two Arabic men had passed themselves off as Hilal and an embassy associate and attempted to take her. This meant that someone else valued the sheik's daughter as much as the king did and knew Hilal was on his way to collect her.

He closed his eyes. They had overestimated the professor's competence. Trusting a woman with such a delicate matter had been a mistake in the first place. Not that they had an alternative.

There was only one reason any Saudi would go to such lengths to intercept Miriam before he reached her. They needed her for their own gain. There was only one way to gain from a woman, and that was through marriage. The mixing of bloodlines. Someone besides the king was after Sheik Abu al-Asamm's allegiance. Which meant that someone wanted power over the king.

But who? Who would have the intelligence to know of his trip and the woman's whereabouts?

Wouldn't it be ironic if the kingdom's fate was decided by a woman rather than a man? Of course, a single bullet to Miriam's head would decide everything.

The shrill tone of the phone interrupted his thoughts, and he picked it up. "Yes."

"Good evening, Hilal."

"General Mustafa. It would be best for me to call you on your cell phone. Please keep it with you—I've taken care of security. Every six hours, as requested by the king."

"Of course."

Hilal paused. His first call to Saudi Arabia had been directly to the king, but he couldn't interrupt the king every six hours to update him on this mess. General Mustafa was blood brother to the king and the head of intelligence. If they couldn't trust him, they could trust no one.

"She escaped with an American—a student named Seth Border."

"So, the authorities are cooperating."

"Locally, yes. I'm scheduled to meet with the State Department tomorrow afternoon in Los Angeles. Meanwhile the local police have begun a search for the car. We believe she's headed south—several complaints were called in from other motorists. Evidently the man she's with thinks he's in a racecar."

"Don't all Americans?" The general chuckled.

Hilal found no humor in the statement. "The police say they will have the car by morning. With any luck I will be on a plane back to Riyadh tomorrow night."

"Good. Then this should be a simple matter."

"Perhaps. Perhaps not. It bothers me that she managed to escape the two men who tried to intercept her."

There was a pause. "You going after them?"

"I have a car; I have a police scanner. Freedom has its advantages, General. I'll call back in six hours."

Hilal hung up the phone, picked up his briefcase, checked the room by habit, and left for the garage.

Omar paced across the carpet, slapped the flat of his palm against his father's desk, and stormed back.

"I told you! I should have gone. Now these idiots have let her run!"

"These idiots were *your* men," Khalid said.

"And now there's an American helping her. I told you she would marry the first fool who made eyes at her. She's a whore!"

"She may be a whore, but she just happens to be a very important whore." Khalid's voice held an edge that Omar had learned to fear, a biting tone as easily felt as heard.

Khalid settled back in his chair. "The fact that Hilal himself has gone means the king suspects something."

"The king always suspects something. His days are numbered and he knows it."

They faced each other in silence for an endless moment.

"Who is this American?" Omar asked.

"Just a student. Someone who came into the bathroom at the wrong time."

"That's what they said? They were fooled by a man who just happened to walk into the women's bathroom by mistake?"

"No. They said the man seemed to know they were coming, but we both know that's not possible."

"What's his name?"

Khalid gave his son a lingering look. They both knew that no man alive was better equipped to deal with the situation than Omar. He knew how to kill, and he knew how to put a man in a position to kill.

"Seth," Khalid said. "Seth Border. That's all your men were able to uncover before they left the scene. Evidently the police showed up in some force."

"That would be Hilal's doing. By now he's working with the authorities." Omar sat and stared at the man who would be the next king of Saudi Arabia. In the end, men like his father always depended on men like him, didn't they? On killers and enforcers of the law. True strength was always found in the sword. Even the prophet had known that.

"I can tell you that no idiot escaped from my men. Whoever this American is, underestimating him would be a mistake," Omar said.

Khalid stood, walked to the window, and crossed his arms. He took a deep breath. "You will need to marry her in America if you can," he said. "With Hilal involved, bringing her back could be a problem. We have to move quickly." Khalid faced him. "And if she does not cooperate, then she must be silenced."

"Killed."

"Either marry her or kill her. But we can't have her telling the world stories that put our necks on the line."

Omar grunted. He wanted to reiterate the foolishness of not sending him in the first place, but he'd made the point already. Khalid could only be pushed so far.

The phone rang. Khalid picked it up and spoke quietly.

The decision was now behind them: Omar would leave immediately. He would track down the woman and the American with her, and if he had to, he'd kill them both. Not before marrying the woman, of course. No, he would have his bride either way. Hilal might pose a problem—the man had always been a snake. Perhaps it would be best to leave him in a gutter as well. If Hilal knew the truth about Miriam—and there was no guarantee he didn't at least suspect it—he wouldn't hesitate to try to kill whatever came between him and protecting the king.

Khalid dropped the phone in its cradle.

"General Mustafa?" Omar asked.

"Yes."

"And?"

"Hilal called ten minutes ago. They've already identified the student's car and expect to take Miriam into custody by morning. She's headed south."

Omar felt a chill walk down his back. "By morning. The soonest I can be there is tomorrow afternoon."

"Yes, I know."

"And what do you propose to do about this problem? If Hilal gets to Miriam before I do—"

"Then you'll have to kill him," Khalid said. His face was red, and a blood vessel stood out on his temple like a worm working its way toward his eye.

Omar stood and walked for the door. He stopped halfway and turned around. "There's no question about General Mustafa's loyalty?"

"No."

"How often will Hilal call him?"

"Every six hours. We will know what he knows before the king does."

Omar frowned. "Tell my men to wait for me in Los Angeles. Keep them apprised of Hilal's progress."

"Los Angeles?"

"I'll call from New York; if there's any change, I'll make necessary adjustments then." He paused. "In the meantime it might be helpful to prepare the sheik for the worst. We need his loyalty even if his daughter is killed."

Khalid smiled. "You are telling me how to arrange my business now?"

Omar dipped his head very slightly. "Pray to Allah for us, Father."

13

Miriam sat in the speeding Cougar and watched the endless string of oncoming headlights. They'd spent an hour speculating who was after her and what course would be best for them.

They'd made their way to the southbound Interstate 5 toward Los Angeles. Although they saw no indication that the authorities were in pursuit, Seth insisted that the farther they traveled from Berkeley, the safer they would be. Judging by the labyrinth of freeways and endless lines of cars, Miriam honestly didn't think anyone had a hope of finding them. She'd traveled American freeways, of course, but during the few months of her schooling two years earlier, she had remained mostly sequestered in the hotel suite down the street from Berkeley's campus.

After a flurry of discussion, Seth settled into an introspective state, drifting between deep thought and filling her in on America, as it really was, he said.

They stopped once for petrol. He gave her a short tour of the gas station, explaining what the different candies were and why he preferred the red licorice strips over the black ones and why mixing a fruit drink with candy for health reasons made no sense because the candy was bad enough on its own. So were most of the nuts.

They came out with two tall bottles of cold Dr Pepper, two bags of red licorice, and two bags of beef jerky, which he assured her was just as hard on the body as the other "junk" they had purchased. Being consistent seemed important to him.

She assured him that she knew most of this—not only had she spent a summer in California while attending Berkeley, she had made several trips to European cities and read a thousand magazines published in the West. Still, he did have a unique perspective that struck her as refreshing.

Seth took advantage of the stop to change into a pair of black corduroys and a faded orange T-shirt that seemed to loosen him up considerably. She shared no such luxury. The white dress she'd worn to the party was holding up well enough, but the disparity in their dress made her feel disadvantaged. She was entirely too proper for this bold man beside her.

Miriam finally decided that Seth should know the whole truth of her predicament. It took another hour to tell him of the events that had led up to her leaving Saudi Arabia—all of them, ending with Sita's drowning.

"So you were forced to watch?" Seth asked, horrified. "That was your father's purpose. How . . ." His voice faded and he closed his eyes for a moment, furious.

"Now you see why I fled? Not every corner of the world enjoys the freedoms you do."

He faced her and for a second she thought he was going to challenge her. But then his face softened. "I'm sorry. That's a terrible thing to have to see." He shook his head. "I can't imagine what the girl's mother must be going through."

"Like many women, Sita's mother is fundamental to the bone, but she is still a mother who lost a fifteen-year-old daughter to her husband's own hand. Her devotion is beyond me."

Seth stared forward and swallowed, fighting emotion. Her savior had his soft side. Or was it patently American?

"When you grow up in a country like this, it's hard to understand the suffering others face," she said, looking away. "Perhaps Americans have it too easy."

"You think so? Not all Americans. Have you ever been slapped around by your father, Miriam?"

What was this? "I've received my share of beatings."

"Not a week went by that I wasn't beaten by my father when I was a child."

"You?" She felt surprisingly appalled by his admission. Perhaps because he was an American, and she'd never imagined mistreatment in America.

"Never mind. It was nothing."

"I tell you about Sita and you tell me never mind?" she asked.

He considered that for a moment. "My father was an alcoholic and despite repeated intentions to the contrary, he habitually abused both my mother and me. Not all of America is as pretty as it may seem. My childhood was pretty ugly."

"I'm sorry. Please forgive me—"

"It's okay. I can't complain." He forced a grin. "I may not be the most well-adjusted human being you'll meet, but I have more than my share to be thankful for. Not being born in Saudi Arabia for starters."

"Ha! I don't think you understand. You would do well in my country."

"That's right, I forgot. I'm a man, right?"

"You forgot your gender? Perhaps you're really a woman in disguise."

He smiled, breaking the tension for the moment. Silence filled the car, and they traveled south for a while without feeling the need to break it.

It occurred to Miriam that for the first time, she was traveling America the American way, with an American. Two thoughts crowded her mind. On one hand, despite the danger that surrounded them, the adventure of racing down the highway with a true-blooded American was quite thrilling. On the other hand, the fact that the American was indeed a man triggered conflicting emotions. She had never been *alone* with a strange man, much less been stuck in a car with him for many hours.

Miriam looked over. The dash lights highlighted Seth's profile—a smooth jaw and blond hair that was decidedly messier now than when she first met him. His ragged features were appealing in an American sort of way. He possessed the kind of air she'd always imagined a free-willed spirit might have, handsome yet purposefully detached from his own charm, somewhat of an enigma in light of his intelligence. Despite his fumbling back in the rest room, this man had a sharp mind—his every word was saturated with that fact.

Miriam removed her stare and smiled, thinking of their narrow escape from the university.

"What?" he asked.

"Nothing," she said.

"That's not a nothing smile. That's a *boy, isn't he a strange one* smile."

"Maybe. You think you know women so well that you understand their thoughts with a glance?"

"Maybe."

"Maybe I should slip a veil on. I feel naked here with you reading my mind."

That gave him pause. How many men had seen her face well enough to judge her thoughts? Very few.

"A princess with an exceptional wit," Seth said. "Fascinating."

"When you look at my face, do you like what you see?" Miriam asked.

"What do you mean?"

"You're one of only a few men who have seen my face. It seems to have made enough of an impact on you to influence your assessment of my thoughts. I'm just asking if you see anything else in it." She said it knowing that the question would throw him, and she took no small pleasure in throwing a man of such intellect.

"Yes." He avoided her look and glanced in the side mirror although there were no cars behind them at the moment. "You're a woman. A princess. Remember?"

"A princess? I've seen more than one princess who would only look appealing next to a toad. On a good day." She looked at the road. "You'll forgive me, but in my country an unmarried woman doesn't hear that she is beautiful. Even the married ones hear it only from their husbands and then only when their husbands aren't busy telling their other wives how pretty they are. I think a woman is born with a singular desire to hear that she is beautiful, don't you?"

"Yes. Well . . . yes. I think so. Sure. Makes sense. Innate desire for the sake of the perpetuation of the species."

She glanced at him. "I had never thought of it in such scientific terms," she said.

"No. Sorry, that's not what I meant. It seems reasonable."

"Perhaps it's more a matter of love than reason," she said. "Have you ever been in love?"

"Love? Love as in what kind of love?"

"Evidently not. Love as in I would give anything to be in Samir's arms right now, hearing him whisper my name and telling me how beautiful I am. Love."

"Samir?"

"Yes. Samir. The driver I told you about."

"You're in love with him?" He grinned softly. "There's a twist. So while people in high places are plotting your marriage, you're secretly in love with another man. A forbidden man."

"Yes. Desperately," she said.

"Desperately in love with a forbidden man. A princess with enough backbone to stand the great kingdom of Saudi Arabia on its end."

She laughed, delighted at his assessment. He possessed an uncanny sense of her country, as if he'd been there himself, even though he'd insisted his understanding came only from books.

Seth cleared his throat. "So where I come from, a man madly in love with a woman in danger would be running to her defense. Where is Samir?"

Miriam turned on him. "What do you mean? He can't come after me! They'd kill him!"

"That wouldn't stop a man in love."

"And *you* know this?" she mocked, surprised at her sudden anger. "He doesn't even know where I've gone. When it's safe, he will come out for me; I can promise you that. In the end, nothing will separate us."

"Okay. Sorry. I was just asking."

She faced her side window and thought about the way Samir had looked at her as he made his promise. What if he *had* left Saudi Arabia in search of her? What if at this moment he was in San Francisco, hurrying to protect her? What was she doing running in this wild man's company? Six hours earlier she hadn't known Seth existed. He smashed into the lavatory and kidnapped her because of some strange vision that he refused to explain to her. And now she was trapped in a roaring car with him. What if Seth was actually an American agent working with Khalid?

She closed her eyes. *Slow down, Miriam. He is your protector. He's as innocent as you. Without him you would be back in their hands.*

Her mind filled with a flurry of images. Omar, King Fahd, Salman, the sheik, Samir, Sultana. Dear Sultana. Where are you, Samir? What had she started? It had taken her enemies exactly two days to catch up to her in Berkeley.

"What are we going to do?" she asked.

He didn't answer.

"Please, Seth, perhaps we should go back into San Francisco. What if Samir is there? I've never been anywhere outside of San Francisco. What are you going to do, just drop me off at a bus stop in Los Angeles and expect that I will find my way?"

"Don't worry, I'm not going to drop you off at a bus stop."

"Then what?"

"I'm not sure."

The absurdity of it suddenly struck her full force. "This is crazy!"

"Yes. Yes it is. You're not only a very pretty princess; you're a very smart one. That much I can—"

"Stop it. I'm serious! You're driving me to nowhere without a clue about what you're doing. Maybe you should let me out of the car."

"At the next bus stop?"

He had a point, of course.

"Look, I didn't exactly plan on rescuing a princess today. Forgive me if I don't have my handy-dandy *Ten Most Efficient Strategies to Deliver a Distressed Princess to Safety* handbook in my back pocket. Maybe if you'd given me some notice."

She stared at him, her mind scrambling to make sense of his jargon.

She understood his basic intent. He was as lost as she and covered his insecurity with this wit of his.

"That doesn't mean I don't have any ideas," he said. "I'm sure there are people who handle this sort of thing for a living at the State Department. I'm assuming their offices are closed at the moment. I'll call them as soon as the sun breaks the horizon. In the meantime, going back toward San Francisco would not be smart; there are people back there who don't like you, remember? And before you forget, I'm as much a hostage to this situation as you are. These people are after you, not me."

She couldn't disagree with his thinking. In some ways he reminded her of Sultana with all of his ironclad logic. Sultana should consider leaving the kingdom to marry this man—they would make a deserving pair.

"You're right. I'm sorry, I've been through more than I'd planned in the last few days."

"No, really, it's okay."

"You're really here because of the vision you had," she said. "If not for the vision, you would be home."

"I didn't say it was a vision."

"You refuse to call it anything. So I'm calling it a vision. You saw a man coming for me in the bathroom. Where I come from, we would call that a vision from God."

"Of course. Mohammed was famous for his visions. Anytime he needed something done—a new wife or the leveling of another village—he just had himself another vision, right? And if the vision happened to contradict an earlier one, it was okay because this was God speaking, and who could question God? It may have worked for the holy prophet, but that's not what I would call what happened to me. It has nothing to do with God. I'm sure there's a perfectly rational scientific explanation for what I saw."

"You're insulting the prophet? This is the American way of tolerance? And your prophets are superior to Mohammed?"

He paused. "I'm sorry. Really, I'm not trying to be disrespectful. And for the record, I don't have any prophets. Here we have the freedom to follow Mohammed or Jesus or Jimmy Jones—or, most reasonably, none of them—and still keep our necks. I'm not saying your prophet is any worse than Jimmy Jones. I'm just saying that whatever happened to me couldn't have been like what happened to Mohammed. In my understanding of the matter, his visions were a highly motivated fabrication—what I saw was not."

"So now you're not only an expert on love, but on my religion. When was the last time you actually read the Qur'an?"

"Two, two and a half years ago."

She humphed. "You should examine something more closely before speaking so flippantly. Mohammed never claimed to be perfect, but his revelation was certainly from God."

"Then God has a short memory and tends to contradict himself frequently."

Heat flared up Miriam's neck. "How *dare* you speak so flippantly! You haven't touched the holy book in two years and yet you can say this?"

"I don't need to touch the book. I had most of it memorized, sura for sura, by age twenty-one. Certain things tend to lock themselves in my mind, poetic abstractions being chief among them. As you know, the Qur'an is very poetic. So is the Bible. They both fascinate me."

He knew the Qur'an? The revelation made her blink. "You can't possibly understand Islam, living here in America."

"Actually, I know this may sound arrogant and I apologize in advance, but I think I understand both Christianity and Islam quite well. They have a surprising amount in common."

"How could they? They are like black and white."

"Both believe that there is one God, an all-knowing creator, which I happen to agree with. Both believe that Jesus was born of a virgin and was sinless. Both believe that the writings of Moses, David, the prophets, and the gospels were divinely inspired. The primary differences between Islam and Christianity come in contradictions between the Qur'an and these other writings. Muslims simply explain it away by saying the gospels and the Christian Bible have been altered since their writing, something not even Mohammed claims in the Qur'an."

He had his facts right, but his dismissal of the Qur'an infuriated her. "And perhaps you've read a bad translation of the Qur'an. A twisted English version."

"Actually, I read and understand Arabic. Language is like mathematics—both come easy to me. I admit that the translation I memorized was in English, but I understand it was quite accurate."

He understood Arabic? She spoke a sentence in Arabic.

He answered in English. "Yes, most Westerners do have difficulty with Arabic. But I'm not most Westerners. And really, forgive me for taking Islam to task, but to question is the nature of man, right? Every religion has its place. Christianity has its place; Islam has its place. They hold societies together and answer man's unanswered questions and such. But I have to reject both. Christianity on philosophical grounds, and Islam on both philosophical and historical grounds. Whatever happened to me back there, I'm definitely not ready to attribute it to religion."

"Then what? Why *are* you here, Seth Border?"

He hesitated. "I'm here because I saw the future."

"But you won't call it a vision. You see a difference?"

"Maybe not. I just wanted to make the distinction. Just because we don't understand how something works doesn't mean we have to pawn it off on some deity. The world was once flat because the church said it was flat, remember? Have you ever considered the possibility that time is the same way? It's a dimension that we don't understand, so when someone sees now what happens later, he's finding a way to step beyond that dimension. It may be as simple as that."

"Simple? Stepping beyond a dimension. Oh, I see. How silly of me. Then at least tell me what stepping beyond a dimension feels like. Indulge me."

Seth glanced at her, somewhat self-conscious, she thought. "I'm not saying that's necessarily what happened. I'm just telling you that it might have been what happened. It's possible."

"Then tell me."

He ran his fingers through his curly blond locks. "You ever been in a dream that feels real?"

"Yes."

"It felt like that. But so fast that it didn't interrupt anything I was seeing in the present." He paused. "Make sense?"

"Sounds like a vision," she said.

"But different," he said.

They drove in silence for a long time after that. Miriam lost herself in thoughts of Saudi Arabia—the best of her beloved homeland. The beaches of Jiddah, the sands of the desert, the palaces dripping with wealth. In some ways it wasn't so bad to be a woman with the run of a palace, was it, veil or no veil? Sultana would slap her for even thinking it. Miriam would slap herself.

Still, loneliness was nearly as bad as captivity, and tonight, for the first time since her whirlwind escape, Miriam felt lonely. For Haya and for Sita and for Sultana. For Samir.

Dear Allah, what had she done?

Seth pulled into a rest stop at 2 A.M. and suggested they get some rest. Sleep came almost before she closed her eyes.

The sun was shining when Miriam awoke. She sat up groggily, searching her memory for where she might be. A car door slammed shut and she spun to her right. A large man had shut his door and was walking from a white Jeep. He glanced her way and then made his way toward a building to the far left of where they . . .

Seth! He was gone.

And then he wasn't gone. He was walking toward the car, hands in his pockets, hair in his eyes. The wild man who had memorized the Qur'an and stepped beyond time.

He opened his door and plopped in. He looked tired.

"Morning, Miriam. Sleep well?"

"Well enough. You don't look like you slept at all."

"Never could sleep in a car." He shrugged. "I got some."

"Where are we?"

"We're on the way to freedom. Two hours this side of Los Angeles. Twenty minutes outside of Santa Clarita."

She just looked at him, lost.

"I called a friend of mine back at the campus," he said. "Professor Harland." Seth grinned and shook his head. "Boy, did we cause a ruckus. He said the place was crawling with cops within half an hour. By the sounds of it, Baaron's not too happy."

"Did your friend help you?"

"Yes. It seems the police know about you. He asked them what to tell us if we called. They suggested that we go to the State Department in Los Angeles. They will have someone there to take you into protective custody. An old acquaintance of mine from the NSA—Clive Masters. A curious development actually. Either way, I'm pretty sure we can trust Clive."

She furrowed her brow. "Why should we trust anyone?"

"This isn't Saudi Arabia, Miriam. This is America, the land where people like you on the run from oppressive governments escape to. Harland talked to Clive, and they're both urging me to take you in. I can't think of any reason why they're wrong."

"And what if the police turn me over to authorities from my country? You have no idea what they'll do to me."

"Why would they? Besides, we're not going to the police; we're going to the State Department. They won't turn you over. You're seeking asylum."

She just looked at him.

Seth diverted his eyes. "I won't let them. They're not going to lie to us. If they do, I'll get you out."

"How?"

"I don't know. I can always use the bathroom trick."

He grinned and she smiled despite the anxiousness she felt. His demeanor had changed, she thought. His eyes didn't hold hers with as much confidence as they had last night. He looked at her several times, but then glanced away.

"I think you'll be safe, Miriam. Besides, unless you've got some other brilliant plan you've kept from me, I don't think we have any alternative. We can't just take off across the country like Bonnie and Clyde."

She cast him a questioning glance.

"Bonnie and Clyde were two famous . . . lovers who ran from the law. Old story," he said, looking away again. "You said you had some money on you. You mind me asking how much?"

"Five," she said.

"And I've got ten. I was thinking you could use a change of clothes, but I guess we'll have to make do."

"Clothing! That's a wonderful idea. There's a store nearby?"

"Santa Clarita. But fifteen dollars isn't going to buy us food and clothes."

"Fifteen dollars? I said that I have five. Thousand."

He looked at her sideways. "Five *thousand?*"

"Yes. I didn't want to leave Hillary's house without some change."

"Okay. Change is good. Well then, we'll just have to go shopping, won't we?"

"Yes, that would be good."

Miriam ran her fingers through her hair and then twisted the rearview mirror to look at her face.

"The bathroom's in there," he said, nodding at the building.

"Thank you." She opened the door.

"Hurry back."

"I will."

Five minutes later they pulled back on the highway and headed south. She asked Seth if she could listen to the radio, and he obliged her with a tour of the airwaves. She felt a little like a child with all of his enlightenment, but he did seem to know music. And watching him enthusiastically expound on why Frank Sinatra and a band called Metallica were really cut from the same cloth, she was once again struck by his strange appeal. A kind of appeal that fit his explanation of Bonnie and Clyde.

The mall was still closed in Santa Clarita, but Seth insisted the twenty-four-hour Wal-Mart across the street would work just fine. Same basic clothes, but with different labels for different folks, he said. Most of the threads probably came out of the same sewing lines.

He parked in a near-empty lot and walked her through the doors of the huge store.

"Ladies' clothes up twenty-three paces, and to the right five paces, across from photography and this side of lingerie," he said. "All Wal-Marts follow one of several basic formats, and this one I know. I'm going to the left, where I hope to find a couple of toothbrushes and some paste for whitening the teeth and refreshing the breath."

She looked at him, trying again to catch up to his use of English. It wasn't that she didn't understand him; it was that his choice of words took her off guard.

"Is that okay?" he asked.

She glanced up the aisles. "You're going to leave me alone? What if I get lost?"

"You won't. If you do, ask someone in a blue vest where the check-out counters are. Trust me, you'll be fine."

She hesitated. It wasn't like she'd never shopped before. "Okay."

He walked several paces before turning back. "And please try to hurry. I know how critical these moments of garment selection can be for some women, but Harland suggested we hurry and I think he makes good sense."

She didn't respond.

"Good," he said. "And for the record I would go with the blue jeans and the white top any day over a dress. Considering our situation, that is."

She stared at him, taken aback. "How did you know I was considering blue jeans or a dress?"

"You were considering that?"

"Exactly that. Nothing more."

"Hmm."

"Now you're seeing into my closet? What else can you see?"

"I'm not seeing into your closet. I'm not really sure what I saw."

"But you did see something?"

He hesitated, as if just coming to the realization himself. "Yeah, I guess I did."

"Hmm," she said.

Seth turned and ambled toward the pharmacy section. They walked out together ten minutes later, Seth holding a bag of toiletries and another bottle of Dr Pepper, and Miriam dressed in blue jeans and a white blouse.

14

HILAL DROVE SOUTH in the Hertz Mercedes, tuned to the scanner and drifting in thought while the police slowly tightened their net.

They had failed to locate the Cougar, but the American, Seth, had used his Texaco gas card at a station near Kettleman City. He was indeed headed south. And so was Hilal. They had passed Santa Clarita and were headed into the maze of freeways that covered the Los Angeles basin like a spider web.

He reached up and tested the scanner, which had remained silent for a few minutes. Static sounded, indicating a clear signal. A new Kenworth tractor-trailer rumbled past on his left, hauling three large Caterpillar generators. The West knew one truth that flew in the face of Islam, he thought. It was the simple belief that the individual's rights were supreme. Personal freedom. America had been built on the notion, and despite the slow erosion of those rights, the evidence of their impact was everywhere he looked.

Although King Fahd wasn't ready to open up his palaces to the common man, he understood the power of freedom more than most in Saudi Arabia. The militants, on the other hand, would negate personal freedom in the name of the prophet. And in truth, Mohammed himself had overridden his people's rights in the name of Allah. Overseeing the barbaric beheading of nearly a thousand Quraiza Jews in groups of five as punishment for refusing to convert certainly qualified. As did the slaying of whole tribes for their refusal to accept him as Allah's prophet.

But the world had changed. And unless Saudi Arabia changed with it, she would be washed into the sea. His was the job of protecting the kingdom from just that. And if it meant the death of one woman named Miriam, so be it. Not that he had any intention of killing her at this point—she was, after all, the king's daughter. On the other hand, if she refused to cooperate, he would have to.

Hilal sighed. It was a complicated world.

The scanner burped to life. "Units near 5 and Balboa respond to a possible sighting of a vehicle matching the description of a brown Cougar on the bulletin. Sky reported vehicle exiting the freeway, westbound on Balboa."

It was them! *Balboa.* The exit was directly ahead.

Hilal glanced in his mirror and eased the Mercedes into the right lane. His pulse quickened. So his gamble had paid off. A soft smile curved his lips.

The scanner squawked again. "Copy 512. Will take that. We're ten miles south on 5. There's not much out there past the truck stop."

A short silence. Hilal sped under a sign that told him Balboa exit was one mile off.

"Confirm. Looks like the truck stop. Sky's headed south and will be out of visual shortly. What's your E.T.A.?"

"Give me fifteen minutes."

"Fifteen minutes."

Hilal instinctively felt for the bulge in his jacket and touched the gun's cold steel. He had fifteen minutes.

❧

The truck stop sat alone on the north side of Balboa, roughly three hundred yards from the highway.

"You haven't experienced America until you've sat in a smoky truck-stop diner and choked down their greasy hash browns," Seth said.

"How long will it take to reach the State Department?" Miriam asked. He'd said they were scheduled to meet a representative there at eleven. It was now eight.

"Two hours. We have an hour to burn." They climbed from the car. "Let's eat some grease," he said, winking.

They walked through a dimly lit hall lined with video games and pinball machines into a diner. The gentle odor of grilled bacon and eggs filled the place. A woman wearing a red-checkered apron smacked some chewing gum.

"Two?" she said.

"Two," Seth replied.

The woman seated them in a booth that faced the parking lot. Seth's brown Cougar sat next to a Toyota sedan—otherwise the lot was empty. Miriam scanned the menu. The loneliness she'd felt last night had fled. She felt surprisingly safe in Seth's company. Only a few days ago she'd been standing in the Souq with Sultana, hiding behind a veil, plotting her impossible escape. Now she sat across from an American named Seth, trying to choose between the greasy hash browns and the banana splits on the back cover. If Samir were to come to America, she was sure they could build a good life together in this country.

She looked up and saw that Seth was watching her.

"So. What do you want?" he asked.

"The hash browns are potatoes?"

"Sliced up and fried."

"You recommend them?"

"I do."

She smiled at him. "Then I want hash browns."

"Me too." He set aside his menu.

"You are very fortunate, Seth Border."

"Why's that?"

"To live in such a beautiful, clean country."

"Don't let the trees fool you, my dear. I hear there are goblins in the forest." He suddenly grinned, as if embarrassed. He was being colorful again, part of America's charm, she thought.

"And by this you mean what?"

"Well actually, I was just making an offhanded comment that behind the plastic smiles you see everywhere, I promise you'll find greasy mugs that will make the hash browns we just ordered seem dry by comparison. The ugly side of human nature is not exclusive to Saudi Arabia."

"And are your women oppressed here like they are in my country?"

"No, I think you beat us in that category. But in the plastics department, I'm sure we have the edge."

"Plastic. As in fake," she said. "You are a very cynical man; has anyone told you that? I've spent half a day with you in your car, and honestly I don't know what you believe in."

"I believe in lots of things. God for instance."

"God? But you despise religion?"

"I believe in God because only an idiot could look at the intricate balance of nature and believe it was not designed. Believe it or not, some people still believe a watch can form itself out of sand given enough time. They call it evolution. And you wonder why I'm cynical. From where I'm standing, I'd have to be a fool *not* to be cynical."

She smiled, amused by his wit.

"Excuse me," she said, sliding out. "I would like to freshen up."

"Back in the hall next to the pinball machines," he said.

Seth watched her walk toward the hall, dressed in her carpenter's jeans and white shirt, and could not deny the strange feelings that had overtaken him during their drive south. He was attracted to her, but it was more than that, wasn't it? In an uncommon way they were the same, Miriam and he. They were both uncommon. In other ways they were very different—from different planets altogether. He had no business feeling anything toward her beyond what a good Samaritan might feel.

Yet here he sat, his belly light and his pulse on edge. He couldn't remember ever feeling so taken by any woman in his entire life. Why?

She disappeared into the hall and Seth picked up his coffee cup. The notion that she was a princess on the run from some sinister characters intent on harming her seemed absurd now. Like something he might read in a book. Rapunzel, Rapunzel, let down your hair. But the events of last evening were nothing out of a book. He would deliver her to safety in a few hours and then . . .

And then he didn't quite know what.

Seth took another sip of coffee and looked out into the parking lot. A black Mercedes had parked at the far end of the building. He yawned. The lack of sleep was starting to catch up to him. Before he did anything, he would have to sleep. Deliver Miriam to safety and then—

The knowledge struck then and he jerked upright. It deposited itself in his mind, like a foregone conclusion, without reasoning. A man with black hair was shooting Miriam in the bathroom.

Seth sat rigid, immobilized by what he'd just seen. Had this just happened? Or was he seeing into the future again?

A second conclusion popped in his mind, next to the first one. Now there was a man in the bathroom standing over two bodies. One of the bodies was Miriam's and one was his. Both were dead. The twin realities lodged in his mind, static and unchanging. He saw the waitress approach in his peripheral image, slow motion. She was saying something.

A third image dropped into his mind. A third conclusion. One in which he was in the bathroom standing next to Miriam, facing the Arab with a policeman in the door. He blinked.

In the first scene he wasn't present and Miriam was dead. In the second he was present but the police officer wasn't, and they were both dead.

In the third . . .

Seth scrambled from the table and tore for the hall. The waitress back-pedaled to avoid a collision. His heart slapped against the walls of his chest. He had to get into the bathroom. What he'd just seen wasn't *the* future, but three *possible* futures! That had to be it! The only one in which Miriam lived was the one in which he was in the bathroom with the officer. Which meant he had to get to the bathroom!

Of course, the only future in which he ended up dead was one in which he was in the bathroom. If he didn't enter the bathroom, he would live. He knew that like he knew the theory of relativity. If he *did* enter the bathroom, he might die.

He was seeing possible futures. More than one. Three different outcomes, depending on who entered that bathroom. Evidently, he had influence over which future became the real future. Was that possible?

For the second time in less than a day, Seth slammed his way into the ladies' room. He pulled up, panting and sweating. Miriam stood to his left, face white and stricken. A skinny Arab with sharp features stood opposite her, gun in hand.

For a brief moment, neither of them moved. Seth couldn't go after the Arab, of course. The man had a gun. Suddenly the gun was pointed in his face.

"Lock the door," the man said evenly.

Seth wasn't sure he could turn to lock the door. His muscles had frozen.

"Lock it!"

The crack of the man's voice jerked Seth back to reality. He turned, twisted the deadbolt, and faced them again.

The Arab shifted the gun back to Miriam and spoke in Arabic. "Whom were you to marry? If you think I won't kill you because this man has stumbled in here, you're as big a fool as he. Tell me whom you were to marry."

So, she'd told him about the plot to overthrow the throne without revealing who was behind it.

"Tell me!" the man screamed.

Miriam jumped.

A grin split the man's face. His nose was sharp enough to pass for an ax, and his cheekbones pressed against his skin like knives.

"You are frightened, Miriam?" The smile vanished. "I can understand. You are a Saudi Arabian citizen, and your actions in this plot threaten the life of our king. For that you will die. And your running won't save you. You've been gone for only three days and already I've found you."

Miriam looked frantic, not the self-assured woman Seth had come to know in their flight from the bay. She believed him.

"If you tell me who is behind this, the king might find it in his heart to overlook your flight."

"I'm running from the marriage," she said softly. "Not from the king."

"Then you have nothing to fear. Tell me who's plotting with Sheik Al-Asamm."

The Arab would kill them both. Seth had already seen that much, and the knowledge had turned his muscles to lead. The only future he'd seen in which they both survived was the one with the police in the doorway. But what control did he have over the police arriving?

And then another future dropped into his mind, like a nugget of gold from the sky above. It was a police cruiser; an officer slumped over the wheel of his cruiser, dead; Miriam toppled in the rear seat, dead. "What?" he stammered. Both Miriam and the Arab looked at him.

It was an involuntary note of surprise, not a question, but he continued because it seemed that they expected him to. He spoke in English.

"If there's no Miriam, there is no marriage, regardless of who's behind it. You're going to kill her anyway, aren't you? But as long as she has information you want, she's more valuable alive than dead. So she won't tell you who's plotting with the sheik, right?"

The man stared at him. "He speaks Arabic?" he asked Miriam, still speaking Arabic.

She didn't respond.

The man nodded and smiled again. He switched to English. "So you are as intelligent as they say you are. And quite perceptive. But like so many Americans, too brave for your own good. What do you suppose that I'm going to do with you now? Hmm? Do you know who is behind this marriage?"

A small idea came to Seth. A very small one, like the light seeping past the hinges of a locked door.

"You're planning to kill me," he said. "I know too much. And I would be a witness to your murder of Miriam. But you have three problems. The first is that Miriam's death will come back to haunt you. There's more to this story than you know right now. If she dies, Sheik Abu Ali al-Asamm will be freed from his bond with the king. That may not seem like an insurmountable problem in your mind, but it will be, I can promise you. I can promise you because I've thought it through and in *my* mind it's an insurmountable problem. And you already know that my mind is five or eight times as powerful as yours."

He let that drop and watched the man's blank stare. There was no truth to his words, but they were having their intended effect of confusing the Arab. Seth continued before he had the time to lose his nerve.

"The second problem you have is that the police are on the way. Even if you pulled the trigger now, I'm not sure you'd have the time to get your big black Mercedes down the road before they cut you off. And your third problem is that neither Miriam nor I are in a hurry to die. In fact, you have us pretty much terrified here. See? So we're going to use every trick you've ever thought of and a few you haven't to throw you. Problem is, you're already having difficulty deciding what is a trick and what is not a trick. Am I right?"

The man stared, as if he'd been immobilized by this alien before him.

"Thought so," Seth said. "You're—"

"Shut up!" The man reached into his breast pocket and pulled out a small black cylinder. A silencer. He began to screw it on the barrel of his pistol. "You may think you know some things, but there are many things you clearly don't know, or you wouldn't waste your breath with empty threats. I have diplomatic immunity, and I'm dealing with a fugitive from our justice system. The police are powerless to arrest me, you fool."

"What's your name?" Seth asked, fighting panic now. He knew the man was right. He could kill Miriam and walk out untouched.

"His name is Hilal," Miriam said.

"Hilal." He had to stall the man. He'd seen a future in which both he and Miriam survived, at least up until the point the police showed up. He had to assume that the futures were possible futures and that he could influence them.

"I can see the future, Hilal," Seth said.

The man tightened the barrel. "Very good." He faced Miriam. "I'll give you one last chance to tell me. If it's true that you have no argument against your king, then you will reveal his enemies. Your silence is proof enough of guilt."

"Please, stop being silly and put that thing down," Seth said. What on earth was he saying? "I've seen the future and you don't kill us here. You're not that stupid; it's far too dangerous. I nearly knocked a waitress over getting in here—there's probably three or four sets of ears pressed against the door right now, listening to every word we say. You may be at liberty to walk into rest rooms with a bazooka and blow people away at will in your country, but this is the United States, my friend. Now lay the iron down and let's negotiate terms of surrender here. How much money will you give me?"

"I'm offering you your life, not money, you imbecile!"

"Exactly. But as I said, neither of us is eager to *give* our life. Maybe for some dough we would be willing to spill the beans. All we really want is to live together happily ever after. Miriam came to the land of the free to find herself a real man, and she's done it already. Allah has smiled on her. Let us go with a million dollars each, and I personally will tell you exactly who's plotting against your king and how he plans to do it."

The gun wavered in the killer's hand. Seth's talk was unnerving Hilal. But that could push him to pull the trigger just as easily, couldn't it? Hilal's right eye twitched and suddenly Seth knew he was going to pull the trigger. The Arab was too smart to buy any of this nonsense. The exchange had bought a few minutes, but this man with the sharp nose was far from stupid.

Seth's entire body felt as though it was on fire. A buzz ran through his bones. He was trapped somewhere between full-fledged panic and a dead faint. But he had to move, and he had to move now. So he forced himself to do the only thing that came to mind in that moment.

He walked up to Hilal and slapped his face with an open palm.

"Stop this!" Seth said. "Don't be a fool!"

Hilal's eyes widened. He stood speechless.

It occurred to Seth, sweating before the killer, that he had just signed his own death warrant. Hilal's gun was still trained on Miriam, but at any moment it would swing his way and a slug would smash through his chest.

"You're acting like a child," Seth said. "I can give you what you want, but you have to stop pretending to be Rambo here."

The color flooded back into Hilal's face, which twisted into fury. He swung his gun around.

"Police!"

Someone pounded on the door.

"Police, open up!"

Hilal froze. With a practiced flip of his wrist, he spun off the silencer and slipped both it and the gun into his breast pockets. "You will be sorry for this," he said.

Then, as if this sort of thing were the stuff of everyday play, he strolled over, twisted the lock, and pulled the door open. "Thank God, you are here," he said. "I kept them as long as I could."

A state trooper stood with one hand on the butt of his gun, trying to make sense of what he saw. "Is everything okay here?"

The fear that had gripped Seth only moments before turned to terror looking at this state trooper. He'd seen the man before. In his mind's eye. Dead. With Miriam dead behind him.

That had been the fourth future he'd seen.

"You're Miriam and you're Seth?" the trooper asked.

"Yes," Miriam said.

"I'm sorry, you're going to have to come with me. There's a warrant out for both of your arrests." The trooper looked at Hilal, still unsure about the Arab's presence. "Who are you?"

Hilal pulled out a small wallet and flipped it open. "I'm the legal guardian of this woman, on assignment from King Fahd of Saudi Arabia. I would be grateful if you would take her into custody immediately. We've wasted enough time."

"I don't care how much time you think you've wasted. I wasn't told a thing about meeting you here . . ."

The trooper kept talking, but Seth heard nothing else. Another outcome to this scenario had dropped into his mind. Another possible future. Then two futures. Then six of them, all at once, like a string of posters, each one different, depending on the choices made.

Then a hundred possible outcomes, a barrage of the unseen, seen now by him.

Miriam survived the next ten minutes in only one of them.

Hilal was talking to the cop now. He was cooperating. At least for the moment.

Shaking with terror, Seth shoved his hand into his pocket, wrapped his fingers around the superball he carried by habit, and stepped forward. It was pure lunacy, but he was beyond reason anyway. This was the one future in which he and Miriam survived, and he had no alternative but to try to facilitate that future.

"Where do you think you're going?" the cop asked as he barged toward him.

"You want to arrest me? I'm coming to be arrested," Seth said.

He stepped through the doorway and spun around to present his arms behind his back. Halfway through the spin he released the ball from his pocket. He wasn't sure how he knew precisely when to release it; he only knew that if he did release, precisely as he had, it would roll just so toward the diner.

And it did.

Seth faced Miriam now who stood with wide eyes. Hilal smiled softly, just inside the door to his right.

"Just walk to the car peacefully," the cop said. "I'm not gonna use cuffs. Ma'am, if you'll please come with—"

A scream ripped through the air. Followed by a hollow thud and the horrendous crash of shattering plates.

"Call an ambulance!" someone cried from the diner. "Hurry!"

The cop spun and took a single step in the direction of the diner before stopping himself. But Seth was already on the move. Without warning he stepped into Hilal and gave him a hard shove. The Arab back-pedaled and slammed into a stall door that sprung open, accepting his flailing body.

Before Hilal hit the toilet, Seth had Miriam's hand in his. "Run!"

She ran behind him, through the bathroom door, right past the cop who had spun back and was palming his gun.

"Stop!" the officer yelled.

"Run! He won't shoot us," Seth said.

They crashed through the exit doors and sprinted for the Cougar. Thank goodness it wasn't valuable enough to lock. Seth threw Miriam's door open and managed to climb in himself before the cop made an appearance at the door, weapon trained on the Cougar.

"Stop!" he yelled again. He snatched up his radio, calling for backup. Seth knew he wouldn't shoot, not at a Saudi princess and a student whose only real crime was running out of a bathroom. Besides, they were next to gas pumps.

"Go! Hurry, go!" Miriam shouted.

"I'm going!"

The Cougar's tires squealed on the truck stop's apron.

"Believe me, I'm going."

"Did you hurt anyone?" she asked.

"No. The waitress will have a few bruises, but she'll live."

"How do you know?"

They peeled onto Balboa and roared for the freeway.

"I just do."

15

YOU . . . YOU SAW THE FUTURE," Miriam said. "You really saw the future again?"

Seth veered down an exit. "I'm cutting across to 210. We have to get to the State Department. The police know what the car looks like; if we don't change things up a bit, they'll pull us over before we get downtown. I'm not sure I'm ready for a full-on chase."

"I don't understand." Miriam pulled one knee up on the seat and sat sideways to look through the back window. No pursuit in sight. "We're going to the State Department; why don't we just let the police take us?"

"Because . . ." He paused and glanced at his mirrors. "Because, in all the outcomes I saw that included the cop, you ended up dead."

She stared at him. "I . . . what do you mean, dead?"

"I mean slumped over in the backseat of his car, with a hole in your head. Hilal's obviously not the timid type."

"You said outcomes. You saw more than one future?"

"Yes."

"How many?"

"Many. A hundred."

Her mind spun. What he was suggesting was impossible. To see into the future was possible, of course. Many mystics and prophets had seen visions, including Mohammed himself. But this idea that one could see more than one future—she'd never heard of such a thing.

"Why did you throw the ball?"

"Because the future in which I threw the ball was the only future in which you survived."

She turned from him and stared ahead. It was absurd. He drove on, somber.

"I don't understand it any more than you do," he said. "I only know that prior to a few days ago, I'd never experienced anything remotely similar to clairvoyance. Then my mind short-circuited or something and I began to see glimpses. Now I'm seeing what I know are possible futures and I'm seeing more than one at a time. I was sitting at the table and I saw Hilal. How else would I know to bust in like that?"

"And you saw me dead? You saw many possible outcomes of the situation, including the arrival of the police, and the only one in which I wasn't killed was when you threw the ball?"

"Yes. At first I knew I had to stall Hilal until the cops came. If I did that, you would survive the bathroom. But then I saw that he would kill you anyway, in the car. The only way to survive was to distract the cop long enough to escape, and the only way that was going to happen was if I threw the ball just like I did, so that the waitress would fall on it."

"But . . ." It still made no sense to her. "What if the ball had bounced somewhere else? Then the waitress wouldn't have fallen."

"Right. Which means that I'm seeing what actually *will* happen, not what might happen. Small distinction maybe, but pretty mind-blowing. I didn't *make* a future to save us; I *chose* the one that saved us. I knew that if I released the ball it would roll where it did because I had already seen it."

"And what if none of the futures had provided an escape? You couldn't do something to change it?"

He shook his head. "I don't know. Maybe not."

The notion made her mind hurt. She sighed and put her face in her hands. Twice now he had saved her. She couldn't be sure about the intentions of the first two men at Berkeley, but the look in Hilal's eyes was unmistakable. She'd seen death too many times. The realization made her feel weak. She removed her hands and looked at him.

"You haven't . . . seen anything else?"

"No. No, I don't have a clue what's next. I just see in these spurts. We're going to the State Department."

His face was pale. A bead of sweat ran past his temple. The agnostic in him was shaken, she thought. Allah had sent him to save her—it was the only thing that made sense. As a Muslim she'd always been taught that whatever happens is Allah's will. Islam was fatalistic in that way. So this stranger had been put in her path to save her from certain death. At least for the moment.

Miriam gazed out the window, suddenly awed by the truth of it. Her fleeing had not been in vain. Surely she'd been *meant* to flee. Maybe Samir was on the way to rescue her at this very moment, and Seth was keeping her until then. She breathed a prayer for the will of Allah and for her safety.

"This is crazy," he said.

She couldn't disagree.

"This is plain nuts. I'm only seeing into the immediate future—a few minutes or so. This'll make the propeller heads go ballistic. Do you have any idea what this means?"

"It means that Allah is speaking to you."

"No. Actually, the moon-god can't speak. He's dead."

"Pardon?"

"What this means is that God can't exist. He's—"

"No, about the moon-god," Miriam said.

"Al-ilah. The moon-god to the locals. One of over six hundred deities worshiped in Arabia during the prophet's lifetime. It's where some believed he first got the idea for his religion, although I can't say I agree. Just a passing comment." He said it all staring ahead, lost in his own calculations, hardly knowing what he was saying, she thought. His own convictions were so distant from her own that he slaughtered them by rote.

He glanced at her and seemed to sense her horror at his accusations. "Sorry. I'm not trying to pick on your god, but this isn't a god speaking. Not your god nor anyone's god. In fact, that's the point."

She wanted to reach over and slap him. Him with all his brains and his big mouth. What did he know?

"I thought you believed in God," she said.

"I did. But now I can't, can I? By definition, an omniscient God *must* know the future. If God knows *the* future—if he has seen into the future and knows what will in fact happen—then the probability of there being another future, other than the one God knows, is zero. By definition there can only be one future. Follow?"

She thought about it. "No."

"If God knows that I'm going to cough in exactly ten seconds, then I'm going to cough in ten seconds, right?"

"Unless he changes his mind."

"And he would *know* that he's going to change his mind. He would still know the end result, regardless of what caused it. Right?"

"Okay."

"That's the future an omniscient God would know, the one that will ultimately happen. That's what it means to be God."

"That's what you just said."

Seth paused. "But that means that any *other* future has a probability of zero. That there's only one *possible* future and that's the future God knows."

"I think you're repeating yourself."

"But, I've just seen more than one actual future! I didn't just see *one.* I saw many and I know for a fact that they were all possible! Therefore there can't be a God who knows only *one.* Yet a God, by definition, knows *the* one." Seth looked at the horizon. "Unless there is no God. I do believe I've just become an agnostic. Perhaps an atheist."

"This makes no sense," Miriam said.

"Either there is a God who already knows precisely the *one* future that will occur, deeming man's ability to affect the future nonsense. Or there are many real futures for man to choose, unknown by any intelligence. No God. I am living the latter, so as of now I am not sure I can believe in the existence of God, an agnostic at least."

"I understand your logic, but it all falls apart when you bring more than logic to bear. Have you considered the fact that you only seem to see these futures when you are with me?"

He blinked. It obviously hadn't occurred to him.

"Except for the first two, you're right. That's true. So maybe you affect me somehow." He looked at her and smiled. "You make my mind . . . I don't know . . . crazy."

"Perhaps it's women. They do that to you."

"Women?"

"Yes, of course. Your exceptional understanding of women and love, remember? It's advanced to the point where when you're with one, you can actually know what they are going to wear and say before they do. You're nothing less than the supreme male."

He blushed. As he would say, she'd scored, but she hardly felt satisfied by it. The fact was, despite his tendency to take a sword to her beliefs, she felt safe with him. Though misguided in spiritual terms, he was true to the bone. Genuine.

"The woman has a brain after all," she said, smirking in spite of herself.

"Touché, as we would say," he said. "Not bad, Princess. Not bad at all."

"And this woman with this brain thinks your logic, though impeccable, is still somehow flawed."

"An oxymoron," he said.

"Nevertheless, my heart tells me it's true. Do you trust my heart?"

That threw him completely, she thought. They were sparring—he with his mind, she with her heart. No, not with her heart, because her heart belonged to Samir. Both with their minds, then.

"I'll have to think about it," Seth said.

"Then think with your heart," she said.

They drove for over an hour, switching freeways several times, slowly closing in on their destination. Although Saudi Arabia covered as much ground as the entire western United States, her population was no larger than this one city. Los Angeles. Seth made passing remarks about the massive metropolis, but for the most part they were cynical and hard to grasp. Miriam felt distant from this crowded land. Lonely again.

Samir, Samir, my dearest Samir. Where are you, my love?

A knot rose into her throat. If she had more time, she could have planned to flee with Samir. But there hadn't been time. She had to leave the very day she did, or end up married to Omar. Perhaps once the Americans gave her safe harbor she could contact Samir.

She had left most of her money at Hillary's house. Maybe her father could send money with Samir. But what would the sheik do? He was in his own bid for power. He'd sold her into the king's house for power in the first place. How could she ever trust him? No, she would have to make contact directly with Samir. Maybe through Sultana.

"Okay. Here we are," Seth said, interrupting her thoughts. "That gray building across the street. See it?"

"Yes."

Seth pulled into a parking spot, muttering that the vacancy of the spot was a miracle. She was tempted to ask him how miracles could exist without a God, but she knew he'd used the word only as a figure of speech. He turned the key off and sat staring at the building.

"What if they aren't friendly?" Miriam asked.

"Harland was sure they would be. I don't see any reason why they wouldn't be. You're here to ask for political asylum—they can't just pull out their guns and shoot you."

"You could choose better words."

"Sorry."

"I'm not worried about being shot. But being sent back to Saudi Arabia would be worse than being shot."

"I won't let that happen," he said.

"No? And why should I trust you?"

He looked at her, slightly dumbstruck. "Because I've saved you twice already. Or maybe because I actually care about what happens to you."

"Do you?"

Apparently he hadn't expected the quick comeback.

"Yes."

She looked at the doors across the street. "Then I'll trust you, Seth Border." She opened her door and stepped out.

They walked in, an inconspicuous couple, she thought. Seth was just another American citizen, dressed in his corduroys, black canvas shoes, and orange T-shirt, wearing his hair slightly disheveled, which she'd noticed during their drive was not so uncommon, at least in California. She felt natural in the blue jeans and white blouse, not because she was accustomed to wearing them, but because they made her feel like a woman. A free woman, walking into a public building with an unmarried man.

The thought gave her a surge of confidence. She'd done it, hadn't she? Even if they did take her now, she had found her slice of freedom. She would have to return here with Samir one day.

They stopped inside the swinging doors and gazed over a large lobby crowded with people from a virtual melting pot of races. Seth took her arm and guided her toward a desk under a large sign that read INFORMATION.

She was aware of his hand's warmth on her elbow, only the second man ever to touch her skin. For a brief moment she felt naked, walking beside him, face and arms uncovered. *You're being silly, Miriam. You've been tied up in the black sack so long that you don't know what it means to be touched innocently by a man.*

A woman with black-framed glasses who wore her hair in a bun eyed them from the information counter. Three security guards stood behind her, legs spread and arms folded, at ease.

Her mind returned to the touch of Seth's hand around her arm. Here she was, about to give herself up to the Americans, and her mind was distracted by the touch of a man. Absurd and juvenile, but true.

The first time Samir touched her had been in Madrid, in a park—she couldn't remember the name. His fingers had lightly brushed her right cheek, and a gentle wave of warmth had spread right down her spine. She'd thrown her arms around him and wept, rather forward perhaps, but she felt powerless to stop herself. They'd sat, trembling in each other's arms for an hour. She'd learned then that love was like a drug. Although they hadn't found an opportunity to be alone again on that trip, the intoxication of that one hour had melted the two remaining days into a dizzying, forbidden pool from which she thought she would never emerge.

Feeling Seth's fingers on her elbow now was like putting her toes back in that pool, she thought.

What has gotten into you, Miriam! You may be a woman on the outside, but you're a foolish girl—

Seth suddenly stopped. His grip on her elbow tightened.

"What is it?" she asked.

His eyes were wide, fixed on the guards. They blinked.

"What? Seth?"

He turned toward her and forced her around. "Just walk. Don't look back, just walk."

The urgency in his voice said enough. She walked. Stride for stride with him, tense from head to toe now.

"What—"

"Don't speak."

She swallowed.

At the door another guard she hadn't noticed lifted his radio and spoke quickly. His eyes met hers and she knew he recognized them. The guard walked toward the door to cut them off.

Seth stopped. His hand trembled at her elbow.

"You're frightening me," she said. "There's a problem?"

"We have to get out of here!"

"I thought—"

"Don't move! Don't speak, don't breathe."

"Please—"

"I'll be right back. Please, Miriam, don't move. If you want to live out the day, do not move."

Seth left her side, stepping long for one side of the atrium. The guard saw him and stopped. Miriam's heart beat steadily. She glanced back—two of the guards from behind the counter walked toward her. Don't move? She should be running! Don't move, he'd said.

She turned back to him. "Seth?"

Seth had reached the wall. She saw the red box on the wall and knew it was a fire alarm before he pulled it.

A shrill bell clanged to life. For an endless moment the bustle of the room seemed to freeze in time. Seth spun around and yelled above the bell. "There's a bomb in the building set to go off in thirty seconds. Please exit immediately in an orderly fashion!"

Contradicting his own advice, Seth ran. "Out! Everyone out!"

Bedlam broke out. Seth raced for her, and around him a flood of humanity rushed for the door, set in motion by Seth's sprint. Screams joined the bell and Miriam fought the impulse to join them.

Seth reached her. "Hurry. Follow me!"

They ran for a side door with FIRE stamped on its surface. The guards cut across the room to intercept. But to do so, they had to cross the traffic of running bodies. Seth and Miriam reached the side door well ahead of the closest guard.

A gunshot detonated over their heads. "Freeze! Stop where you are!" Whether the guard addressed the entire mob or her, Miriam didn't know. Whatever the case, the action dumped panic into the room. Screams broke out and the rush for the door became a stampede.

Seth and Miriam crashed through the fire door. Seth took five long steps toward the front of the building and slid to a stop. The street was filling with people.

"Run!" Miriam panted.

He grabbed her hand and spun her around. "This way!" They sprinted to an alley and then behind the building, where a couple dozen cars sat parked. Seth pulled up just around the corner, panting.

"What about your car?" Miriam asked.

He released her hand and looked frantically from car to car, muttering through clenched teeth. "Come on! Come on!"

A male voice yelled around the corner and Miriam stole a quick glance. A guard had exited the building and was running toward the alley.

"They're coming!"

"Try the cars! Find an unlocked car!"

This was his plan? "An unlocked car?"

"Unlocked!"

He ran to the nearest car and yanked on the latch. Locked. He ran to another. "Come on. Help me!"

Miriam ran for a blue Mercury Sable and pulled on the door latch. The door sprang open. She spun to tell him, but he was already racing for her.

"Get in!" He was whispering frantically now. "On the floor."

She clambered in and flattened herself on the front seat. She didn't know how he expected her to get on the floor—the steering wheel was in the way and . . .

A knee or a hand pushed into her back and she grunted.

"Shhh!"

He was climbing over her. His full weight crushed her and she nearly yelled at him. But she quickly decided that he would never climb over her unless it was his only option. She gasped for air.

The door thudded softly closed behind her. Silence smothered her. She pushed up on her elbows to give her lungs room to breathe. His body was dead weight.

"Don't move!" he whispered.

"What do you mean don't move? You're *crushing* me!"

He was silent for a moment, as if considering this information.

"The guard's in the parking lot," he whispered. "He'll see me if I get up."

"You're . . . suffocating me."

Another silence. It was true, she was positioned wrong for breathing, but her shock didn't help. On the other hand, she thought she really might suffocate under him. Imagine, she wouldn't die by drowning at the hands of the mutawa, but by suffocating under the body of an American.

"Should I move?" he asked.

"Y-yes. Off my back."

"What if he sees me?"

If he didn't move, she would suffocate for sure. She swung her elbow back as much out of self-defense as anything. It landed in his side and he grunted.

Now he moved. His weight shifted from her back to her legs and she nearly cried out with the pain of it. At least she could breathe. His knees found the seat between her legs, and then his weight eased altogether.

They remained motionless for a long minute, breathing hard. Then his body began to tremble and it occurred to her that the poor man must be supporting himself in a strenuous position.

"Should I look?" he asked.

"Yes."

He eased himself up.

"I think we're clear," he finally said. He reached forward, shoved the passenger door open, and scrambled out over her, all elbows and knees again, apologizing profusely with her every grunt.

He spilled out onto the gravel, sprang to his feet, and gave her an awkward look as she struggled to sit. He scanned the lot quickly and then ran back around to the driver's door. He climbed in and shut the door.

"Sorry. You okay?"

"No."

He grinned sheepishly. "But you're alive."

"Barely. There's no key."

"Who needs keys?"

Evidently not Seth. It took him less than a minute to pull out three wires and press two together to start the car. Thirty seconds later they eased out of the alley and pulled onto the street. Behind them a number of fire trucks and police cars had arrived with lights flashing. The Cougar was blocked in by two cars.

Seth sped down the street, smirking like a boy, leaving the chaos behind.

"Boy, that was close," he said.

"Thanks to you."

They drove a block in silence, Seth checking the mirrors every two seconds.

"Actually, that's not fair," she said. "You got us out of the building, although I'm still not sure why we ran."

"I got us out. But you found us wheels." He paused. "They were going to turn you over to Hilal."

"You're sure?"

"Pretty sure. Yes, I'm sure."

"You saw that in the building, but you saw no way of escape once we got to the alley. So your gift has its limits."

"It's sporadic. But I think it's gaining strength. I'm seeing more and I'm seeing longer."

They turned onto a side street and then onto another. Still no sign of pursuit. Miriam began to relax.

"Now what?" she asked.

He looked at her for what seemed like an inordinate amount of time and then faced forward, took a deep breath, and let it out slowly.

"Now we run, Princess. Now we really run."

16

HILAL EYED THE DIPLOMATS around the conference table, thinking that debating protocol while the woman and the American fled was a waste of time. The State Department's cooperation was critical now, but not at the expense of allowing Miriam to disappear. The fact that she had escaped him once infuriated him enough.

He closed his eyes, aware of the heat at the base of his neck. The American had handed him an insult unlike any he'd ever been dealt. The man's words ran circles through his head still. Stupid, absurd words that he had no business listening to, much less considering. And yet he had. Dealing with Seth Border was in some ways as important to him now as dealing with the sheik's daughter.

" . . . if it makes any difference to you, Mr. Sahban."

Hilal looked at the man who'd addressed him. Peter Smaley, deputy to the secretary of state, had flown in from Washington with Iona Bergren. Bob Lord, the undersecretary for State Department affairs, sat beside them, waiting for his response. The only other person in the small conference room was Clive Masters, on loan from their NSA. Within a minute of the meeting's commencement, Hilal had judged them accurately and placed them in their respective roles, he was sure of it. Smaley was here to administer the meeting and make sure that Saudi-American relations were not threatened by this event. Lord was here to play the antagonist—the individual-rights activist who would rather see a hundred Arabs die than one American. Iona, the woman, was the most understanding of the Middle East's sensitivities despite her gender. And Clive Masters, the NSA operative, was the killer here. Of them all, he was the only one who gave Hilal some pause.

"Forgive me, my mind was elsewhere," he said. "Could you restate the question?"

"Bob has suggested that we pull back and let them surface," Smaley said.

"We are dealing with a time-sensitive issue here," Hilal said. "I'm not sure you appreciate the difficulty this puts my government in. You do not sit back and let a coup surface."

Iona cleared her throat and leaned forward. She looked to be of Mediterranean descent, pretty with olive skin and a rather large nose. She would be an interesting one to become better acquainted with.

"You are saying that the princess herself confessed to being an integral component of a planned coup? Why would she confess this?"

Amazing how intelligent a woman could be if given the opportunity. Saudi Arabia would have to change one day. "I believe she thought it would dissuade me from taking her back."

"And you believe her?"

"I have no doubt."

"Seems rather assuming," Bob Lord said. "And either way, if you know about the coup, you don't need her to deal with it. Arrest the parties involved. We certainly don't need to bring in gunslingers to hunt down a couple of people who've done nothing more than run for their lives."

"She has broken our laws, Mr. Lord. And your assumption that we can simply arrest the suspected parties in Saudi Arabia shows your ignorance of our society. Even if we did know who was behind the coup—"

"You said Sheik Abu Ali al-Asamm was behind it."

"He is naturally an accessory. But the coup would not come from him," Hilal explained patiently. "And if arresting the sheik made any political sense, we would have done it twenty years ago instead of adopting his daughter. He's too powerful to arrest. We need his allegiance, not his head. It's the man among our own that we must expose, and I am convinced the woman knows his identity."

They were silent for a moment.

"You'll take the princess back and torture her for this information," Lord said.

"Our government is at stake, Mr. Lord. We will do what we must. And if she can't be returned, then she must be . . . dealt with here."

Lord just stared at him.

"I'm sorry, I don't understand how anything beyond her apprehension's in our interest," Smaley said.

"It's in our interest because it effectively cuts off this coup attempt," Iona interjected. "Even if it doesn't expose the parties involved."

Hilal gave her a soft smile. "Precisely. It also gives my government leverage with Sheik Abu Ali al-Asamm."

At the far end of the table, the NSA operative chuckled. He didn't say anything, he just stared at Hilal with pale blue eyes and nodded through a soft chuckle. Clive Masters was no idiot. His hair was a sandy red and his skin was unusually white—a strange sight with his gray-blue eyes. Disturbing even. He would have to watch this man.

"Explain," Smaley said.

Hilal turned from Clive Masters. "The sheik will be distressed to learn that his daughter has been killed. Naturally, so will King Fahd, her adopted father. We will approach the sheik and explain our suspicions that she was killed by the man whose marriage she fled. It may be in the sheik's interest to reveal that man's identity and look for favor with King Fahd, which we will be pleased to extend."

"So the woman's death becomes a bridge back to the sheik," Lord said.

"Precisely."

"But this assumes that the United States is interested in keeping your king in power at the price of an innocent woman's life."

Iona turned to the deputy secretary. "It's not as simple as keeping the king in power. It's a matter of regional stability. I'm confident that the secretary would agree. Where Saudi Arabia goes, goes the Middle East. The United States can't afford a coup in Saudi Arabia. Period."

"I wasn't aware that you were so partial to the House of Saud," Lord said. "Their track record on human rights isn't exactly stellar."

Iona looked at Hilal, evidently deciding how frank she would be with him in the room. Publicly supporting a government that still delivered amputations as punishment for theft and stonings as punishment for adultery had always been difficult for the sensitive Americans.

"Please," Hilal said. "Off the record, I know as well as you that certain practices in my country are, shall we say, outdated. The desert has a way of trapping us in time. But the next king of Saudi Arabia will not be as progressive in his thinking as King Fahd; I can promise you that. In fact, the only reason we are here today, in search for a woman on the run, is because some fundamentalist considers the king *too* progressive to deserve power. We are in a battle against the extreme elements of Islam, my friends. Miriam is a pawn of those extreme elements. Dealing with her is not so different than dealing with a terrorist."

"Terrorist?" Lord objected. "She's no Bin Laden. She's a refugee seeking political asylum. We have laws to consider here."

Iona still studied Hilal. "I am partial to the House of Saud only to the extent that the alternatives are less appealing," she said. "I think that's the administration's policy as well. Moving Saudi Arabia into the twenty-first century is a tedious task, but as long as the movement's forward rather than backward, I'm okay. If a militant were to seize control of Saudi Arabia, a dozen neighbors would swing their way. So in some ways the minister makes a good point. Track record on human rights aside."

She looked at Lord. "However unfair it may seem, the fate of your innocent princess may have more bearing on the fate of the region than you would guess. I'm not sure I'm ready to gamble the stability of the Middle East to protect one woman."

Lord's face darkened a shade. "What are you suggesting? That we kill this woman?"

"I'm suggesting that we avoid a bloodbath in the Middle East, Bob. We're the State Department; that's part of what we do. You may think of her as a refugee seeking political asylum; I see her as a criminal on the run. We have an obligation to help our ally bring her to justice."

"Justice in this country doesn't come at the end of a gun."

"No, but justice in the Middle East does. And I don't recall mentioning a gun. I'm simply laying all of our cards on the table."

Hilal couldn't have put it better. As far as he was concerned, the discussion here was over. It was time to go after the couple. Regardless of what the Americans did or did not do, he would hunt them down. He could use the intelligence the Americans would generate, of course. For that alone, perhaps this meeting was worth the time after all. But either way, he could not allow Miriam to remain a free woman.

"And what about the American? Who is Seth?" Smaley asked.

"He's a student from Berkeley," Iona said. "Mr. Masters?"

Clive Masters faced the group, amused by the banter. Smaley and company weren't necessarily slouches, but the Saudi diplomat, Hilal, had them hogtied and properly disciplined. "Diplomat" was the wrong word for the man. He was a killer, pure and simple. And judging by his hard eyes, a good one. The king of Saudi Arabia would employ nothing less.

"Seth Border," Clive said, shifting in his chair. "The man you're after just happens to have an IQ that makes Einstein's look normal."

"I wasn't aware we were after a man," Lord said.

"Well, if you're after the woman, you're after the man. I don't know how the brightest mind in the country happened to team up with our Saudi princess, but I can tell you that it's him, not her, who you need to go after. You find him, you find her. And I was just curious, sir," he said, looking into the Saudi's dark eyes. "How exactly did Seth manage to stall you in that bathroom?"

If the Saudi registered the slightest surprise, he didn't show it. The man had Freon ice in his veins.

"If I were in your shoes, I would have killed her then. But Seth pulled some trick, didn't he?"

Smaley cleared his throat. "I'm not sure what you're suggesting, Clive, but this isn't a run-and-shoot operation. We're dealing with complications that require a measure of caution. You're here because of your past association with Seth, but that doesn't mean that you go after them with a bazooka."

"A bazooka? Not exactly the weapon of my choice. I was merely pointing out, Peter . . ." He paused there for the simple reason that the deputy's facade annoyed him. Before they'd gone their separate ways, they attended the FBI's Quantico school together. Small world. They'd virtually tied for the highest academic scores the bureau had ever given before or since. But not all bright minds see eye to eye. Some are cut out for the grind and gore of detective work, and others make better politicians. Clive had gone on to receive a doctorate in psychology and had put in five years as an FBI profiler before moving on to the NSA. Peter had pursued a career with the State Department.

Now, twenty years later, they found themselves on opposite sides of the same coin. The perfect diplomat and the perfect detective.

Clive continued. "I'm saying, Peter, that if our friend here had killed the woman in that bathroom, as he probably intended, we wouldn't be here trying to keep the Middle East from blowing up. And we all know that if the House of Saud *is* overthrown by militants, sooner or later the Middle East *will* blow up. But he didn't kill her, did he? And frankly, I'm just a tiny bit curious how our fugitive managed to pull one over an accomplished . . . diplomat's head."

Lord looked at him like he'd just tossed up on the table. Thank God the rest weren't so naive.

"Try to control yourself, Clive," Smaley said. "Whatever you might think, not everyone's a gunslinger."

"Perhaps if I had been in my own country I would have taken care of the problem," Hilal said, staring Clive down with those black eyes of his. He dipped his head slightly. "But I am not. Now it will be your job. And by the sounds of it, you are well qualified."

The man was either sucking up or insulting him, and Clive wasn't ready to decide.

"Can you bring them in?" Iona asked.

"Do you want her dead, or do you want her brought in?" Clive asked.

"Brought in," Smaley said. "Preferably."

A faint smile curved Hilal's lips.

"They're headed east in a blue Mercury Sable reported stolen from the alley behind this building," Clive said. "They have a two-hour head start and, according to the clerk at the Wal-Mart they stopped at, they're loaded with cash. Seems simple enough. We put out a new APB, cast a broad net, and try to anticipate his next move. Run-of-the-mill. But Seth Border's not exactly run-of-the-mill. If he hadn't given the slip to three different parties, you might guess that his mind is geared more for breaking the light barrier than for leading a chase. But you'd be wrong."

"A simple yes or no would do," Smaley said.

"I'm not sure it would, Peter. As I've explained, in a case like this the best way to get to the girl is to get to the man. But I'm not sure it's in our best interest to end Seth Border's life. He's not exactly an easy human being to replace. We can't kill him."

Smaley smiled. "I didn't know you were so soft-hearted. Your friend may be a genius, but we have the stability of a region to think about. I'm sure you can figure out a way to outwit him. Live up to that reputation of yours."

His old rival hadn't lost his touch. Clive gave him a polite nod. Give credit where credit is due, but owe no man anything.

"In the meantime, we will keep you informed," Smaley said to the Saudi. "You may tell your government that you have our full cooperation."

"Then I'm sure you wouldn't mind allowing me to follow the investigation on a real-time basis," Hilal said. "I would like to be updated on the hour."

The snake was going after Miriam on his own, Clive thought wryly.

"Of course. Now if you'll excuse me, I have a plane to catch." The deputy secretary stood. "Please keep me informed." He cast a glance at Clive and left with Iona.

Hilal stared at Clive in the brief silence that followed. Clive stood. "You'll excuse me as well, gentlemen, but I have a fugitive to catch."

"He's very quick," Hilal said, holding his stare.

"How so?"

"With his mind."

So, the Saudi had been outwitted after all. Lord watched them with a raised brow.

"And if you were he? Where would you go?"

"I don't know your city. But I would get out of the city."

Smart man. "You wouldn't go underground?"

"It would be difficult to go underground with a Saudi princess. Yes?"

"Yes." Clive walked for the door.

"I believe that he may also be unusually intuitive," the Saudi said. "Perhaps clairvoyant."

Clive turned back. Clairvoyant? Hilal was a Muslim. Evidently a mystic. He could see how facing the man *Scientific American* had called the next Einstein might feel like going up against Elijah himself. Either way, Hilal was right about Seth: He would be an elusive prey.

But then Clive had built his reputation on tracking elusive prey. As of yet, he'd cornered every man he'd gone after in this country. Granted, Pascal Penelop had taken seven years and Al Cooper three, but both were now behind bars alongside another twenty-three fugitives he'd collared.

"Thanks," Clive said. "I'll keep it in mind."

He left, knowing he'd see Hilal again.

17

THEY ARE IN A BLUE MERCURY SABLE, believed to be headed east out of the city. The police have issued an order to stop the car when it is located."

Omar stared down at the smoked-glass window high over Century Boulevard from the tenth story without acknowledging Assir. Sa'id stood to Omar's right, hands held at his waist. These two had failed once, but they would not fail again.

An orange-and-yellow plane floated by the window on its final approach to LAX. SOUTHWEST AIRLINES, the tail read. It looked like a lizard to him.

He'd left his thobe in London's Heathrow Airport in favor of a dark gray silk suit. With his trimmed beard, he looked more Mediterranean than Arabic—intentionally so considering his mission. He'd been in the United States a dozen times, and he'd learned early that Arabs from Saudi Arabia tended to draw attention, especially if they placed the title of Prince before their names. There was a time for attention, of course, particularly in nightclubs frequented by women.

But this time he was after only one woman. She was a Shi'i Muslim, she was rightfully his property, and he would have her at any cost. Or she would die in accordance with the law.

He remembered watching his first stoning as a boy of seven. They had pulled the woman out of a wagon and pushed her roughly to the ground. The wagon was piled high with stones the size of a man's fist. After a short pronouncement of guilt, thirty men started throwing the stones. It had been a harrowing sight at first, seeing the stones bounce off her body as she waddled around on her knees. She was in her abaaya and veil, of course, but that only made the stoning mysterious. He tried to picture what was happening under those garments and then picked up a rock himself. He had to lob it as hard as he could to even reach the woman. Amazingly, it landed on her head and bounced off. The black cloth darkened with blood. His father laughed and handed him another stone. The woman passed out four times and was reawakened each time before she finally died.

He later learned that she was seventeen and her crime was flirting with a man.

The flight over the Atlantic had given him time to stew over the matter of his bride, and with each passing hour his anger swelled. This chase wasn't simply about his right to claim what belonged to him—it was about the future of Saudi Arabia. Not the future of who ruled the kingdom, although that, too, was at stake. But more importantly, the future of a sacred culture in which man was ordained to rule the woman and ensure the worship of Allah. The future of Islam *itself* was at stake. What would the prophet Mohammed have done if one of his wives had fled? Or Aziz?

Aziz would have had her head! He would have chased her to the corners of the desert and dragged her back by the hair to be made an example of.

The world had changed in the fifty years since the first king's death. The world had placed Islam under assault. Not that Omar had ever been such a devout Muslim. But now one woman flagrantly mocked an entire way of life. He would not tolerate her gross affront to Allah and his prophet.

And she was Omar's woman. He couldn't stomach the thought of returning without her.

Omar turned from the window. "This is from General Mustafa or from the scanners?"

"Both. The lead investigator on the case is making his way toward San Bernardino."

Mustafa had filled them in on Hilal's meeting with the State Department. The fact that they'd brought in the NSA to track down his wife both pleased and angered Omar. On the one hand, they could be instrumental in leading him to her. The agent on the case reported to Hilal on the hour, and whatever Hilal learned, Mustafa learned. This was good.

On the other hand, no one had a right to the woman but him. The fact that Hilal was going after the woman as well was not as large of a concern as the American agent's involvement. If Hilal found Miriam first, he would have to be killed, but the prospect of killing the king's man was like child's play next to killing the NSA agent, if he were to find Miriam first. And Omar would have to kill him, wouldn't he? He couldn't allow the Americans to take her into their custody and coddle her. They would return her to the king. His marriage to her would be lost.

"Then we go to San Bernardino," he said, moving toward the door.

Either way, Omar's plan was now straightforward. This Clive would lead him to Miriam and he would be the jackal, to close in after she'd been found. To steal the prey. To make the prey his wife and then to extract payment for her insult to Allah. To Islam.

To him.

Samir stood at the gates to the great mosque in Mecca, dressed in a traditional white seamless ihram. He stared at the three-story cloth-covered cube known as the Ka'bah, which sat in the sun sixty meters off, black and oddly plain considering its reputation as the most holy place on earth. Allah gave it to Adam after expelling him from the Garden of Eden and then later led Abraham to it. Through the ages many idolatrous people had bowed at its base, to any one of a hundred gods that had been worshiped in Mecca before the prophet Mohammed claimed it as his own. The pagans would come here to worship before dawn, stripped of their clothing and wailing loudly. The mystery that lay behind that black cloth felt to Samir like a physical force that squeezed his chest every time he came to the holy mosque.

The courtyard boiled over with several thousand Muslims on pilgrimage. Mumbled prayers rose to the sky, a steady groan to Allah. But Samir wasn't concerned with their prayers; he sought his creator's guidance for his own dilemma. And only now, eyes fixed on this most holy of holies, did he finally know the will of Allah.

Not once did the suras in the Qur'an call Allah a God of love. But the teachers were right, he thought—it was because God's love was self-evident. One doesn't need to say that the Ka'bah is black if everyone already knows its color. Mohammed had no need to expound on the love of God because love was at the very heart of Islam. So then Samir's own life would have to be a life led by love.

And there could be no greater love than the love he felt for Miriam. Nothing mattered except her now.

Samir left the mosque and walked quickly toward the limousine that waited on the main street. His love for Miriam was as genuine as the beating of his own heart. He'd never exposed himself to any other human being as he had to Miriam. The memories of their innocent touches in Madrid haunted him still.

What Miriam didn't know about him would undoubtedly shock her. On the other hand, she probably suspected his true identity already. In Saudi Arabia, where flesh was so deliberately covered, one tended to take note of the flesh they saw. Miriam had seen his bare chest and upper arms only three times, once by mistake when he was changing shirts in the garage, and twice when she'd pulled his thobe aside in innocent curiosity. He'd never exposed himself beyond this, of course. That would wait for marriage. But she'd seen more of him than any woman had. And tracing his chest with her index finger, she'd wondered aloud how a driver came to have such strong muscles. He'd made a joke about lifting all her heavy bags in and out of the car, and they'd laughed hysterically as only lovers can laugh at the slightest hint of humor.

Miriam wasn't a dull woman. Her intelligence had first attracted Samir to her, before he'd even seen her face. Surely she would know that her true father, the most powerful sheik among the Shi'i, would not entrust his daughter to a common man. But he doubted Miriam knew that the man she'd fallen in love with was well-known in small circles as a warrior. An exceptional one, worthy of the task given him.

The sheik had spared no expense in training him to be Miriam's protector. Now, for the first time, he would put that training to good use.

He opened the rear door and slid into the limousine. The sheik sat against the opposite door.

"Drive," the sheik said.

The driver pulled into the street.

"So. What has Allah told you?" Al-Asamm asked.

"Allah has told me that he is a God of love."

The sheik looked at him. "You will go?"

"Yes. I will go. For love."

The sheik nodded and smiled gently. "You'll be interested to know that the Americans are after her as well. Hilal, Omar, and now the Americans."

"Good. It will only make my job easier. You're receiving the information still?"

"Yes. You'll know what they know. But we're running out of time. They can't be allowed to reach her before you do, Samir. Hilal, at least, will kill her. And there's no telling what Omar will do out from under my eyes. He won't kill her, but he may maim her."

"I won't let that happen. You trained me to protect her—I will do just that. And I have the advantage—your daughter knows me. As soon as I'm in a safe position, she'll come to me. She loves me."

Samir looked out the side window at the faithful streaming for the mosque and breathed a prayer for her safety until he arrived.

"And I love her," he said.

18

MIRIAM SAT BESIDE SETH, her mind spinning with the realization that something special was happening to them. In the few days since she'd learned of her betrothal to Omar, her life had not only been turned upside down, it had been turned inside out, as Seth said.

She'd fled on this wild impulse that Sultana had inspired in her—that was the upside-down part of this situation.

Then she'd been thrown together with this unlikely character sitting beside her now, and that was the inside-out part. He was the living antithesis of everything she knew, from his haphazard dress, to his whimsical outlook on life, to this madness about seeing into the future. She found him unexpectedly fascinating, which was just as inside out. He should repel her, not attract her. Not that she was truly attracted, at least not in any romantic sense of the word. No, definitely not!

The entire matter both frustrated her to the bone and thrilled her in a way that confused her. If only she could get word to Samir, he would come; she knew he would. He would come for love.

The car veered into an alley to the right, sending her leaning hard to the left. She threw a hand out to keep from falling into his lap, inadvertently shoving Seth into his door. His head knocked against his window.

He grunted.

She pulled herself quickly back to her side. "You're driving like a madman!" she said.

He glanced in the mirror and slowed, eyes wide, sweat beading his forehead. His mind was on the chase—she doubted he'd even heard her.

"Are you listening?"

"They know that we're in a blue Sable," he said.

"They do? How do you know?"

"Because a dozen police cars within a mile of us are looking for a blue Mercury Sable as we speak. There was one coming our way back there, which is why I turned when I did. We'd have been pulled over if I hadn't."

She looked ahead at the approaching cross street. His knowledge of what was about to occur—these possible futures, as he put it—flew in the face of her fatalistic Islamic world-view, but she could hardly deny that he could see things. Of course, he understood no better than she, despite all his curious intellect.

"How do you know we won't encounter any police on this street?"

"I don't. I can only see what happens in the next few minutes or so. But I'm pretty sure that if I take a left up here, I can get on 10 headed east without being spotted. It's a future in which we don't get stopped. At least for a few minutes."

"If you can see into the future, why can't you just see what we need to do to escape and stop all this nonsense?"

"That's not the way—"

His eyes widened for a brief moment, and he slammed the brake pedal to the floor. The car jerked to a stop, and she crashed into the glove box.

"Ouch!"

He stared ahead. "See, that's what I'm talking about."

"You're going to kill us!"

He snatched an open hand up to motion her to silence. She looked ahead through the windshield. Nothing but cars crossing ahead and a teenager with yellow hair walking across the alley mouth, staring at them.

"What?" she whispered.

"A police cruiser must have turned onto that street ahead," he said in a low voice. "Onto Atlantic."

"I thought this street was safe," she said.

"So did I."

Miriam wasn't sure what to think of these antics. One minute he knew what was happening—or might be happening—the next he didn't. A chill spread over her skull.

He faced her. "I can only see what happens to us in different futures, depending on what we do now. And depending on what other people do now."

His eyes shifted past her, lost in bright blue astonishment. "It's fluid. Whatever happens in this moment changes the next. But . . ." He looked forward. The rush of the cars crossing the street fifty meters ahead of them sounded distant behind their breathing. Miriam stared at Seth, struck by the thought that she was looking at a miracle. Under his tossed blond curls, behind his clear green eyes, Seth's mind was encountering the future. Like a prophet. Like Mohammed.

He spoke softly, as if to himself. "What I saw a few minutes ago has already changed by what other people have decided to do beyond those minutes. I can stay ahead of them, but only for as far as I see out. A few minutes ago I didn't see the police car spotting us on Atlantic. But two minutes have passed and now I do. He must have just decided to turn onto Atlantic, and in doing so, he changed the future. So then I saw a future in which, if we'd proceeded onto Atlantic, we'd be seen. But now that we've stopped we've changed the future again. The police car will only stay on Atlantic long enough to look up the street, see nothing, and then turn up another street. So now we should be okay." He looked at her, a wry smile twisting his mouth. "Incredible."

It didn't make sense, not really. Her mind was bending in impossible directions. Seth eased the car forward.

"You saw all that in the last few seconds?" she asked.

He nodded. "Crazy, huh?"

"But you can't see past a few minutes, so really we could be seen once you turn onto the street anyway?"

"Yes. But, if I'm right, I think I can stay ahead of them. If I could see out even, say, half an hour, they wouldn't stand a chance! Assuming I could keep all those futures in my mind. Incredible."

He started the car forward, turned onto Atlantic, and headed north toward the freeway that Miriam could see arching over the street, about half a mile ahead of them.

"Like right now, we will hit the freeway in less than three minutes. I can see out that far." He looked out the windshield, lost in his own explanation. "And I can see that when we do, we'll be okay. But every second that passes now opens another second that I can see into the future. Just because I don't see any problems in the next three minutes doesn't mean there isn't a problem waiting four minutes out, created by a decision someone is making now. A chopper pilot might decide to fly over the freeway . . ." He trailed off.

Miriam lifted both hands and rubbed her temples. Her heart thumped, unrelenting. Yes, this was indeed inside out. Seth's explanation defied every last shred of her reasoning. Seth wasn't seeing the future as a prophet might, in snapshots of events far to come. He was seeing a steady stream of events as they *might* occur, depending on what *they* did. How many possibilities could he see? She was afraid to ask, afraid it would make the entire notion more ludicrous.

"You're seeing more than one future; that's hard enough to believe. And you're seeing them only a few minutes out. I'm really supposed to believe this?"

"Come on, Miriam," he said with a side glance. "You're smarter than that. This is actually happening. Was I wrong about Hilal?"

"I don't know. We ran off."

"Ouch. That hurts."

"You're hurt?"

"No, your doubting me hurts."

She'd hurt his feelings. "I'm sorry, I didn't mean to offend you. But have you ever heard of seeing a few minutes into the future? Many futures?"

"Seeing many futures isn't a new phenomenon," he said. "In fact it's quite common in the Bible if not the Qur'an. Prophets repeatedly saw multiple futures. If you do such and such, you'll be destroyed by the Babylonians. But if you do such and such, Jerusalem will be saved."

"That's two futures. Not many," she said.

"Two, three, whatever. Elisha told King Jehoash to strike the arrows on the ground. He did, three times. Elisha then informed the king that he would've defeated Aram four times if he would have struck the ground four times, and six times if he had struck the ground six times, et cetera. That's at least six different futures based on what the king might have done. Multiple futures. That's what I'm seeing. Different outcomes depending on what we do."

"You said you don't believe in prophets. Yet you use them as examples?"

"Did I say I didn't believe that some prophets have actually seen things? No. In fact, ancient prophecy has proven amazingly accurate. I just don't believe the prophets received their revelations from an all-knowing God any more than I am now. People have obviously seen things—I'm a living example of that! The question is how and why."

"And what about seeing only a few minutes out? That is also common?"

"The future's the future, one minute or one year. But yes. The Bible is full of seeing only a very short time out. So is the Qur'an. You don't need to pretend that what's happening to me is impossible. Religious literature is full of it already."

"But not both: many futures and only a short time out."

"What do issues of time and quantity have to do with the feasibility of my seeing multiple futures?" He smiled at her, and she couldn't mistake the impression that he was trying to be kind to her, patiently indulging her difficulties.

Either way, he had made his points: One, history and particularly religious literature were full of examples of people who'd experienced a phenomenon similar to his, and, two, he didn't believe the source of his gift was from God because his gift proved that a God who knew *the* future couldn't exist. In a crazy kind of way, it made sense.

Seth turned to the west one block before they reached the freeway.

She looked at him. "I thought we were safe until we entered the freeway."

"We were. We are," he said. "But now I see that a mile down the freeway, a cruiser is headed west. I couldn't see that until just now—it was too far out. We need to delay our entry onto the freeway for a minute."

Even with Seth's extraordinary gift, they were vulnerable. If he made a misjudgment in one minute, they could be caught in the next. And what would happen when he fell asleep? He hadn't slept in nearly two days.

"Do me a favor," Seth said. "I put the Advil in the glove box. Could you dig out a couple? Thinking like this is giving me a headache."

She gave him two and he swallowed them without water.

"Thank you."

They entered the freeway at the next intersection and made their way east, out of the city, where there were fewer prying eyes, Seth said. The fact that this unusual phenomenon had latched itself onto him seemed to have persuaded him that he should be her guide. He said that much, but she suspected he was beginning to enjoy himself. And if not himself, then perhaps her company.

Three times he pulled off the freeway to avoid detection, twice by regular police and once by an unmarked detective's car. So he said, and she believed him. Each time he seemed very pleased with himself for having avoided trouble. Like a man who'd just discovered he could sit down at a piano and play whatever he wished without practice. The power of his gift was understandably intoxicating to him.

They turned north on 15 and then north again on a smaller state highway, leaving the crowded roads behind them. They both settled into an introspective state—Seth undoubtedly mulling over the next few minutes, Miriam considering what she would do if they escaped.

She was on the run. But where was she running to? She could no longer say "America," because she was *in* America, and as Seth pointed out, every police officer this side of Las Vegas was on the lookout for them.

Her mind drifted back to Saudi Arabia. Driving in the car, next to Samir. His gentle eyes smiling at her veiled face, knowing what lay beneath. By fleeing her country she had fled him. What had she been thinking? He might have gone with her. Then it would be he instead of Seth in this car. What if she had lost Samir forever? What if by fleeing for freedom she had instead consigned herself to a prison without Samir?

She cleared her throat. "What will we do, Seth?" She looked at him. "I mean if we do escape?"

"I don't know. I've been wondering the same thing."

"We need to get word to Samir. I would not be here with you if it weren't for Samir. It was my love for him that convinced me to flee Saudi Arabia. The thought of marrying another man made me run. Now I've been delivered in a way I could never have asked for. It can only mean that I am meant to be with Samir."

"I wouldn't say that you're delivered just yet." He paused, visibly bothered. "Why didn't you just run off to Spain with Samir in the first place?"

"I've told you, I couldn't tell him what I was doing. It was far too dangerous. Both sides would kill him if they found out he was involved."

Seth was silent. With a quick glance in his mirror, he pulled off at the approaching exit, headed for a Texaco station a hundred yards off the road, pulled behind the building, stopped the car for a few seconds, and then drove back onto the highway. She wanted to ask him whom they had avoided this time, but she let it go.

"I just think you could have gone about it differently if your objective was to be reunited with Samir," he finally said.

"Maybe. I'm not exactly an accomplished fugitive. Now that I'm here, I realize I have to find Samir again. This whole exercise will be meaningless without him. So, unless you can think of a better objective—"

"Our objective should be to get you to safety. You can worry about Samir later. Right now we have people with guns on our tail—it's not the best time to be getting homesick."

"Don't be silly! You have no idea where we're going. You're just running away, from one minute to the next. I'm only saying that while we are running, we need to make contact with Samir. I would think this would make sense to a mind as perceptive as yours. And I believe it is the will of Allah."

They rode in silence for several minutes. She wasn't sure if he was irritated or just thinking.

"Can Samir leave Saudi Arabia behind?" he asked.

"Of course."

"Then why didn't he? With you, I mean?"

"Now you're questioning his motives? If I didn't know better, I would say you were jealous!"

"Please, no. That's . . . that's not what I meant." But his face had turned a shade lighter, and it struck her that he might indeed be exactly that. Jealous!

She faced the road. Goodness! Was it possible? No, she had to be mistaken. He would know that such a thing would be impossible. Were Americans so quick to find attraction? Had she even sent him one signal that she was the kind of woman who wanted any affection? No! She was *fleeing* men!

Miriam let out a short, impulsive humph.

Seth glanced at her. "Okay," he said, swallowing. "You're right. We should make contact with Samir. I'm sorry, I just . . ." He stopped talking.

"Yes," she said.

For a long time neither spoke. The silence was awkward.

"Then we need to get you out of this country," Seth said. "The State Department obviously wants you as badly as your own government does. They're more interested in keeping peace with Saudi Arabia than in protecting you."

"Out to where?"

"To England, where you should have gone in the first place. They have a history of protecting dissidents."

"I didn't realize I was a dissident."

"You are. You're dissenting from the woman's place in your country. You're intolerant of your countrymen's view on women."

"Okay, then I'm a dissident."

"Miriam, the lovely dissident." He smiled and she smiled with him. "Bottom line is, we need to get you to England, from where it will be much easier to make contact with Samir—assuming he wants contact—"

"Of course he will."

"Okay, we'll assume that. The hardest part will be getting you *out* of the United States. Public transportation is out. The State Department has spotting Arab dissidents down to a fine science. We'll have to get you out through another route. Unfortunately that will take more than five thousand dollars. A lot more."

She bit her lip. She'd been a fool to leave the money at Hillary's house. "How much?"

He shrugged. "Air travel isn't as easy as it once was. We'll have to find a charter and leave illegally. A couple hundred thousand maybe."

"We?"

"Someone has to keep you out of trouble." Seth glanced at her with a twinkle in his eyes. "I'll think of something. What's a few hundred thousand dollars to a man who can see into the future?"

They traveled north, and with each passing minute, Seth seemed to regain his good nature. Perhaps she had misjudged his motives. He was wired and wide-eyed, despite the dark circles forming under his eyes. In thirty miles he didn't change course once—the threat fell behind them for the time being. Instead he spent the time explaining what he was seeing in their futures and trying to manipulate those futures. He could see out six or seven minutes now—the distance of his vision continued to grow—and he could only see futures directly related to either of them, but even those amounted to hundreds if not thousands.

He couldn't say what was happening anywhere else or what would happen beyond seven minutes, but he could see with stunning accuracy what might happen to them in the next six minutes. If he saw two possible futures—one in which she took a drink from the water bottle and one in which she asked for a drink of his soda instead—he would attempt to manipulate which alternative she chose without being obvious, and then he would tell her what he'd done afterward, grinning wide.

"Can you read my mind?" she asked.

"No. I can only see events. But I'm pretty sure I can tell what you're going to say. Speech is an event."

"You can't be serious!"

"As a heart attack, my dear. Believe me, this thing is absolutely incredible."

She had no clue what he meant by the heart attack, but she was too taken by his claim to ask. "Then what will I say now?"

"That depends on what I say, and on what I do, and on a bunch of other variables. But I know what you will say in each case. Including what you'll say now that I've told you. Isn't that wild?"

She hesitated. He was saying that he knew exactly what she would say next. How? Because he had seen her saying it. And what if she changed her mind and said something different? It didn't matter—he knew what she would say, not why.

"That's—"

"Very clever," he finished with her, grinning.

She stared at him, blinking. This was disconcerting. "You're saying that you can influence what I'm going to say? That's absurd!"

"It is, isn't it? But I'm afraid there's some truth to it." He was still grinning.

"I don't see the humor," she said.

"Sorry. It's a nervous smile."

"If you can influence what I'm going to say, then make me say something," she said, defiant.

He paused. "I think you're very beautiful."

She hadn't expected that. He was manipulating her, of course. Somehow in his mind he saw that if he told her she was beautiful it would draw a particular response from her. Probably a thank-you, or something like that. She decided to throw him. Something he could not possibly expect.

"Your eyes are like the . . ." She waited for him to finish.

"Blue waters of the Al-Hasq Oasis," he said.

It was precisely what she was going to say.

"And thank you," he said. "But they can't be as beautiful as yours."

"You know the Al-Hasq?"

"Never heard of it. Did you mean it?"

"Of course. You have beautiful eyes. But then you already know I was going to say that. That's unfair."

"I wasn't aware that we were playing a game. Besides, I'm your savior—how can I be unfair to you?"

She sat back and frowned. "If you can't read my mind, then maybe I should say things deliberately off base, so that you'll have no idea what I'm thinking."

"You're right, you could say all kinds of things that don't match what you're actually thinking. I don't mind at all."

"I've gone from having my face unveiled to my mind unveiled in a few short days. I feel positively naked."

"I can't read your mind—"

"But you can trick me into saying things. You might as well know my mind."

"No, I can only say or do things that will make you say one of the things you were going to say anyway."

She shook her head. "Either way, it's positively maddening."

"Fate. Allah's will, remember?"

She refused to dignify his jab. But then he would have known his comment would elicit silence. Was he trying to shut her up?

"You're trying to shut me up?"

"You're speaking, aren't you?"

True enough.

"I meant what I said," Seth said. "You should know that."

"You've said many things."

"One of them was that you are very beautiful. I meant that."

She looked away. So then she hadn't misread him. How could he be so bold? "And I meant what I said," she replied. "I am in love with another man."

"That's not what I meant."

"But it is what I meant." Was she really so beautiful?

Her low blow seemed to have no impact on him. He simply changed the subject and talked to her about Saudi Arabia, a subject he seemed to know nearly as well as she, despite never having been there. She considered apologizing for the comment, but withheld after realizing that if she was going to say anything, he would have seen it already. Better to keep him guessing. God knew she needed some advantage.

They rolled into Johannesburg as dusk settled on the small town. Seth checked them into separate rooms at a small U-shaped Super 8 Motel off a side street and parked the car in the rear lot. Miriam found her room decorated in orange, like pumpkin. But the sink functioned well enough, and she was grateful for the chance to freshen up after a day and a half on the road. They would need to buy more clothes at the earliest possible opportunity, she decided. If she'd known they would be on the road overnight, she would have purchased several changes at the Wal-Mart.

She'd just finished brushing her teeth when Seth knocked on her door and suggested they get some dinner at the Denny's down the street.

"You're exhausted! Look at you, you can hardly walk straight."

"My mind's too full to sleep," he said.

She glanced down the empty street. "You're not concerned about being discovered here?"

"The last time we were spotted, we were in Los Angeles. We're way off the beaten path. Actually, sleep may be more dangerous than going down to the Denny's. Somehow I doubt I'll be able to see when I sleep."

Miriam looked at his tired eyes. The thought hadn't escaped her. If the police were still on the prowl and Seth was fast asleep, they would be powerless to avoid any search. Maybe it would be best to keep him awake a few more hours.

"Can we go shopping?" she asked.

"Shopping?"

"You expect me to wear this shirt all the way to England? And why do you need to ask? Don't you know my response already?"

"I can't know a response unless there is one. And there can't be a response unless there's a question."

She was beginning to understand.

"There's a large truck stop on the corner. It should have a few overpriced items of clothing. I could use some too."

"Promise no tricks?"

"I wouldn't dream of it."

She stepped past him. "Why do I find no comfort in that?"

19

THIS BUSINESS ABOUT REPORTING every hour was about as sensible as hiring a chaperone for your twenty-fifth wedding anniversary, Clive thought. Especially considering the fact that traffic about the blue Sable that had disappeared into thin air crossed every secure police channel in Southern California. But he dutifully kept the State Department updated—no need to get the Saudis all whacked out of shape. He understood as well as anyone that, despite the House of Saud's poor record on human rights, the alternatives to its leadership in the region could prove disastrous. A successful coup led by fundamentalists would be a nightmare. Hilal might be a snake, but he was a snake in the service of a government the United States knew how to handle.

Knowing Hilal's kind, Clive thought the man was probably after Miriam personally, using the information from the State Department to close in. Well, there was nothing to close in on now, was there? Seth had vanished.

Clive angled the Lincoln Continental into a Diamond Shamrock truck stop on the outskirts of San Bernardino and parked behind a row of purring rigs. A band of teenagers crossed the graveled lot, headed for the store. Gangbangers. Probably headed to some joint to fry their brains. The collective mind of America was headed into the toilet. At some point during the last twenty years, someone had decided that intelligence wasn't such a hot commodity after all, and the rest of the country licked up that nonsense as though it were a melting vanilla cone on a hot summer day.

On the other hand, the mind he was after—there was an exception if ever one existed. He'd met with Seth four times over the past two years, and each time he walked away knowing that he couldn't give up his pursuit of this one. Seth possessed the perfect qualities for greatness in the world of intelligence. Brains were one thing, but genius with a passion for danger was exceedingly uncommon. He'd never imagined that his pursuit would take on a physical nature.

Without looking, Clive found the round walnut in his coin tray and pulled it into his palm. The nut had been rounded from years of rubbing, and he moved it slowly in his hand now. The mind was like a walnut, smooth on the outside and wrinkled on the inside. His task was to figure out what was happening on the inside, where wrinkles made the task more difficult.

His arrangement with the NSA was unusual, but then he had come to them with an unusual list of accomplishments. He was a throwback to the old days when trackers sniffed out criminals with keen noses rather than with fast-flying fingers on a keyboard. More like a bounty hunter in the Wild West than the agents churned out of today's high-tech schools. Not that he had any dislike for his peers who preferred the road of high science; they were an exceptional lot in their own rights. He just preferred the hunt one-on-one, on the road, mind against mind, may the best man win, and may the loser hang until dead. Figuratively speaking. Most of the time anyway.

Clive depressed the toggle on his radio. "Five into one, you have any new information?"

A short hiss and then the voice of Sergeant Lawhead, the clearinghouse for all the uniforms on this one, crackled. "Several blue Sables, but not the right ones."

Clive picked up a map he'd folded to reveal the Los Angeles basin. He'd highlighted the five primary exits out of the region in yellow. Observation points stood along each one, far enough out so that Seth couldn't have slipped out before they'd been activated. If the couple had passed through, they hadn't done it in a blue Sable.

He scanned the street to his right. A Ford Taurus drove by, followed by another, blue instead of yellow. Would Seth have traded cars?

The man he was tracking might be one brilliant son of Sam, but he wasn't a criminal. Minds like his didn't neglect details; in fact, they tended to consume vast quantities of them. One of those details was that in this day of computers, the police could track down a car purchase in a matter of minutes. If Seth bought a used car in some remote lot under his own driver's license, he would trip the wire. And Seth hadn't come into this chase with a fake ID. For all Clive could ascertain, he'd stumbled into it without a clue.

Short of buying a car, Seth would have to steal if he wanted to swap cars. But that would be a last resort. He'd done it once and he could do it again, and in fact twelve cars had been reported stolen in the last six hours. But none of them was Seth—too far out of the zone.

He looked at the map again. Of the five exits out of the city, one headed south to San Diego—out. Seth wouldn't head home for the simple reason that all stupid criminals headed home. He would suspect a ring of cruisers around his house already. Two exits headed north, the Pacific Coast Highway and 5—both out. You don't head back into the pursuit unless you know exactly what you're doing, which Seth didn't. He was no criminal.

That left two exits east. One toward Palm Springs and one toward Las Vegas. Both passed through San Bernardino. Clive toggled the radio. "Any word from the Nevada authorities?"

"Checkpoints on all the state crossings, but nothing yet." A pause. "How about south across the border?"

"No. Border's too tight. He's headed east—Arizona or Nevada."

The radio remained silent. Clive set the receiver down and studied the map. *Where are you, my friend? Hmm? Where have you gone?*

He ran his right index finger over the routes slowly, caressing the paper, tracing every road and judging for the hundredth time its viability as an escape route.

Which road does a twenty-six-year-old surfer-turned-Einstein in the company of a Muslim woman take?

Hilal's assessment came back to him. Clairvoyant? Now there would be a challenge—on the trail of a man who could see the future.

To have escaped Hilal, Seth would have to have been crafty enough, but clairvoyant?

Clive took out his pencil and shaded a red line on the map. A road that headed straight north off 15. Two miles this side of the observation post on 15. It ran all the way north through Johannesburg and dumped into Death Valley. No cover. That would be almost as dumb as heading home. Unless . . .

Clive shifted his attention from the small highway and returned to alternative routes southeast toward Twentynine Palms and Parker. Maybe. He lifted the walnut to his upper lip and absently drew it across the skin under his nose, and then over his right cheek. *What are you thinking, Seth Border? Tell me your secrets. You're out of your league, boy. Give it up.*

To have a mind like Seth's would be like playing God among the mortals, he thought. A lonely existence in which only you have the unique view of reality. Like standing on a ledge staring down at a hidden lake of blue water during a drought, while the rest of the villagers stand beside you, unable to see the water, staring despondently at a dry valley, ignoring your mad pointing.

Well, I've got a secret of my own, Seth boy. I know the lake is there too. Maybe I can't see it like you, but I know enough to know it's there.

Clive lifted the mic. "Sergeant, I want some heat on 395 headed north through Johannesburg. What do you have up there?"

It took a moment for Lawhead to answer. "Small local force. I could send a couple of cars up."

"Couple won't do. I want a roadblock north of Johannesburg, and I want every parking lot this side of Ridgecrest methodically searched."

Static. "That'll take some doing. You want to ease some assets from other observations?"

"No. Move your people up from 5 if you have to. He's not headed south."

"You know something we don't, sir?"

"No. Let me know when you have the roadblock up."

He set the mic down and took up the walnut again. *You may tell the world how to travel faster than light one day, my man. But for now you'll have to settle for trying to outrun me.*

Omar slouched in the back of the BMW, watching the black American landscape drift by in silence. A luminescent clock on the dash read 2:24 A.M. The police had taken their search north of San Bernardino; no doubt Hilal had followed them. As far as he could tell from the radio traffic, there was no particular reason why the authorities believed that the fugitives were here, to the north, but Omar had no choice except to follow their lead. They could just as easily be driving away from Miriam as toward her. The thought clawed at his mind like a relentless demon. Still, regardless of how mad the method seemed, he would follow it.

He closed his eyes and ground his molars. Once they found Miriam, he would take matters into his own hands. The suitcase in the trunk contained enough firepower to assure that much.

He replayed his right of revenge, loitering with each detail. She would not die quickly. If possible, not at all. First he would take her to a safe place. Alone. A hotel room. An expensive hotel room with proper insulation in the walls—he didn't intend to leave her gagged.

She was beautiful; that was all he knew about her appearance. His mind had already sculpted her face a hundred times—she was fair skinned, with high cheekbones and pouting lips. Her eyes were a light brown, like sand, and her eyebrows arched in soft black. Her nose was small and her nostrils would flare with each breath, as much from desire as from fear. Women with spirit walked a fine line between fear and desire. In his arms she would discover both. If she was any less beautiful than the image now firmly in his mind, he might have to fix that.

And the others? The more he thought about it, the more he realized that at the very least, Seth would have to die. The man had defiled his wife. He had taken a woman betrothed to another and fled. Seth had earned his sentence as a matter of principle and morality.

The scanner hissed to life. "One-oh-two to one. We've got a blue Sable with a matching license plate."

Omar's eyes snapped open. Meaning what?

"Come again. You have the Sable in question?"

"That's affirmative. We're in Johannesburg, behind the Super 8 on Main. Unlit parking lot."

"Copy. Stand by."

Omar sat up. "How far is Johannesburg?"

Assir was already studying the map. "Ninety miles to the north."

"Go."

The scanner burped. "One-oh-two, could you give me that tag number?"

The officer read the plate number.

"No sign of activity?"

"The place is dark. We haven't spoken to the manager yet." There was a pause.

"Okay. We're sending three more units your way. Clive Masters from the NSA will give you your orders on the ground. He's an hour out—wait for him. And don't let the car out of your sight."

"Roger that."

"Move!" Omar screamed.

20

Sleep had evaded Seth for two days, and when it finally came at 2:08 A.M., it swallowed him whole, a welcome reprieve from the onslaught of impressions that made up Seth's clairvoyance.

They'd retired at ten after buying the clothes in the truck stop down the street. He'd discovered with surprise and relief that the moment he entered his room, all the future possibilities related to Miriam faded from his mind. He hadn't relished having to walk through all the possibilities that came with her preparation for bed.

The enigma had swelled like a tide through the day, flooding his mind with more images each passing minute than the minute before. His understanding of the future had begun with glimpses of major events, like the threat to Miriam's life at Berkeley. But the precognition had steadily broadened in scope. By the end of the second day he was seeing hundreds, if not thousands, of possibilities extending out further into the future with each passing hour. Simple possibilities that had no bearing on anything of substance.

Entering the restaurant, he'd seen that the hostess might possibly have seated them at any one of eleven tables—it was a slow night. Which table she would select depended on dozens of other possibilities held in the balance. How they responded to her questions; which direction she was facing when they approached her; whether she decided to turn to her right to scratch an itch on her hip; whether the busboy with the overloaded tray took the first exit to the kitchen or the second; whether the man seated in the first booth coughed into the aisle, prompting her to avoid his spew, or whether he coughed into his hands, diffusing his germs over his own table. These possibilities among a couple dozen others flashed through his mind in the space of half a step.

But with them came several hundred other possibilities yet to be realized in the next ten minutes. Possibilities of what they might eat, or what they might say, or what the waitress might suggest to them—all dependent on what preceded the possibilities. He was a prophet on steroids. The labyrinths of the future had been opened up to him; the gauze that kept man from seeing beyond time had been ripped from his eyes. It occurred to him that a person of average mental capacity might have difficulty keeping track of it all.

To many, attributing his newfound prophetic nature to God would have been natural. It would indeed account for the many prophets throughout history. They had only experienced what he was now experiencing on differing scales.

Now, in his dreams, he argued the impossibility of God's existence before a classroom filled with his peers at Berkeley. Yes, only days ago he had believed God existed. But a problem had surfaced. The problem was the future. The very admission that there was more than *one* possible future proved that God did not exist, at least in the way we know existence.

Something was happening at the back of the classroom—a disturbance that interfered with his explanation. Frustrated, he looked up to see that someone had forced his way into the room. He couldn't see who the person was, and he didn't care. The intruder had no business being here while he set the record straight on God. Perhaps it was Mohammed, come to reveal one of the insights he'd borrowed from one of his wives. Or maybe it was John the Apostle, begging to differ in light of his revelation. All to naught, my friends. Two plus two cannot equal nine—not in a cave, not on an island, nowhere.

He turned to take a drink from the glass on the podium. It was empty. He was parched. Cotton mouth. More cotton-mouthed than he could ever remember feeling. He was in a dream, and he knew that he was in a dream, and in dreams feelings were always exaggerated. Of course they were.

But this meant he had to get himself a drink in real life. The commotion at the back of the room was so annoying that he wasn't sure he wanted to continue lecturing anyway. Men in black were fanning out, like ants. Time to exit.

Seth's eyes opened. He really was thirsty. Amazing how that worked. He should get up and—

The images crashed in on his mind then, like a full load of bricks dropped off the end of a dump truck. He jerked up in bed, heart thumping at the walls of his chest. They'd found the car!

A hundred futures streamed through his mind, and in all of them his door broke down under the kick of a boot within the next five minutes.

He spun to the clock radio—2:51 A.M.

Seth threw the covers back, rolled out of bed, and grabbed his pants. He had no clue what was happening to Miriam. As far as he knew, they already had her. He cursed himself under his breath and pulled on his cords, arms trembling. *Think. Think!*

He ran to the window and was about to pull back the shade for a peek when it occurred to him that he would be seen by an officer in the lot. He'd seen that. He was still seeing the future.

Seth stepped back, breathing hard. *Control yourself, boy. Find a future in which you get out before they kick the doors in.*

His mind flashed through dozens of scenarios.

A single scenario popped into his mind—one in which the door was kicked in to an empty room. Hope flooded his veins. He had to find the thread of possibilities that led to that scenario! He had to get out of the room. *Focus! Start at the beginning.*

Still shaking, he took a deep breath and closed his eyes. Focus. Swirling in a frothing sea of futures, a single one popped to the surface. It was the only one he could see in which he got out of the room unseen.

It occurred in precisely ten seconds, when all the officers in the courtyard below had their eyes diverted for a span of three seconds, allowing him just enough time to slip out and into the shadows beside the door.

Seven seconds now . . .

Beyond that . . .

Six seconds.

He didn't have the time to consider the endless possibilities beyond that. *God help me.* There is no God.

Seth ran for the door, shirtless and shoeless. He slipped back the chain, unlocked the door, and counted. Three, two, one . . .

He twisted the knob, eased out onto the second-floor concrete walkway, quickly eased the door closed, and sidestepped into the shadows to his right, beside an ice machine. He pressed himself against the wall and held his breath.

Silence hovered over the cool morning. No sign of the threat below. What if he were wrong? He exhaled slowly through his nose and cracked his eyes.

Three black-and-whites cordoned off the motel. Another car sat kitty-cornered behind them with a group of officers gathered around. Seth scanned the second-story walkway on which he stood. A cop stood at the top of each stairwell, awaiting orders. Streetlights cast pale light on the door next to his—Miriam's door. No room for shadow tricks there.

Panic tickled Seth's spine. He may have gotten out of the room, but escaping was an impossibility. Something else flashed through his mind—a full-fledged firefight with the officers below. But he didn't have a gun.

One step at a time. He closed his eyes. *Just concentrate.*

He still couldn't see any of Miriam's futures. He had to get to her. He saw a myriad of attempts to do so that ended in the same two words. "Stop, police!" In another scenario he managed to reach her back window from the roof. A muzzle flash momentarily lit the back lot. A bullet took him in the head.

And he saw one future in which he dropped into her room from the return vent above her bed.

A bead of sweat snaked past his temple. But how? He was concentrating on events too far down the road—several minutes out. He had to find a way to get out of this nook unseen first.

He saw it immediately.

Miriam's door was to his right. There was a linen closet to his left, on the other side of the ice machine. Attic access was through the closet's ceiling. From the ceiling he could wrench free a portion of the two-foot square ducting, slide over to the next room, and drop into Miriam's room.

And if he saw futures in which he did that, there had to be at least one in which he got into the closet unseen. He saw it. A faint groan of relief cleared his throat.

Blink.

Seth caught his breath. Something had just changed. Everything had just changed! The images of his entry into Miriam's room vanished. Someone had heard him. He had inadvertently changed his future with that one groan.

His mind spun frantically. He'd drawn attention that cut off the possibility of his unseen entry into the closet. Someone who wouldn't have been watching the ice machine had heard his faint groan and now scanned the shadows.

But couldn't he change that?

He searched his mind for another thread—another future.

Cough. Yes, cough.

If he turned his head just so and coughed, he could get into the closet. Because the cough would sound as if it had come from the far corner, momentarily distracting them while he slipped around the ice machine and into the closet.

The rest of the thread popped back into his mind. It had probably been there all along, hidden among a hundred others, but he'd been too distracted to see it.

Time was running out. Seth faced the far corner, took one last breath in a futile attempt to settle the quaking in his bones, and coughed softly.

Without waiting, he slipped out into the open, expecting a cry of alarm at any moment. *Trust yourself, Seth. Walk.*

He walked around the ice machine, opened the closet door, and eased inside. He stood in the darkness and shuddered. He'd just manipulated the future. He had seen one that fit his need and chosen it. With a cough.

No time. He looked up and saw the faint outline of the attic access. In less than a minute he climbed over the boxes of toilet paper, pulled himself into the attic, and found the duct. He couldn't see a blasted thing up here, but in his mind's eye he saw all he needed—a fraction of a second into the future, like a movie playing in his mind. The hardest part was trusting this new sense of his. This seeing in advance. Knowing that if he put his hand right here, he would find the loose piece of duct tape that he could tear free because he'd seen it as part of the future just a heartbeat ago.

He made a ruckus banging through the duct—unavoidable. It only encouraged him to move faster, which made even more noise. If they could hear him, they might think an elephant was stampeding through the place. He dropped onto the grate above Miriam's bed without giving full thought to how his entrance might affect her. With a screech, the grate tore loose and, together, he and the grate crashed down on the sleeping woman.

His world exploded in a flash of new futures.

Miriam's futures.

Miriam dreamed that the roof had collapsed on her, but she knew immediately that it wasn't a dream. She grunted and tried to sit up, but a heavy mass pressed her into the mattress.

A *moving* mass. Breathing hard.

An animal!

She shrieked and shoved herself up in panic. The animal flailed above her, startled by her sudden movement. Miriam swung her elbows and the covers flew. The animal hadn't managed to bite her yet, but it was still there, on her calves, waiting to pounce. Desperate to be freed, she twisted to her back, jerked her legs from under the beast, and kicked furiously, groaning in horror.

It tumbled off the end of the bed, hissing. She snatched her pillow and hurled it at the mass. *The door! I have to get to the door!*

It bounded to its feet, tall like a ghost, draped in the blanket.

"Stop it! It's me!"

She froze. The thing was speaking! Her mind spun crazily.

The figure tore the blanket from its head. It stood there in the dim light, a bare-chested man with disheveled hair, panting.

Seth!

For a moment she just stared at him, numbed. What was he doing in her bedroom? She wore only an oversized T-shirt she'd purchased at the truck stop. A black cotton shirt with an eagle soaring over a shimmering ocean.

"Are you mad?" she demanded.

He threw his index finger to his lips, shoved a hand out to silence her, and looked frantically at the drawn curtains.

"What?" Half of her mind was on his inexplicable entry, the other half on her exposure. He was looking around and whispering urgently, but she couldn't understand a word of it.

"I can't understand a word—"

"They're outside!" he said, aloud this time.

"Outside . . ." Suddenly she understood it all.

Seth jumped up on the bed. "Hurry! We have to get back up into the vent."

"I'm nearly naked!" she said.

He towered over her on the end of the bed. "Where are your pants?"

He was right—if the authorities were outside, they had very little time. She glanced at the chair where her jeans were draped. A bag on the floor held the rest of the clothes she'd purchased.

Before she could move for them, Seth bounded off the bed, grabbed the jeans from the chair, and ran back. He didn't see the tennis shoes in the middle of the floor and tripped on them. He crashed into the bed, face planting into the mattress beside her leg, holding the jeans outstretched to her like a warrior who'd just barely managed to return with the magic elixir.

Miriam snatched up her pants, stood on the bed, and quickly pulled them on.

"These too," he whispered, shoving the shoes toward her.

She yanked them on without bothering to tie them. "My bag."

"Too slow. Where's the money?"

"In my pocket." She grabbed at her jeans and felt the lump. Seth jumped back up next to her, panting from his efforts. He looked up and she followed his gaze. The vent opening looked like a black hole to nowhere.

"I'll shove you up first," he said.

"Are you crazy? We can't go through that!"

"We don't have a choice. Trust me! I know what happens here." He put his hands on her waist and she smacked them away.

"Stop it! I can't fit—"

"We don't have time for this!" he snapped.

"I don't care—"

His lips were suddenly on hers, smothering her words.

Seth pulled back, leaving her in shock.

"Sorry, I had to. I'll explain later."

He grabbed her waist and shoved her up before she knew he was doing it. Limited on options and still horrified by his kiss, she grabbed the duct's lip and pulled herself in. Utter blackness faced her and she froze there, legs still dangling out of the duct. Below he was pushing at her legs, whispering urgently. She scrambled forward.

Behind her, the tin crashed with the sound of his hands, slapping for purchase. He slipped and fell out, and then tried again. This was impossible! She'd come to America to climb through air vents in the dead of night, pushed by a maniac who had kissed her and . . .

"Miriam. Back up! I need your legs!"

She scooted back so that her feet touched the lip. His hands suddenly grabbed her ankles and he hauled himself up. Smart man.

He almost made it too. But suddenly her right tennis shoe came off in his hand. With a mighty crash that she could only guess was his head on the tin, he fell back to the bed.

Miriam was left with the echoes of her breathing.

Thud, bang. Here he came again. This time he made it by grabbing her jeans, although he nearly pulled them off in the process.

"Go, go!"

She went. Scrambling into the darkness. She stopped.

"Where?"

"To the end! Hurry!"

Omar crouched on the hotel's roof, eyeing the police through the rifle's scope. They had reached the hotel at breakneck speed, but not before the others had taken up their positions in front of the Super 8. Cursing under his breath, he'd left Sa'id and Assir in the rental car behind a grove of trees, withdrawn the AK-47 from the trunk, and quickly scouted the perimeter. With so many police, his chances of taking Miriam were minimal.

The authorities had abandoned the rear of the motel for the exits in the front. Reasonable enough. But in doing so, they left the roof access unguarded. He'd climbed the two stories and eased into position here, behind a large air-conditioning unit near the crown of the roof.

Omar had never killed in the United States. Tonight that would change. He had nothing against these particular men. But as fate would have it, they were after something that didn't belong to them. Miriam belonged to him. No man, American or otherwise, would have her. These men were now his enemy. And he had his enemy in the cross hairs.

It was time to even the odds. If he was right, they would conclude that Seth was the shooter.

Omar steadied the scope on an officer bent over the hood of his squad car, pistol trained on the front of the hotel. "In my country you do not interfere in another man's business, my friend. She is mine."

He squeezed the trigger.

The night exploded. Omar shifted the rifle before the man hit the ground. He took down two more officers standing to the rear of the cars before they could find cover, one through the head, the other in the shoulder judging by the way he spun.

Omar pulled back and slid down the roof to the ladder.

"Shots on the roof!" a voice yelled from the front. "He's on the roof!"

Omar shouldered the weapon and scrambled down the ladder. He ran for the grove of trees behind the hotel. The car door opened for him and he slid in, weapon first.

Assir fired the engine.

"Shut it off!" Omar said.

The car died.

"Are you begging for their attention?" He turned to see the motel through the trees.

"We're sitting—"

"Shut up. We don't move until I say we move."

Miriam and Seth had just dropped through a hole into what appeared to be a closet when the muffled explosions sounded from the roof above them.

"What was that?"

"Shots," Seth said. "An Arab is shooting from the roof."

She faced him, two inches from his face in the cramped quarters. "Shooting at whom?"

"The police." His voice sounded strained. "I think one of them is dead."

She was too stunned to respond.

"I . . . I didn't see any way to stop it." He turned from her and gripped his skull. "They think we did it. Okay, I did *not* sign up for this!"

It had to be Hilal. Who else could possibly be shooting at the police? But why would Hilal . . .

Miriam gasped.

Seth spun back. "What?"

"Who is the Arab?"

"I don't know, but another Arab is watching from across the street. I see events, and that includes faces sometimes, but not names, and it's hard to tell—"

"Omar!" she said.

He said nothing.

"Or Omar's people. At the very least someone who doesn't want the Americans to turn me over to Hilal."

"Your father?" Seth asked.

"No. No, he would never send this kind of man!"

Seth turned from her and leaned his forehead against the wall. Voices yelled outside. Boots thumped on the cement walkway. Wood splintered and doors crashed. Miriam swallowed at a dry throat.

A man's muffled voice reached them from the walkway, only feet away. "Rooms are empty. They're gone, sir. A vent cover is torn loose; looks like they escaped to the roof."

"Copy that," a walkie-talkie rasped outside. "Clear the vent."

The officer's muffled voice carried from the room. "Okay, clear the vent, Danny. And watch for fire. This guy's armed."

"What now?" Miriam whispered.

"Now we wait. We have a window in a minute. Then we run to the side alley and down the back stairs. We can't take the Sable."

"So you're still seeing all this. This is madness. Why did you . . . kiss me?"

"Because. I'm sorry about that. Look, a police officer was just killed out there and you're worried about a kiss? It was the only future I saw in which you moved quickly, and we needed to move quickly."

The vents creaked above them.

"I'm saving your life," Seth said. "Time to go. Follow me. Ready?"

"I suppose."

He gripped the knob.

"They won't see us?" she asked.

"Trust me. Three, two, one."

He opened the door and ran to his left. She followed him, glancing at the open courtyard to their right. An ambulance had arrived, lights flashing. Several men were busied around the cars. She and Seth ran unnoticed.

They flew down a flight of concrete steps and spilled into an alley separating the hotel from an abandoned garage next to it. Seth led her across the alley around the rear corner of the garage, glancing each way for danger, although she suspected he knew the route was safe.

"Wait here," he said, turning. "Don't move until I tell you to."

"You're leaving me here?"

"I won't be out of sight. But I've got to do this. Trust me."

To her surprise, she trusted him implicitly. So much so that his departure made her feel exposed. She wrapped her arms around herself and backed into the dark shadow.

Seth walked into the alley and stood gazing out at the street, thirty meters off. A siren burped from the far side of the hotel. Several more sounded from far away. More police. Shouts carried on the air. Surely Seth realized that the place would be crawling with . . .

A figure stepped into the alley, at the far end, backlit by the glow of streetlights. Miriam caught her breath and pulled back.

Seth spread his arms. "Good evening, Officer."

The man stopped.

"Hello, Clive. As you can see, I'm unarmed."

The man lifted a gun with both hands. He scanned the alley. "What did you do with the gun, Seth?" the man said coolly.

"I never had a gun. But then I think you know that, don't you?"

The man walked forward to face Seth, ten meters off. A soft shaft of light fell across his pale face. The redhead looked more amused than concerned.

"Where's Miriam?"

"Safe," Seth said. "I have to be leaving in just a second, but I knew you would be coming and I wanted to tell you something."

"Just like that, huh? You just happened to know it would be me? And you knew I would check this alley? I don't think so. I think I caught you with your shorts down. Or should I say with your shirt off? This is no way to win the Pulitzer, Seth."

"I knew you were coming because I saw you coming before you came. Just like I can see now exactly how I'm going to leave you in this alley. Like a lost puppy."

The man's face twisted to a grin and he waved his gun at Seth. "You may be smart, but I think you're confusing intelligence with science fiction. I'm gonna have to take you in, son."

"You ever hear of precognition? Well, it seems that I've been graced with it as of late. I see the future, my friend, and I see it in all of its possibilities. Or at least in bunches of them. Only a ways out, I'm afraid, but I see every possible outcome ahead of me. That makes me pretty hard to stop. That's why I'm outrunning a thousand cops. Not because I'm a crook. Make sense, Clive?"

Clive's smile faded. "Okay, Seth. You're going off the deep end here. You're not even armed."

"I don't need a gun to leave you panting, Clive. I have precognition. And you should know that gunning down a police officer isn't only stupid, it's not my style. That wasn't me on the roof. You make sure they know that."

"I'm sorry, but I don't believe in precognition—"

"You will. I'm not the gambling kind unless I know the lay of the cards, if you know what I mean. Unfortunately, I don't have the time to discuss it with you right now. We've got fifty seconds before a uniformed officer comes running around that corner. I have to leave before he does. There are hundreds of things I could do to try to escape you and I've seen them all. All of them but two fail miserably. I could shout at you; I could walk up and punch you; I could run to the right, to the left, or straight past you. But I've seen all those possibilities among a hundred others and I know exactly what you would do in each case. Unfortunately for you, I'm going to pick one of the two in which you make the wrong move. You can't stop me. It's going to be like taking candy from a corpse. *Comprende?*"

"You're rambling. The girl's a fugitive. You're coming with me and you're taking me to her. End of story."

"You take her and I'm pretty sure she'll end up in the wrong hands.

The world isn't ready for that. And frankly neither is she. Gotta go, Clive."

The man's face twitched. "Lift your hands slowly—"

"Step out, Miriam," Seth said.

Step out? Miriam hesitated.

"Now, Miriam! We don't have time!"

She stepped out. Clive's eyes jerked to her, and immediately Seth sidestepped over to her. Clive swung his gun to cover her.

"You won't shoot her, Clive, at least not in the next few minutes," Seth said. "I've already seen that it's not one of the possible futures."

He suddenly grabbed Miriam by the waist and pulled her behind the wall. No shot was fired.

Another man's voice echoed up the alley. "Sir?" The officer Seth had predicted.

"Hurry!" Seth whispered. "Run for the end of the building!" She ran.

She could hear Clive's feet running in the alley. A thump. She spun to see that Seth had tipped over a barrel she hadn't seen. He sprinted after her.

"Run!"

She ran. Behind them a hollow crash followed by a grunt and a curse. A shot went off, booming around her ears.

Miriam tore around the far corner of the abandoned building. Seth ran past, grabbing her elbow. "Follow me!"

He chose the most unlikely path, she thought—right under a blazing streetlight, out into the middle of the street. To their left, colored lights turned lazily in the night. Six or seven vehicles flashed red and blue. She couldn't bear to look. They would be seen!

But they wouldn't, would they? Seth led her across the street because, for whatever reason, it was the one way they wouldn't be seen at this moment.

Seth vaulted a hedge and disappeared in its shadows. She leapt blindly after him.

Miriam dropped to her knees and slammed into him.

"Shh! They're coming!" He didn't move.

Clive roared around the corner of the garage across the street and pulled up. She could hear him panting.

"Over here!" he yelled. "You head up the street. I'm cutting back."

The sound of running shoes followed. Then silence.

Seth pulled at her arm. "Come on."

They ran around the house behind them, eased through a back gate, and slipped through the neighborhood, away from the hotel.

21

THE SUN CAST A GLOW over the eastern sky, waking the sleeping valley to another day. Two patrol cars remained at the hotel, one in the front with a forensics team just now finishing up their work in the hotel rooms, and one in the back next to the abandoned Sable. A tow truck waited with amber lights flashing, preparing to impound the evidence.

Clive leaned against the door of the Sable, studying the hotel roof. He rolled the walnut between his fingers and squeezed it tight. The crime scene read like a book. Seth and Miriam had slept in different rooms—the manager could vouch for that. At some point in the night, presumably after the police had arrived, Seth had somehow managed to slip into the linen closet, work his way up to the ducts, tear loose a piece of duct tape—a move that could have been made only from the outside of the duct—wiggle into Miriam's room, and return with her. They'd then managed to slip out of the closet and make the alley without being seen. A handful of personal items, most of which came from the local tourist trap, and the car were all that remained.

Signs of an unplanned journey littered the car: Dr Pepper bottles, empty chip bags, and half a dozen books covering everything from nuclear science to a comprehensive history of New Guinea. Two Dean Koontz novels.

They hadn't taken their toiletries with them. Crest. Johnson and Johnson dental floss. What kind of man picked up dental floss on the run? A man with a woman.

Clive had been over the sequence of events in the alley a hundred times, retracing each step by impossible step. They'd scoured the streets and alleys surrounding the motel. Nothing. The search had extended to the limits of Johannesburg. Still nothing. Seth and Miriam had simply vanished.

There was a simple secret to the art of chasing down criminals: Follow the path of least resistance. Almost without exception, criminals took this path. They were not the most brilliant lot. If common sense dictated that they should duck behind a building instead of running out into the open with flailing hands, ninety-nine times out of a hundred they would duck behind the building.

That's where they could be found: behind the building.

Standing in the middle of the alley, waiting for the adversary as Seth had done, was not a move brimming with common sense. It was, in fact, downright idiotic. But Seth wasn't an idiot.

"AK-47," a voice said.

Clive looked up to see Whitlow, the LAPD detective in charge of the physical search, approach from his left. The officer held a small, clear evidence bag with one of the shell casings from the roof between his thumb and forefinger.

The detective was a city chump, used to back-alley chops and drug deals. Not a bad man, just a bit far from home in Clive's judgment. He removed a Dodgers baseball cap and scratched his head. "Common enough rifle around here. No telling where he got it."

"He wasn't the shooter," Clive said. "We have another interested party here."

Whitlow forced a grin, replaced his cap, and put his hands on his hips. "So says the detective from the NSA."

"So says common sense," Clive said. "You find a weapon? No. And he didn't have one. Someone else took that weapon."

Whitlow studied him for a moment. He looked at the roof. "How exactly did this guy get away from you? He was unarmed and with a girl." He glanced at Clive without turning his head. "Seems kinda odd."

Odd? "Impossible" might have been a better word choice. Only one explanation made any sense at all: Seth's explanation. He knew what was going to happen before it happened. He knew exactly which course of events would allow him to escape, exactly when to tip the barrel, exactly where to run to avoid detection.

But that was impossible. Still . . .

"Let's just say that our man is pretty clever, Detective. You know who he is?"

"Seth Border. Some student from Berkeley."

Clive smiled. "A student from Berkeley with an IQ of 193."

Whitlow frowned. "Sounds high."

"High? Einstein's IQ was estimated to hover around 163. The man we're after just happens to be one of the most intelligent human beings on this planet, my friend."

Whitlow nodded, smirking slightly. "He's still flesh and blood, right? As long as he bleeds, we'll get him."

Clive considered the man's statement. They had managed to approach the hotel with Seth inside, hadn't they? While Seth slept. Every man had his weakness, and if Seth had by some strange act of God been doused with precognition, then sleep might very well be his downfall. He couldn't know the future while he slept. Even if he could, he couldn't run. If Seth was right, that's how they'd found him.

They had to exhaust Seth. A man couldn't stay awake much longer than two days, maybe three, without help from doctors. According to the hotel office, Seth's light hadn't gone off until after 2 A.M. He might be wide awake now, pushed by adrenaline, but what goes up, must come down.

"And how would you get him?" Clive asked Whitlow.

"They can't be far. We're setting up a perimeter now—there aren't a heck of a lot of choices out here in the country. The highway south is sealed off. That leaves twelve possible roads out. Shouldn't be impossible to find a yellow Ford Pinto on one of twelve roads. The car was reported stolen a few minutes ago." Whitlow grinned. "Like I said, we'll get him."

Clive knew it all except for the report of the stolen Pinto. He'd drawn up the plan himself. A *yellow* Pinto. Like renting a neon sign that read COME AND GET ME. Didn't make sense. Nothing made sense.

"If someone else doesn't get him first," Clive said. He shoved the walnut into his pocket and straightened to leave. "I want the entire grid blanketed, not just the roads. He may try to hole up, and we can't let him do that. Any sign of them and I want to be informed. We go in quiet. You got that? I want this guy smothered."

"You got it. Where you going?"

"To talk to our Saudi friends." Clive stepped away. "Don't forget about the other shooter."

❧

"We look like a lemon driving down the road," Miriam said. "They'll spot us from Saudi Arabia."

"Hold on."

The Pinto's tires ground over a dirt road ten miles north of the hotel. Seth eased off into a deserted driveway, rumbled over a knoll, and angled for a rickety barn that looked as if it had been abandoned for a century. Two large doors hung cockeyed off rusted hinges and baling wire. He threw the car into park, managed to pull open the left door, and plopping down behind the wheel again, drove the car into the barn. He turned off the ignition.

"We had to get off the road," he said. "They're clamping down pretty hard."

She looked around at the dimly lit interior. Dilapidated bales of hay sat in a heap next to what had once been a stall. An old tractor sat rusting, cocooned in cobwebs. Smells of mildew and oil laced the air. Silence swallowed her.

Seth's door banged, and she turned to see that he'd gone to pull the door closed. She climbed out. It wasn't so different from a stall at home, she thought. At least in the smell, which was enough to momentarily pull her mind back to Saudi Arabia. Straw covered the floor—at one time someone had kept animals in this place. Horses and cows. No camels.

She turned to Seth, who stood by the car. "So we're safe here?"

"For a while." He walked over to the stall and wiped his hand along the rotting wood.

"How far are you seeing?"

"I'm not sure. Longer. Half-hour. It's expanding."

They'd stolen through the sleeping town in the early morning hours, cutting this way and that, hiding in the shadows for a few minutes before darting across streets. The yellow car came from a house on the edge of town, and Seth had taken it for the simple reason that it was unlocked with keys in the ignition. Rust had nearly consumed the right rear fender, and the tailpipe hung precariously low, but none of this seemed to bother him.

They'd passed the first hour doubling back and driving virtual circles in the deathtrap. She'd seen a new side of Seth, a brooding brought on by the death of the police officer back at the hotel. It was a horrible tragedy to be sure, but she'd seen much worse. He evidently had not. Americans were not as accustomed to death, she thought. This was a good thing—one of the reasons she had come here.

With the dawning of the sun, Seth's brooding had been replaced by exhaustion. He'd slept less than an hour, he'd said. This was not good.

She had no idea where they were now, and she doubted he knew either. He was simply playing cat and mouse, driving where he knew they wouldn't be.

A shaft of light cut through two loose planks on the wall, illuminating a sea of floating dust particles. Seth looked at her with his lost green eyes and for a moment she felt sorry for him. She had led him into this. Apart from the next half-hour's myriad futures that he could see, he was as lost as she. An enigma, to be sure. A stunning creature with that mind of his—American to the bone and yet so different than any man she'd ever met. The only man other than Samir who had kissed her. She was no longer sure if she wanted to slap him or thank him.

Seth lifted his eyes to study the rafters, but she kept her gaze on him. He was still shirtless. She let herself look at his chest and belly. He was as strong as Samir, she thought. Taller and perhaps broader in the shoulders.

Samir, my love, where are you?

"I think they're using their manpower to cut off the roads," he said. "They'll get around to searching this place, but for now they'll assume we're on the run. We have some time."

"You *think* they're cutting off the roads? You can't see it?"

"Well, things are a bit fuzzy right now. I'm not exactly at my best." He sighed and squatted down by some hay bales. "My mind's wasted."

"And you can only see half an hour out. That's not exactly comforting."

He looked up at her and caught her stare. "But I'm seeing all the possible futures of the next half-hour. At least to the extent I can wrap my mind around them. I'd say we have a definite advantage."

Miriam crossed over and sat next to him. To their right, the old tractor sat, half buried by the gray cobwebs. To their left, the Pinto sat, pale like a ghost. The silence hollowed out her chest.

"Thank you," she said.

"For what?"

"For saving my life. Four times now. I'm indebted to you."

"You're not indebted to me," Seth said. "I'm here because I need to be here. I want to be here."

"I'm scared, Seth." She was. She was suddenly terrified. The last few days had flown by with such speed, filled with so many new sights and mysteries that adrenaline had overridden her fear. The adventure of it all was giving way to terror. An army of American police had them surrounded, and now that one of their own had been killed . . . How would Seth and she ever escape?

She hadn't prayed in two days.

"You're a long way from home," Seth said softly.

His statement was meant to comfort her, but it didn't. A lump rose through her throat. If Seth were a Muslim, they could take solace in Allah together. But he hardly believed in Allah. In fact, he seemed particularly disposed against the prophet, an absurdity in light of the fact that he himself was a prophet.

Her vision blurred and she looked away. *Dear God, what have you done to me? Sita died slowly under the water. Now I will die slowly too in this strange land.*

Seth leaned his head back on the hay and closed his eyes.

She needed Samir now. A strong man to hold her and comfort her.

She gritted her teeth, suddenly furious. Her people had robbed her of her womanhood with their impossible interpretation of Islam! She should be free to be loved by a man and free to love a man of her choosing. Now she had been forced to flee the only man she had ever loved because of their madness! Because of Sita's death and because of Omar. Because she had been turned into a dog by the men of her country.

I am lost.

Seth cleared his throat and spoke quietly. "When my father used to beat my mother, we would run into this closet we had in the hall. I sat in there and cried with her. I didn't want to see. There was nothing I could do. I was too small. A week after I turned thirteen I did something—I hit him hard enough to break his jaw. That's when he left."

He lifted his head and looked at her.

"In some ways I feel like that boy again. I know what you mean; I feel lost too. Powerless."

It occurred to her that he was seeing into her heart. He couldn't read her mind, but he *could* see what she might say in the next half-hour. It was enough.

Rather than feeling stripped by his probing mind, she felt oddly comforted.

She swallowed. "You aren't powerless," she said. "You might be the most powerful man alive right now."

He nodded slowly.

"You've been God's gift to me," she said.

"But I'm as powerless to heal your wounds as I was my mother's."

She understood what he was saying. He really cared for her, didn't he? This mad scramble had become more than an effort to deliver her to safety. There was a bond developing between their hearts. Not like the bond between Samir and her, really, but another kind, perhaps as strong. A friendship. And yet he was a man.

The thought flooded her with warmth and desperation at once. Something had been pulled from her eyes—a hidden veil that had distorted her vision. But what she saw now wasn't what she wanted to see.

"You're a very special man, Seth. I would be desperate without you."

They looked into each other's eyes and she felt the unreasonable impulse to embrace him. Not in a romantic way, but as a friend. But then she was immediately horrified by the thought. He was a man!

He settled the issue for her. His arm reached around her shoulders. He pulled her to him and kissed her hair. "I'll take care of you," he said. "I promise."

They smiled at each other. "No woman deserves the life you've been dealt," he said. "Don't ask me how, but one way or another we're going to have to change that."

His eyes held a subtle light that she could not mistake for anything other than true attraction. The kind that mere friends did not share. She hated it. She loved it. She hated that she loved it. So she said the only thing that came to mind.

"Thank you. I owe you my life. And I can promise you that Samir will be as indebted."

He frowned, nodded, lowered his arm, sighed.

"I have to get some sleep while I can," he said. "You think you can stay awake?"

"Won't that put us in danger?"

"It's either that or throw water on my face to keep me awake. I've got to sleep at some point, and I know I have at least thirty minutes now, so I might as well take advantage of it." He shifted his weight and settled back. "Wake me in thirty minutes."

Miriam stood and walked for the tractor. She could use the time to pray, she thought. Maybe she could find some old clothes around this barn.

"Sleep," she said.

"An old barn," the pilot's voice crackled. "There are marks on the grass that I can swear were not there twenty minutes ago when I made my last pass."

Clive skidded to a stop on the graveled shoulder. "Do not, I repeat, do not approach. Are you close enough for any occupant to hear you?"

Static. "Ahh . . . negative, sir. I don't think so."

"How far north?"

"Ten miles give or take."

It was just the kind of place Clive himself would choose to hole up in for a couple hours of sleep. He hadn't expected a break this soon—for that matter, this might not be a break at all. But in the absence of any other affirmative ID, this would do. If Seth was there, he would be asleep. Otherwise his precognition would have alerted him already.

"Okay, we go in quick and we go in quiet. I want ten cars on the main road ASAP. Stay high and out of their sight. I'll be there in fifteen minutes."

"Copy that."

Clive dropped the mic and pulled the car through a U-turn. "Sleep on, my friend. Sleep like a baby."

22

KHALID BIN MISHAL sat in the elaborately decorated Bedouin tent, eyeing his host carefully. A silver teapot steamed between them, spreading an herbal aroma gracefully. Sheik Abu Ali al-Asamm nodded knowingly.

"We walk a fine line, my friend. If the king doesn't already know of my involvement, he at least suspects it. There is a reason Fahd has survived so long, and it has nothing to do with good fortune."

"Of course he suspects your involvement. You've made no secret about your leanings. They were why he approached you to adopt your daughter in the first place."

"There is a difference between 'leanings' and an actual attempt to seize power."

Khalid took a sip of the hot tea and felt the liquid hit his stomach. "Regardless, he knows you have the sentiment of a large group of people. His hands are tied. The streets would erupt if he detained you."

"Don't you mean kill me?" the sheik said with a slight grin.

Khalid ignored the question.

"My identity, on the other hand," Khalid said, "is the real issue for the king. If he discovers I am behind a plot to dethrone him, I will receive my death sentence."

"And he would learn this from whom? He would need proof to move against a prince with your power."

"He would learn it from Miriam. She's demonstrated her evil nature plainly enough already."

The sheik flashed a stern glare. "Don't mistake a strong will for an evil nature. You are talking about my blood."

"I mean no insult. I would say the same about my own son. We all have our weaknesses."

Al-Asamm looked toward the door, jaw firm. They were cut from the same cloth, father and daughter. Today, Miriam was the problem; tomorrow, this man could be the problem. Khalid would keep that in mind when he became king.

"The point is, Miriam has become a problem. I would like to propose that we continue without her," Khalid said.

"Impossible," the sheik said sternly. Then he smiled and relaxed diplomatically. "I may be a pliable man when the time calls for it, but I can't change a hundred years of history and dismiss our tradition in a single stroke. Without a bond of marriage or blood, my hands are tied. My people won't join me in support for you without a bond. You need the support of several million Shi'i, not just me."

Khalid knew as much. The desert was made as much of tradition as sand. "And we *will* have our marriage. But be reasonable. The time to strike is now, before the king expects it. We can simply claim that your daughter has married my son in America. We both know that your daughter will return wed." Or dead, but it went without saying.

"If my people discover I have deceived them, even I will lose their trust," the sheik said. "Impossible."

Khalid sighed. "Very well. But you should know that we're in a very dangerous position." He paused and delivered his final thrust. "I'm afraid that the king's men will attempt to kill Miriam in the United States."

"And risk losing my loyalty? I don't think so."

"Unless he were to blame it on me."

The sheik stared at him, unprepared for this thought.

"If the king wouldn't do it, then Hilal would," Khalid said.

"Then you will have to find her before Hilal does." The sheik stood and walked toward a bowl of fruit to the side. "What is the latest word from your son?"

"If not for the American's interference, he would have her already."

"Will he succeed?"

Khalid hesitated. His son had contacted him several hours ago. He'd shown a resourcefulness that surprised even Khalid. He'd always known that Omar was a ruthless warrior, even a wise one. But his quick decision to shoot the policeman was a brilliant stroke. He had forced Hilal to make an accounting of himself, freeing Omar up to close in undetected.

But the man who'd abducted Miriam was proving to be a challenge for the local authorities. They had brought hundreds of officers into the search, which lessened the likelihood that Omar would bring her out alive. Khalid's instruction to his son had been unmistakable. If he could not take Miriam into custody, neither could Hilal.

"Yes, I believe he will." Khalid smiled. "Your daughter is proving to be quite smart for a woman. She has your blood."

The sheik turned around. "Of course she does. I wasn't aware that gender was a factor when it came to intelligence."

These desert dwellers, they were impossible! Not even Mohammed had allowed the testimony of a woman to stand on its own. Did time change the truth of his teaching?

"Of course not," he said and took another sip. The tea was cooling and it was time to leave.

"You must know something, my friend," the sheik said. "The die has been cast. We may carry out our plans, but in the end the will of Allah will prevail. His ways are sometimes . . . mysterious. I will bring the full weight of my influence to bear on my daughter, but she does have a mind of her own. I won't resort to barbarian extremes."

Khalid blinked. What was he saying?

"I trust that your son will win the love of my daughter, but if he does not, I will not allow her to be maimed or killed." He waved a dismissing hand. "But I'm sure you assumed nothing less."

"Of course. I assure you that she's in good hands. If there's one thing Omar excels at beyond the sword, it is courting a woman." He said it with a wedge of heat rising up his back, but he said it gracefully. "He has the blood of his grandfather, Aziz, in his veins," Khalid said, grinning.

"That's what I'm afraid of."

They looked at each other in an uncomfortable silence.

"No matter," the sheik said, breaking the moment. "She will love whomever Allah wills her to love." He reached for his cup of tea and raised it. "To the will of Allah, my friend."

"To the will of Allah."

Omar lay in the grass, scoping the barn below, poised for a shot. A line of police cars waited down by the road, out of the barn's line of sight. No fewer than twenty policemen crept over the meadow toward the red building. If Seth and Miriam were in there, they would not escape. So, Clive Masters was proving to be an efficient tracker, better than Omar would have guessed.

This was not good. Once the Americans had Miriam, his job would become significantly more difficult.

He had two options. He could begin shooting now and send the police scurrying for cover, which would give Seth a chance to escape. Perhaps the safer option.

Or he could affix the silencer, wait until the police were closer to the building, and then carefully shoot one in a way that made it appear as if the shot had come from the barn. Risky, true. He might miss and Seth might not escape. On the other hand, the police would once again have to consider the possibility that Seth was armed and dangerous. They might also think the shot had come from Hilal.

Omar lifted the scope and scanned the surrounding hills. The snake was out there; Omar could almost smell him. He would have heard the report and would be waiting. Another reason to use the silencer.

His scope caught a pinprick of light and Omar adjusted his sight. The profile of a rifle materialized through the grass, five hundred yards off.

Hilal!

Omar put his cross hairs on the form beneath the grass and tightened his trigger finger.

The silencer! He rolled to his back, pulled out the tube from his breast pocket, screwed it on, and then rolled back into position. The police were no more than thirty yards from the barn now.

Now, Omar. Now!

He swung the rifle toward Hilal, acquired the target, and squeezed the trigger. His rifle coughed quietly. The rifle across the meadow jerked from view. He would not kill Hilal yet—he needed the information the king's man passed back to Saudi Arabia. But he couldn't allow Hilal to kill Miriam.

Omar spun his sights to the lead officer in uniform and dropped him with a long shot through the chest.

For a moment the rest stopped, stunned by the sight before them. Perhaps they assumed the officer had fallen for cover.

Omar was about to put another round in the man's fallen body when the officer rolled slowly. His moan carried through the valley.

"Man down! Man down!"

Pandemonium swept through the men strung out along the field. Several retreated in a quick sprint; the rest dropped for cover. Omar hugged the earth and slowly pulled back.

The rest he would monitor by radio.

Seth was snoring. Miriam dusted off the old boots she'd found and watched him rest, his mouth half open, chest rising with each breath, lost in a sleep he'd descended into just under half an hour earlier. She'd discovered the leather shoes along with a blue plaid farmer's shirt in the toolbox behind the tractor. The shirt was missing its top four buttons and the shoes were splitting at the toes, but she had no doubt that Seth would be delighted with them.

The wind moaned outside. Or something moaned.

Miriam smiled, set the boots and shirt on the Pinto's trunk, and walked toward Seth. Time to . . .

Seth jerked up, eyes wide. "Huh?"

"Man down! Man down!"

Miriam spun toward the door. Someone was outside, yelling!

Seth was on his feet already. "In the car!"

Miriam grabbed the clothing from the trunk and piled through the passenger door.

"How long did I sleep?" he demanded.

"Less than thirty minutes!"

Seth paused, hands on the steering wheel, staring intently ahead. "That's not good. I should've seen them."

"Go!" Miriam twisted around, expecting police to barge into the old barn at any moment. Seth sat still, jaws flexed. "What are you doing?"

"Thinking. Don't worry, I can see now. He's not dead."

"Who's not dead?"

"The policeman who was shot outside." Seth's face looked strained. "Man, oh man, this is gonna be like threading a needle by candlelight."

He suddenly fired the car and stomped on the accelerator. The Pinto roared for the far wall. Miriam threw her arms over her head and ducked. With a mighty crash the car slammed through the brittle wood, sending splinters flying.

Seth fixed his eyes dead ahead. They flew over the grass, picking up surprising speed. Miriam turned and saw that they'd left at least a dozen policemen by the barn.

The Pinto screamed unabated. They skirted a pond and then slammed through a picket fence. Still Seth did not ease their speed. She looked at him and wondered if he were going too far this time.

"It's amazing how easy it is to elude the mortals when you see clearly," Seth said above the engine's roar. "It's like playing tag with children who are blindfolded. They don't have a chance!"

But she knew he was wrong. Seth had his weakness and it had almost betrayed them back there. If the police were this good, their troubles weren't over. Not even close.

Seth took the car into a wooded area and slowed. For five minutes he threaded his way amid thickening foliage. "Helicopter," he said. "We have to keep them blind."

He stopped by a large oak and they climbed out.

"We have to hurry. There's a house a mile to the south. They have our car."

She lifted an eyebrow. "Our car? Here." She tossed the boots and shirt to him.

"Where'd you get these?"

"In the barn, while you were snoring."

He grinned. "Now you're talking." He pulled the boots and shirt on. "Come on!"

They ran south. A helicopter beat through the air above them and then turned north. Sirens wailed to the west, from the barn. The manhunt was in full swing. But Seth jogged south, unconcerned.

"How did they find us?" she asked.

"I don't know."

"How did you not know?"

He didn't respond right away. She knew, of course. His mind needed rest. If he didn't find rest soon, they would be caught. But there was no time for rest.

"I need rest," he said.

"The next time we might not be so lucky," she said.

This time he didn't respond at all.

❦

Clive picked up a piece of straw and absently sniffed at it. Wasn't so different from the scent of his walnut. He tossed the straw and fingered the walnut. Lights from three police cars parked just outside the doors turned lazily, lighting the barn's interior in hues of red and blue. Two spotlights lit up the red tractor like a prize tomato. They scoured the grounds, but he knew evidence wasn't what they needed. This was a new game—of a kind he'd never played before.

The hay on which Seth had slept was still warm. He had slept here; Clive was sure of it. The officer's yell outside must have awakened him. With true precognition, once gone, Seth would be virtually impossible to catch. The helicopter would complete its search and the men would sweep the grove of trees, but Seth would be long gone.

And yet Clive now knew not only one of Seth's weaknesses, but two. The two Achilles heels. The first was obvious. Sleep. The lack of sleep would eventually catch up to Seth and leave him unguarded.

The second Achilles heel was the future itself. If a particular event wasn't part of the future, then Seth could not know it. If Seth had left Clive in the dark, there had to be a way to bring darkness to Seth's world of futures as well. A way to blind him, besides sleep. By removing futures.

The idea gnawed at Clive, faint and unformed, but just there, under the surface, begging to be uncovered.

"He's here, sir."

Clive sniffed at the walnut. *Where are you hiding, Seth?* He crossed in front of the bright lights and walked up to the Mercedes that had pulled up. Hilal was sitting against its hood.

"Good morning," Clive said.

"It could be better," Hilal returned. For a man who'd spent the last hour defending himself under a barrage of questions, the Saudi showed no signs of humility. He'd persuaded them that he had nothing to do with either shooting—something Clive had never suspected. Hilal had no reason to open fire on the police; they were on the same team. If Hilal wanted to kill, he would be after the girl.

"Let's get one thing straight," Clive said. "The State Department may insist we give you some rope, but that doesn't mean you run around the countryside, shooting up the night."

"You're assuming you would know about it, if I did? Please, don't insult me."

"You've been warned. Tell me, what really happened in that bathroom?"

Hilal flashed a coy smile. "So. Now you're interested. The man told me precisely what was going to happen. I think he actually knew. He threw the ball."

"Which ball?"

"The one the waitress fell on. It came from his pocket."

That hadn't been in the report. "You saw it?"

"As plain as day, as you would say. He let it roll and then ran, as if he knew precisely what would happen. Tell me what happened in the alley."

Clive's stomach felt suddenly emptied. If Seth could do this trick of his at will and actually manipulate events . . . God help them.

"I'm sure you know what happened." The man probably knew more than most of them. He struck Clive as the kind who would be listening in on more than his share.

"This man has a gift," Hilal said. "He's escaped certain capture five times now. Miriam is still alive. I would say that you have a problem."

"Really? I thought it was your problem. And I wasn't aware that killing Miriam was our first concern."

"You have a dead police officer."

"Yes. Quite convenient for you."

"Please. We both know that I had nothing to do with the shootings. As I've said, I am not the only Saudi who wants this woman."

"Someone who vanishes as quickly as Seth?"

"Someone whose identity is a mystery to both of us. Someone who has been trained in my country as an assassin. Someone who would shoot at me. Americans aren't the only ones who've perfected the art of killing."

"You? And where were you when you were shot at?"

"Watching."

"Uh-huh."

Hilal stood and crossed his arms, looking back toward the barn. He was right about the shooter, of course, but Clive had no doubt that he would kill an American officer as quickly as the presumed assassin had.

"So. How do you plan to deal with this problem?" Hilal asked.

"How would *you* catch a clairvoyant who knows every step you're going to make before you make it?"

Hilal paused. "I would anticipate him."

"Very good. It always comes down to a battle of wits, doesn't it?"

"In which direction is he headed?" Hilal asked.

"You're listening in on our conversations—why don't you tell me?"

Hilal shoved his hands deep into his pockets and turned away to face the night. "We are both looking for the same party. I suggest we work together, my friend."

"I work alone," Clive said.

Hilal faced him. "And so do I."

He'd had enough of the Saudi. And he had a phone call to make. "He's headed north. We've issued a nationwide bulletin. This whole valley is sealed, but that hasn't stopped him so far. My guess is he'll try to take her out of the country. It's what I would do, and I can only assume he's thinking as well as I. Most fugitives wouldn't, of course, but, as you've so eloquently pointed out, he's no ordinary fugitive. He's headed out of the country and for that he'll need money. A lot more than he has, if we are to accept the preliminary conclusions of the Berkeley investigation. Seth's not a criminal. He's not a killer and he's not a thief, despite having stolen three cars."

"Three?"

"I doubt he's still on foot. As I was saying, he may not be a thief, but he *is* a gambler. You figure it out. And remember, he's an American citizen. You touch him and you'll deal with me."

Clive turned and walked for his car.

"Mr. Masters," Hilal called.

He stopped. Looked back.

"This other shooter, I would not underestimate him. The next bullet might be intended for you."

Clive nodded.

He walked to his car, slid in, and closed the door. The Continental's dash lights glowed a soft green. What was it like to know that if you tossed a ball just so, a waitress would fall just so and create just the right kind of distraction to allow for your escape? It would be like knowing that if you tipped over a barrel at just the right time, the man behind you would trip over it.

A solitary thought had drifted in and out of his mind since his first encounter with Seth in the alley. Now it had taken up permanent residence. Like a tumor.

He picked up his phone, dialed the number, and massaged the walnut.

"State Department."

"Peter Smaley."

"I'm sorry, but Mr. Smaley—"

"Just put me through, friend. Tell him it's Clive Masters with the National Security Agency. He'll take the call. And if he doesn't, I'll go over his head."

The woman hesitated. "Hold, please."

It took them three minutes to track down Peter Smaley at whatever party he was attending that evening.

"Hello, Clive. I have guests waiting so we'll need to make this quick. What's the problem?"

"The problem is, we've bitten off more than we anticipated."

"Come on, now. Don't tell me you're actually getting a run for your money—"

"He's clairvoyant, Peter."

A beat.

"Maybe we could talk about this tomorrow. This isn't a good time—"

"He's not only clairvoyant, but he sees a number of possible outcomes and he knows what to do to make any of them actually happen."

"Clive. You're talking nonsense."

"I'm telling you this only because I want my bases covered, Peter. My next call is to the secretary of state."

That got his attention. "Hold on." The deputy secretary's voice carried through the covered phone. "Excuse me, gentlemen, I'll be right back." A door closed.

"For Pete's sake, Clive. This isn't exactly the kind of call I would expect from you."

Clive rubbed the walnut and glanced back at the flashing lights. "I want you to imagine something. Imagine that you're in a battle. You're a general, directing the battle. But you have an advantage. You already know exactly what your enemy will do, to the last bullet. And you know exactly what to do to stop him anywhere you want to. You know because you've seen every possibility, every move and every countermove, and you have the luxury of mapping out the course of battle precisely as you choose. What would you say about such a general?"

There was a short pause. "I would say that he is unstoppable. And I would say that I feel a bit silly talking to you about it. It would be an embarrassment to both of us if anyone were to overhear this."

"Imagine something else with me, Peter. Imagine an assassin sent in to kill the president. A unique assassin who could see a thousand possible approaches to the White House, and know with absolute certainty which one would succeed. What would you say about such an assassin?"

"This isn't amusing, Clive. There's no way this side of Hades you're telling me that this fugitive you're after is some kind of clairvoyant who could walk up to the White House—"

"I'm not saying as a fact that he is. And I'm not pretending to know how it's possible. But, in my estimation he's exactly what I've described." Hearing himself say it, Clive wondered if he'd just thrown away his career. It sounded absurd, at the very least.

"You're actually suggesting that I pass this on?" Smaley asked.

"We're courting a man who may either be the greatest asset or the greatest liability the United States has ever seen. I know it, and now you know it. So do the Saudis. Yes, I suggest you pass it on. Tonight."

Smaley's voice softened. "God help me, Clive. If this is some kind of . . ." He stewed for a moment. "Has anything like this ever been done?"

"Clairvoyance. Not exactly an unknown phenomenon. The Bible's full of it, if you believe. Haven't you ever read the prophets? Same principle here. But actually no, I've never heard of anything quite like this."

Smaley was trying to get his mind around the idea—that was a start.

"I hope you don't mind my saying that I sincerely hope you're all wet on this, Masters."

"Would it be the first time you harbored such sentiments?"

Smaley ignored the jab. "I'll call you as soon as I have a reaction. You have any idea where he is now?"

"No. But I'm pretty sure I know where he's headed."

"Then for Pete's sake, do your job. Bring him in or whatever you have to do. This is getting ridiculous."

"Have you heard anything I just said? This isn't like tracking your common terrorist."

"And you're no common tracker. You're telling me you don't know how to catch this guy?"

Clive closed his eyes. "I have a pretty good idea. You just do your job. I'll expect a call by morning."

He disconnected and dropped the phone on the seat.

23

THEY DROVE THE VOLKSWAGEN BUG Seth had lifted from the farmhouse for less than an hour before ditching it by a deserted shack. They would have to go on foot, Seth said. It was the only way past the roadblocks.

They walked slowly. Dragged was more like it. Not only did Seth lack the energy, but there was no hurry—they had to wait for darkness.

His precognition continued to expand from seeing thirty minutes out, to seeing one hour, to two. More futures, generations of futures that added up to millions. He couldn't see them all, of course, only those he intentionally isolated. But the constant bombardment daunted him and, more importantly, tired him and drove him to a bad headache.

If he were able to see only what *would* happen instead of what *could* happen, the matter would have been a simple one. He explained it to Miriam this way: "How many different words do you think I could say right now?"

"As many as you know, I suppose," she'd responded.

"Say a thousand, for an easy number. I could say any one of a thousand words right now, and for each one, you might respond differently with a thousand choices of your own. If I focused hard enough, I think I could see each word and each of your responses. That's a million possibilities in one generation. Extend that out a few minutes and you get the idea. That's just the possible futures of our talk."

The fatalism of Islam seemed absurd in the face of this fluid future he saw.

They skirted the first roadblock at ten o'clock, a full half-mile from where the cars had set up the checkpoint on Route 190. In fact, they could have walked within two hundred yards of the police and not been noticed, Seth informed her with a tired smile.

He led her due north, through a field and over a fence where they would find another unlocked car, he said. If they took certain back roads, they would be safe for at least as far as he could see.

It was then, walking in the dead of night beside Seth, that she finally understood the full weight of his gift. They were virtually invincible, weren't they? As long as Seth was awake and thinking—as long as there was at least one possible avenue of escape among the thousands of possibilities—they could simply choose it and walk on, unharmed.

In this moment, she would rather be here, walking with him, than anywhere else in the world. Except in Samir's arms, of course. A warmth rose through her chest. It was like walking next to an angel. This strange prophet sent by Allah was her guardian angel.

She looked at him in his oversized shirt, hair loose, jaw firm in the moonlight, and she smiled. He smelled musty, a blend of straw and sweat—but to her it was the scent of man, and it only reinforced her sense of security.

He looked at her, his eyes sagging. "What?"

"Nothing."

She slipped her arm through his and walked on, as content as she could remember feeling. She could feel his skin on hers, along their arms, and that was good because here in America you didn't have to be a fifteen-year-old bride to be touched by a man. An image of Sita floating underwater flashed through her mind and she felt a momentary stab of pain.

You are a woman and he is a man, Miriam. What would Samir say to this display of affection, however platonic? And you know that Seth is falling for you. No, she did not know that. It was her fantasy. Miriam pulled her arm away. Horrors, what was she thinking? She was losing her mind with his.

Seth seemed too exhausted to react.

They found the car exactly as he'd predicted. An old white Cadillac with a shredded vinyl roof. It was unlocked.

"The owners are probably in the basement right now, praying someone will come along and swipe this beast," Seth said. He looked at her. "Ready for a ride?"

"I was born ready." It was a phrase he'd used earlier and she liked it.

He grinned wide. "Born ready, huh? I didn't see that one coming. Let's go."

He was too busy considering the future of their escape to dwell on what she might say. That was a good thing. It also meant he was making mistakes. They had to rest.

They drove north to the outskirts of a town called Ridgecrest, where Seth pulled the beast, as he'd taken to calling the car, into a graveled parking lot adjacent to a large steepled building. A church. He eased the car around the back and parked behind an old shed. He simply could not go on.

"We're past the roadblocks, and it's dark. We should be okay. If I don't get some rest, my body's going to start shutting down on its own."

"What if you don't wake up?" she asked.

"Nothing's happening in the next three hours. Three hours past that and the sun comes up. The sun comes up, I awake. Always been that way; always will be that way. Relax, Princess. It's time for sleep."

He leaned against his door, and the heavy breathing of sleep took him within minutes. She wasn't so fortunate. The window felt like a stone to her head, and Seth kept grunting in his sleep, as if fighting unseen demons. In a groggy fit of frustration she leaned toward Seth and rested her head on his arm.

She finally slept.

The heat woke her. A suffocating blanket that smelled of oil. Light streamed in through the window, hot on her thigh like a magnifying glass . . .

Miriam jerked up. It was day! The Cadillac was surrounded by a sea of cars. They'd been found!

She spun to find Seth leaning against the window, mouth hanging open in a snore, dead to the world.

She hit his thigh. "Seth!" she whispered.

He didn't budge.

She pulled her fist back and slammed it into his arm. "Seth!"

"Huh!" He jerked up, eyes wide. A trail of saliva hung from his gaping mouth. He clamped his mouth closed and swallowed. "What?"

"Look!"

He gazed around, blinking. "Cars."

"Who . . . who are they?"

A lopsided grin suddenly split his face. "It's Sunday."

Sunday. Christians went to their churches on Sundays instead of Fridays, when Muslims went. They were in a church parking lot, swallowed up by the cars of worshipers.

Miriam blew with relief and leaned back. "Do you see anything?"

She wound the window down to let some of the desert heat out. He wasn't answering.

"Seth?" She faced him. "What is it? Do you see anything?"

"Yes. I see that in exactly twenty minutes, a cruiser's going to roll into this parking lot."

"Twenty minutes! That was close! We would still be sleeping if I hadn't awakened."

Seth had fixed his eyes on the church.

"Seth?"

He broke free from his trance and threw his door open. "Come on! I want to show you something."

"Now? No, Seth! We have to leave!"

"Don't worry, we have time. Trust me, this will be worth it."

She glanced in the mirror, madly straightened her hair, and climbed out. "Where?"

"To church." He reached out his hand and she took it.

They approached the square building from the rear. The sides were a cream-colored corrugated tin—not exactly Miriam's picture of a Christian church. A wooden steeple with a bronze cross provided the only clue that this building was a place of worship rather than a warehouse.

"I don't like this, Seth," she said as he hurried her through a back door. "We don't have time for this. We don't know who these people even are."

"Sure we do. They're your typical Californian Christians attending a ten o'clock service. You'll find them sincere and loving for the most part—not so different from good Muslims. They won't be on their knees, praying toward Mecca, of course, but I can promise you they won't bite. Who was the greatest prophet?"

The hall they'd entered was deserted. A melody reached faintly through the walls. Children were laughing somewhere. "Mohammed," she said.

"That's not what some of your most influential sheiks teach in Islam. Mohammed was the final prophet—conveniently—so his revelation supersedes all the writings that came before him. But Mohammed sinned. The prophet Jesus did not sin. He was the only perfect man and as such a greater prophet than Mohammed. This is the teaching of Islam. Well, this is like a temple built in honor of the greatest prophet, Jesus. Maybe Muslims should come more often."

She couldn't tell if he was serious or not. "Just because Jesus was a great or even the greatest prophet doesn't mean his followers today are walking in the truth. Any man who rejects Mohammed, the prophet of Allah, is condemned."

They passed a split door, the top half open to give her a view of a room filled with young children playing around plastic slides and miniature houses.

"The doctrine of any good Muslim. But then you're condemning the followers of the only perfect prophet to have ever lived, because another prophet claimed to have a more current vision. That prophet routinely changed his mind, contradicted himself by habit, took young wives for his pleasure, and forced conversions with the very liberal use of the sword."

She stopped in the hall, furious at his barrage. "I want to leave."

Seth turned back. Confusion flashed through his eyes.

"I won't let you so casually destroy what is sacred to me," she said. "You may think you have a perfect view of what is true, but you're only one man. There are over a billion Muslims who disagree with you."

"I'm sorry." His face lightened a shade. "You're right; that was a low blow. I'm just . . . why do people blindly accept what they are taught? No . . . never mind." He closed his eyes and took a deep breath. "I'm just digging myself a deeper hole. We can go if you want."

She nearly turned around to leave. A sudden roar of laughter filtered through the walls. The worshipers were laughing. The absurdity of her situation suddenly spun through her mind. She was in America, on the run from the whole world with this most unique man whom she'd decided just last night was her guardian angel, and where had her flight brought her? To a Christian temple. She was standing in a carpeted hall, listening to sounds that belonged at the camel races, not in this place of worship.

"I really have no intention of trashing Islam in the face of Christianity, Miriam. I'm not even a Christian. Believe me, Christianity is as inconsistent as Islam for reasons of its own. I've never been a person to run from the truth, that's all."

"That's all," she said with a little disgust. Even now, in his apology he challenged her. So she was running from the truth? She looked into his green eyes. He didn't see the offense, as deeply as she felt it. In fact, he was undoubtedly well-meaning. Seth to the rescue, here to save the world from deception.

She walked toward him. "Just remember that *your* truth may not be the only truth." She walked by him and headed for two large doors she assumed were the entrance to the sanctuary. The sight slowed her down.

"We really can leave," he said, stepping up beside her. But a glint lit his eyes. He caught her warning glance and grinned. "And I'm not smiling because of you. Not that you don't make me smile; you do. I've just seen a few things that are amusing."

"But you didn't see that your comments would offend me," she said. "You're slipping."

He considered that. "You're right. I was distracted."

He pushed through the double doors and she followed.

They entered through a side door, into an auditorium with perhaps a thousand cushioned chairs that faced a stage carpeted in blue. A man she assumed to be their teacher stood behind a dark wood podium, dressed in a blue suit, addressing the seated Christians who were mostly dressed in bright colors. The men wore ties; some wore suits like the teacher. The women wore dresses of red and yellow and every other imaginable color. A man stood behind the teacher, wielding a silver trumpet, and next to him a woman sat behind a large grand piano. In the corner, a younger man stood behind bongo drums. They were to a man, woman, and child smiling, as if the teacher had just said something funny or done a trick.

For a brief moment Miriam wondered if they'd strayed into a rock concert by mistake. She'd never been to one, of course, but she'd imagined they might look like this. The man behind the bongo drums suddenly hit them a few times, and laughter rolled across the auditorium.

"I'll be right back," Seth whispered into her ear. When Miriam turned, he was already walking away. Up the aisle.

"May I have your attention, please!"

A streak of heat ran down her spine. What did he think he was doing? She instinctively took a step back.

"Please, I need your attention," Seth called out.

A thousand heads turned to stare at the shaggy-headed man walking the aisle, dressed in a blue, plaid shirt unbuttoned nearly to his belly, tails flopping around black corduroys that swallowed used-up leather work boots.

"Thank you," Seth said, making his way to the front. "I have something to say that I'm positive will interest you. You're the pastor, sir?"

The man in the blue suit stood speechless for a moment. But only for a moment. "Yes, I am. And what's your name, young man?"

"Seth. And yours must be Frank. Frank Goldberg. I know that because I saw you telling me. I also know by the things you might say and do in the next three hours that you're a very honorable man. An exceptionally kind man. The world needs more men like you, Frank. Most pastors would be horrified about now, worried sick by this rude disruption. Even so, I know you can't take all day with me, so I'm going to cut to the chase."

Frank stared at Seth, not at all put off. "Sounds reasonable. Start cutting, Seth." Seth was right, Miriam thought, Frank Goldberg was an exceptional man.

Seth hesitated, and for a moment Miriam thought he might have reconsidered. Perhaps the pastor had so impressed him that he had decided to walk out and not subject him to whatever game he had in mind.

"Do you believe in God, Frank?"

The pastor smiled. "You might as well ask if I believe in the wind."

A voice spoke softly from Seth's right. "That's right, Frank. Speak the truth."

"Excellent!" Seth said, turning. He faced the man who'd encouraged the leader. "Wise counsel, Bill. I know that you're Bill because I heard the pastor call you that after the service."

He faced the leader again. "And do you believe that an all-knowing God exists, Pastor Frank?"

"Without a question."

"So if God exists, then he knows what will happen in the future, is this correct?"

"Yes."

"Very good. I would be disappointed if you said anything less." Seth walked across the floor in front of the stage and slowly scanned the congregation. "*I* know the future, Pastor. That's why I'm here. I am a prophet."

The silence descended heavily, as if made of lead.

"Now, I don't know what kind of church you are here, whether you are the kind that believes in prophets or not. From my readings it's apparent that half of Christendom avoids the miraculous like the plague and the other half runs around trying to catch the disease. You may be either or neither, but it doesn't matter, because I intend to prove myself so that you'll know I'm not some quack off the street."

Seth cleared his throat. "We'll start with you, Bill. You will be going to Dairy Queen for lunch to celebrate your son's victory in his baseball game last night. Am I right?"

Bill glanced at the pastor, eyes wide.

Seth swiveled to his right. "And you in the third row with the large black Bible."

A teenager with red hair looked around.

"Yes, you. Unfortunately I don't know your name because no one actually uses your name in the next several hours. But I do know that there's a piece of paper between pages 564 and 565 in that Bible you're holding. The paper has a note to a girl named Jane, signed by someone named Josh. But your name isn't Josh, is it?"

"That . . . that's my brother."

"Well, show us the note, friend."

The redhead hesitated and then opened the Bible. He withdrew a note and his eyes widened. A gasp ran through those seated near him.

"I saw that note fall out of the Bible about an hour from now. No need to embarrass your brother by reading it."

Seth paced to his left. "There are so many things I could tell you, but this is rather boring, isn't it? I can see that unless I do something really spectacular, half of you are going to be arguing that it was all a fake about an hour from now. I could tell you that James wears Fruit of the Loom, size 34, and that Suzi is going to . . . well, I shouldn't say that out loud. How about if I just say that your sound man, who's on the line with the police at this very moment, is going to cough . . ."

A man in the back of the auditorium coughed.

"Right now," Seth said.

They all turned to see a middle-aged man with black hair staring back, cell phone pressed to his ear. Gasps rippled through the room.

"Good. So now you will at least listen to me when I tell you that we have a problem with the existence of a God who knows the future."

Seth turned back to the leader, who was actually smiling. He seemed to be enjoying this.

"It *is* comforting to see real evidence of what you've read and talked about for years actually present itself before the entire congregation, isn't it, Pastor?"

The leader didn't respond. Wise, Miriam thought.

"Let's pretend for a moment that God exists. If God knows everything, then he knows precisely which future *will* happen. He knows, for example, exactly what I *will* say next. Correct?"

The pastor was quiet and his smile had softened.

"Indulge me, Frank. For the sake of argument. I have a point here."

"Yes," the leader said.

"So if God knows precisely what *will* happen, is it possible that something different might happen? That I might say something other than what he *knows* I will say?"

"We do have a free will. And God is not boxed; he can change his mind."

"Okay, we'll assume that God not only exists, but can change his mind. But after both God and I have exercised our free will, I *will* say something, and God knows what that something will end up being. Do you follow?"

"Yes."

"So really there is only *one* future. The future that God knows *will* happen. Regardless of how it comes to pass, it will come to pass. If God exists, he surely can't be deceived. Isn't that right, Frank?"

"That's right," a chorus of brave souls answered for the pastor.

"Because whatever God *knows* to be the future, *will* be the future."

"That's right," more joined in.

"God can't be deceived. He knows the future," Seth said.

"That's right."

"And there's nothing anyone can do about it."

"That's right." The chorus had lost a few members.

"You can pray and beg and cut yourselves to the bone and nothing will change what God already knows *will* end up happening."

Silence this time.

Miriam saw his logic, crystal clear. It wasn't so different from Islamic fatalism.

"I'm sorry, my friend," the pastor said softly. "But if you think God doesn't respond to the praying of the saints, you're sadly mistaken."

"No fault of yours, Frank," Seth said. "I'm just the bearer of bad news. It requires only simple logic to realize that if God knows what will happen, it *will* happen. Are you suggesting that something other than what God knows will happen, might happen? If the saints pray hard enough, for example?"

"That's blasphemy!" an older man shouted, standing from his seat. "You're undermining the entire reason for prayer!"

"Easy, Bob," Seth said. "By the way, Bob, chances are very high that you're going to take a spill on your Harley on the way home. I would use Forty-second Street, if I were you."

Seth had the entire congregation in a corner now. A pang of sympathy ran through Miriam's chest. Seth was only doing what Seth did, but didn't he realize he was hurting these people? They were comfortable in their beliefs, right or wrong. Why challenge . . .

What about you, Miriam? Are you simply comfortable in your beliefs?

Seth spread his arms. "But I've got good news, my friends. That fact is, there is more than *one* future. I mean real futures that are not limited to the one an all-knowing God might know. And, in fact, we *can* change the future. Or at least choose it." He paced like a lecturer now.

"I know that there's more than *one* future because I can see many possible futures. And I know we can choose different futures because I'm actually choosing them and seeing the future change."

He lifted a finger.

"But the very fact that there is more than *one* future means that there is no all-knowing God who knows the *one* actual future. Which means he is not all-knowing. Which means he cannot actually exist."

Seth looked directly at Miriam. "Which means he can't be the God of Abraham or Jesus or Mohammed."

Half the people, those who had followed Seth's logic, sat with mouths parted, minds spinning. The other half erupted in anger. Miriam had no doubt that in her own country they would take Seth out and string him up for a beating.

"Enough!" Frank's voice boomed over the loudspeakers. "That's enough!"

The room settled to a murmur.

"My friend, I realize that you mean well," he said to Seth. "And frankly, we all ask the kinds of questions you've been asking us today from time to time. But it doesn't mean we all end up with the same conclusions. Believe me, I see your logic. It presents us with quite a conundrum, doesn't it? What you need is an—"

"Encounter with God," Seth finished.

The pastor looked amused. "Yes. Precisely. You have quite a gift, young man."

"But you must admit that my gift at least casts into question God's existence," Seth said. "If there is a being who knows exactly what will happen, then really that's the *only* future that has more than a zero chance of happening, and you or I are powerless to affect any other future than the one he knows. Free will is a figment of our imagination. I can't accept that. I believe man has free will, which means no God."

"God may not function like you or I, Seth," the pastor said softly.

For the first time, Seth seemed caught off guard. He stared at the pastor for a few seconds, as if lost.

"You'll have to forgive me," he said. "I've just seen a few things that worry me. I have to be going. But before I do, I would like to leave you with a simple demonstration. As difficult as it is to imagine, some of you will still be arguing after the service that I was a quack. If I do what I am about to do, only one man will be so unreasonable. His name is John and he'll argue that this was all a setup even though I've just told you that he's going to say that."

Seth jumped up on the stage and crossed to a pile of brown, leather-bound books. He picked up a stack—maybe six—and walked back to the edge of the stage.

He took the first book and tossed it out. It landed with a flat slap, twenty feet from the stage. He took another book.

"I would like to throw this second hymnal and have it land on top of the one I've just thrown. I see that in ninety-two attempts, only once will it do so. I see each throw and each result. But I'm going to skip the first ninety-one throws because I know they won't work. The ninety-second will. Bear with me; I have to wait a few seconds for the unwanted futures to pass." He waited five or six seconds in silence. "Here it is."

He tossed the book. It bounced off the carpet, six inches from the other, flipped over, and came to rest on top of the first one.

"And so on," he said and began to toss books, punctuated by pauses.

Plop. Plop. Plop. Some bounced off the carpet, one glanced off the nearest pew, and one flew in a high arc and landed directly on top of the others. In the end all six books sat in a crooked stack, one on top of the other.

"And for artistic flare, the last one on its edge," Seth said and tossed the last book. It flew through the air, flipped end over once, and landed on its edge atop the pile.

"And that, my friends, is not magic, and it certainly isn't the result of prayer or the doing of God. That's simple logic at work. I have to leave you now. Thank you for your time."

Seth walked quickly for the back, winked at Miriam, took her arm, and led her from the auditorium. The doors whooshed closed on the swell of voices that began to sweep across the congregation behind them.

"Why did you do that?" Miriam asked. "Don't you care about those people in there?"

"I doubt questioning their understanding of the truth will hurt them, do you? The truth will always prevail." He paused. "Besides, I did it for you," he said. "Because I could. Because I do care. Because I didn't want to single out Islam as the only religion that makes no sense to me given what I know."

24

SAMIR EXITED the Los Angeles International Airport terminal Sunday morning, carrying only a single, medium-sized bag. He'd been in the United States only once before, a five-day visit to New York for Sheik Al-Asamm. It was two years after he began working as a driver for Miriam, while she was still twelve and he only twenty. The sheer volume of new sights and ideas had sent him virtually running back to Saudi Arabia, begging the sheik never to be sent again.

Since that time, he'd been to Paris and Madrid on a number of occasions, but they hadn't affected him like New York had, whether because he was older or because those two cities were more reserved he did not know. He'd also been to Cairo, of course—many Saudi men went to the more liberal capital of Egypt for their pleasures. Samir had never understood the blatant disregard for Islam's morals that was almost always associated with such trips, but he had seen the evidence himself. And he despised it.

Not that he had been without his pleasure in Madrid or Cairo, but he always confined his pleasure to what was permissible according to the Qur'an. And always in the company of one person whom he loved more than any other man, woman, or child in the entire universe.

Miriam.

I have come for you, my love.

He hailed a taxi and was soon riding down Century Boulevard, headed for the car-rental agency. His plan was really very simple. He would allow Miriam to find him, and then he would take her away from this nightmare. He needed nothing but his own love and the will of Allah. And a little help from the others, of course. But they were already helping, far more than they could possibly realize.

In the last hour alone they had told him where to find her.

Whatever information the Americans turned up on the ground, they passed on to Hilal, who in turn told General Mustafa, who informed not only the king, but Khalid and the sheik. Hilal knew a third party was after Miriam, but he didn't know it was Omar. Omar knew everything that Hilal knew, but he was not aware of Samir's involvement. Only Samir and the sheik knew the full picture. In fact, because they knew about Omar, they knew more than the American, Clive Masters. And it was appropriate, Samir thought. Only he was here because of love.

The taxi driver swerved and cursed bitterly at a passing bus. By his accent the man was from Pakistan. Likely a Muslim.

"You have lived long in America?" Samir asked.

"Three years. I'll be lucky to survive another three with these crazy drivers."

"That's a comforting thought for your passenger."

The man laughed. "You get used to it. This is your first time to the States?"

"Second. I've been to New York."

The man nodded.

"You are a Muslim?" Samir asked.

"Yes. There are many Muslims here."

"And you are a good Muslim?"

The man glanced in the rearview mirror. "A good Muslim, yes. I try my best. It's not easy to be a good Muslim in America."

"Then you should go home to Pakistan."

The man nodded, but the wind was out of his sails. "Perhaps."

They drove on in silence.

Samir looked to the east. Somewhere out there in this vast landscape of lost souls Miriam was running for her life. Afraid, abandoned, and desperate. He took a deep breath and begged Allah for her safety. *One more day. Give me one more day.*

They had missed Seth and Miriam by five minutes, and Clive knew it might just as well have been a week. Some proactive parishioner had called the police and reported a lunatic was threatening the pastor. Ten units had searched the streets of Ridgecrest for the next hour and turned up exactly what he expected them to: nothing.

Clive stepped out the church's entry doors and walked quickly for his car. With any luck, none of this would matter soon. He was putting the final touches on a plan to upstage Seth. The only way to deal with Seth was to put him in the dark; Clive knew that like he knew the walnut in his pocket was round. And if he was right, he was closing in on a way to do just that. Sleep was not Seth's only weakness.

The first step was to track Seth's movements and establish, with as much confidence as possible, his destination. For that he needed more manpower. If he could determine the destination, Clive thought he had a pretty good chance of getting there without being seen in Seth's futures.

Peter Smaley had called an hour earlier and initiated a conference call with Secretary Paul Gray and NSA Director Susan Wheatly. Clive had talked to Susan before. The straight shooter took a personal interest in his unique position with the agency. It was his first time, however, to speak with the secretary of state, who was understandably upset about having to tolerate Saudi diplomats running amuck in "this crazy manhunt down there." The secretary understood the sensitive nature of the country's relationship with Saudi Arabia better than anybody, but it didn't mean he had to like it.

Clive patiently retraced the events of the last three days and then gave his estimation of the situation.

"You're saying that it's Seth who presents the bigger problem to us," Susan had observed. "Not only because he's assisting the princess, but because of this . . . this ability of his."

"Yes. And I'm suggesting we make bringing him in the top priority."

"You have over a hundred members of various law enforcement agencies directly involved now. And the rest of the country on full alert for this guy," the secretary said. "Sounds like top priority to me."

"I want more. He may try to take her from the country. I want all ports closed to private flights unless they've been thoroughly searched. I want to bring in Homeland Security and I want to set up interstate roadblocks. I'm suggesting we view Seth as a terrorist on the loose with an atomic weapon. And then I want you to give me final authority over all resources. Nobody moves or talks without my saying so. That's top priority."

The phone went silent for a few seconds.

"You really think a college student from Berkeley is that dangerous?" Susan said.

"I think he's the most dangerous man on the planet at this moment."

Now, an hour later, Clive waited for their response. His patience was a formality—he already knew what the answer would be.

He slid into the car, fired it up. Hilal hadn't shown himself since their talk last night—he was probably headed for Nevada already. The man had become an enemy of sorts. He had the will and the means to take both Seth and Miriam out. Clive wanted them alive. At the very least, he wanted Seth alive. No man had done what this man had done to him. No man could do what Seth was capable of doing. Killing him would be a mistake of the worst kind.

His phone rang.

"Yes."

"You have it, Clive," Smaley's voice said softly. Amazing how his attitude had changed since Clive interrupted his dinner the previous night.

"Okay. I call the shots?"

"You run the show in-country. The border is being handled."

"Good enough."

Smaley breathed into the phone. "I have to say, I'm pretty skeptical about this . . . theory of yours."

"Okay."

"So. If you had to call it now, where would you say he's headed?"

"Las Vegas," Clive said.

"Las Vegas," Omar said, dropping the phone on the seat. "Drive."

"How do they know?" Assir asked.

"They don't. But neither do we. The agency man believes they're headed for Las Vegas, and Hilal believes him. So we go to Las Vegas. We stay with our plan. Sooner or later the American will make a mistake, and we will be there."

After two days of cat-and-mouse games, it felt good to have a destination. At every juncture, Omar had been just ahead of Hilal. He'd watched the meeting between Hilal and Clive Masters through binoculars at nearly a thousand yards and received the pertinent points of their conversation an hour later, when Hilal had reported his suspicions to Saudi Arabia. He'd reached the church before the police, but too late to intercept Miriam.

Now Seth and Miriam's entourage was headed for Las Vegas, and he would beat them there as well.

Omar lay his head back on the leather seat and closed his eyes. If the hunters were right about Seth's gift, then there was only one way to trap the student, and the agency man would be the one to do it. But no matter how the scene played itself out, Omar would witness the end. He would be the vulture. And Miriam would be his prey.

His wife would be his prey.

25

SETH CALLED THEM the "eyes from the sky." Helicopters. They were unquestionably the most annoying and most threatening factors in the route they had chosen through Death Valley. Given the Cadillac's white paint, finding cover in the endless brown landscape was like trying to hide on the fifty-yard line during the Super Bowl. If not for Seth's three-hour sight into the future, they would have been apprehended long ago. He'd managed to pull the car into hiding no fewer than six times since their departure from the church yesterday morning.

The other annoying element was the heat. Particularly after the Cadillac's ancient air-conditioning unit quit functioning.

They'd decided Sunday afternoon that traveling at night might be a better idea. The darkness would provide cooler temperatures and hamper the helicopter's search. They'd freshened themselves up at a gas station armed by an old clueless codger, purchased enough junk to fill the backseat, and gone looking for a place to wait out the afternoon. Seth's "old codger" was really just an older man who didn't care what was happening beyond his driveway, and the "junk," as he called it, consisted of critical necessities, like toiletries, food, water, and clothes. The food was arguably unhealthy, and the clothes didn't fit Miriam as she would have liked. But after washing and changing into fresh clothes in the station's rest room, Miriam felt nearly giddy with relief.

They'd found an outcropping of rock off the road, parked the car under it, and done their best to sleep in the stifling heat. Seth certainly needed the sleep. Despite his insistence that all was "peachy," she knew differently.

"You may say you're crisp as a fruit, but you can't hide your tired eyes," she'd said. "You're taking the Advil as if it were candy and your eyes are puffy."

"Don't be silly." He looked in the mirror and then sat back without comment.

"It's wearing you down."

He'd looked past her with glazed eyes. "I'm sure that's what Clive is thinking. He's trying to push us to exhaustion and then close in. But as long as I don't sleep longer than three hours, we're okay."

He picked up a battery-operated alarm clock they'd purchased with their other supplies. What if it didn't work? Or worse, didn't wake him? She decided not to push the issue. He needed sleep, not her concerns.

The issue turned out to be moot. Seth hadn't been able to sleep. They'd resumed their journey after dark, and Seth seemed his energized self again. They'd talked about fashion in terms Miriam didn't know were part of the fashion world's lexicon. His was a unique view of the world, to be sure. And then they'd talked about surfing. How Seth liked to surf! Miriam thought she might like it as well. At the very least, rolling through the waves sounded like a wonderful idea. She'd been to the beach in Jiddah, of course. But always draped from head to foot in the black abaaya and veil. The notion of diving into the ocean wearing nothing but shorts and a T-shirt had never presented itself to her as such an intoxicating idea as it did hearing Seth talk. For that matter, what would it be like to swim in the waves naked? What a lovely idea!

Their progress remained terribly slow, primarily because of the constant detours forced on them by the pursuit. They must have avoided a dozen police cars in one four-hour stretch. By eleven o'clock that night, Seth could barely keep his eyes open. He'd given up in defeat and rolled the car into a ravine well off the road. Clive and his group would not likely discover them before daybreak. They'd both fallen asleep within the hour.

The alarm chirped three hours later. Miriam pulled herself out of sleep's haze long enough to turn it off. She was fast asleep within seconds.

Miriam was the first to awaken Monday morning. She pushed herself up in the rear seat. Seth was gone. She peered over the front seat. Nothing.

"Seth?"

The car moved under her and she looked down to see that she was sitting on him. Alarmed, she clambered for the door, incidentally planting her elbows in his back and on his head in the process. That woke him. He rose groggy and grumbling, but none the wiser.

"We're safe?" she asked.

He looked around, waking. "Safe. What happened to the alarm clock?"

Only then did she remember. "I . . . I think I might have turned it off."

He looked at her dumbly. "That was smart."

"Forgive me. I was depending on your infallible rising with the sun."

He smiled and winked. "Touché."

"Touché."

They devoured three large bags of Doritos, pulled back onto Highway 178, and headed east. Today they would reach Las Vegas.

Seth had explained his plan the night before, and it sounded like something play actors might try in a movie rather than a reasonable course for two desperate fugitives. Nonetheless, she couldn't deny that this city she'd heard so much about seemed to have a certain appeal to her. Riding here next to Seth in the desert, headed for that city of magic and sin, she felt perfectly scandalous.

A voice within kept telling her she was throwing herself to the winds of iniquity even *thinking* such thoughts. She should have her head buried in the Qur'an, begging Allah for his grace. And yet, on the other hand, she'd been to Madrid with Samir and seen the way the men from her country indulged themselves. She was not nearly so liberal as they had been. She was only doing what had to be done to survive for Samir.

Seth had said nothing more to suggest his affection for her. She thought he was only being courteous, because his eyes spoke clearly enough. Although she appreciated his discretion, she was surprised to discover that a part of her longed to be called beautiful by this man beside her. A natural response from someone who had been sequestered away by Saudi culture for so long, she thought. She was indeed a beautiful woman, and he was a compassionate, strong, and very handsome man. Never mind the impossibilities; Seth and she were still human.

Unless it was more than that. Unless she was actually falling for Seth. She looked out the side window and forced her thoughts in a new direction.

The Mojave Desert was not like the great deserts of Saudi Arabia. Sand dunes rose in the distance, but mostly the land was comprised of rocky ground shifting in hues of red and white. Seth drove past a sight called Artists Point, where the rock was green in parts. The Americans called Death Valley—over three million acres of this rugged ground, ranging from almost three hundred feet below sea level to over eleven thousand feet above sea level in the nearby western mountain peaks—a "park."

In a strange way, driving through the desert toward the mysterious city of Las Vegas with Seth at her side felt like a metaphysical passing from death to freedom. There he was again. Seth.

They'd driven for some time without encountering a single vehicle when a sly grin split Seth's face.

"I have an idea," he said.

She looked at him. "This is new?"

He slowed and veered off the road. Gravel crunched under their tires. The desert was flat on either side of the highway here. Rough outcroppings of rock rose from the ground two hundred meters to their right.

"What are you doing?"

"We have some time. I've decided you need to really experience freedom."

"Oh? I thought I was free already. Here with you."

He put the car into park and looked at her. "You haven't even begun to experience true freedom until you have wheels, my dear. In America, wheels are synonymous with freedom. Everyone knows this. Come on."

He opened his door and climbed out.

"What do you mean?"

"Trust me. Get out."

Miriam climbed out. She stood by her door and looked at him over the Cadillac's shredded leather roof. "What?"

"Over here."

She walked around the hood, grinning with him, clueless to his intentions. "What are we doing?"

He held the door and invited her to the driver's seat. He wanted her to drive!

"I can't *drive!*"

"Exactly. That's why I need to teach you."

"Why?" The idea terrified her.

"We may need you to drive. What if I'm wounded and can't drive? We don't know what waits beyond three hours. It just makes sense."

"Now? Out here? We don't have time for this!"

"But we do have time, my dear. I should know. And I also know that you *will* give this a try. I've seen that as well, so you might as well hop behind the wheel and give it a go." He grinned deliberately.

Miriam looked around. "Have you seen me running into anything?"

"What's there to run into? We're in the desert."

"You're not answering my question."

"Okay. Actually there are a few scenarios in which you have a few mishaps, but we'll do our best to avoid those. Come on, don't tell me a princess who risked her life by crossing the oceans is afraid of a little joyride in the desert."

"Mishaps? What kind of mishaps?"

He shrugged. "Nothing noteworthy really. Driving off a cliff. Hitting a truck head-on. Please, I insist."

She looked at the steering wheel. Women were not permitted to drive in Saudi Arabia. Perhaps that was reason enough to try it. She felt a grin pull at her lips.

"You promise me it will be safe?"

"There's always risk in life's most rewarding pursuits, isn't there?"

She walked for the door. "You're impossible," she said and slid in behind the wheel.

Seth bounded over the hood and climbed in, ecstatic.

It took him three minutes to explain the basics, not that she didn't know them, but because she felt comforted by his repeated explanations. This is the brake, used to stop the car; this is the accelerator, used to speed the car up; this is the steering wheel, used to keep the car on the road; this is the radio, used to keep you awake so you don't drive off a cliff.

She turned off the radio and demanded he stay serious. She also insisted he show her how all the turn signals and lights worked. If she was going to learn to drive, she might as well do it right.

He told her to drive out toward the rock outcroppings. The ground was hard enough here to resist tire tracks, and he'd seen what would happen if they took to the road. It wasn't pretty. Miriam put the gearshift into drive and gripped the wheel with both hands, knuckles white.

"Let's roll," he said. He was already trying hard not to laugh, and she wondered what he was seeing.

"Let's roll," she said and pushed the pedal on the floor. The Cadillac jerked forward. She immediately shoved her foot down to stop. Instead of stopping, the car shot out into the desert like a bullet from a gun.

Miriam cried out in alarm. Beside her, Seth was laughing. Cackling uncontrollably, in fact.

"Seth! Stop . . ."

Her limbs froze, fixed by terror. The car screamed forward, headed directly for the rocks.

"Seth!"

Suddenly he swallowed his laughing. "Turn!" he shouted.

He grabbed the wheel and yanked it down. He tried to turn the car, and she resisted his attempts with this rigor mortis that had seized her arms, powerless to change any of it.

She glanced down at the steering column and for some inexplicable reason thought she should hit the lever beside the wheel. She slapped at it. Water sprayed up on the windshield, blinding her to the onrushing rocks.

"The brakes!" Seth yelled. "Stop the car!" He swung his leg toward the pedals and stabbed at the floor, shoving her against her door in the process. "Push the brakes!"

One thought rose above the panic that had immobilized her. The thought that Seth was scared. That he hadn't seen this as a real possibility. That he needed *her* to stop this car because he was powerless to do it without her.

Her limbs came free. She swung her elbow into his rib cage with enough force to take the wind from him. He grunted and released his grip. She spun the wheel to her right, just as the windshield wiper made its first pass on the glass, clearing her view. The rocks loomed twenty meters ahead.

The car suddenly slid sideways. It occurred to her that her foot was on the accelerator rather than the brake. But she decided that it should stay there. She should use the power of the car to take them out of harm's way. Ride it out, as Seth had said once.

The back of the car swept around in a great half-circle, wheels spewing debris back toward the rocks. They came to a near stop, engine still roaring, and then shot back out into the desert, away from the outcropping.

Miriam blinked. Exhilaration flooded her veins like a rush of cold water. She eased off the accelerator. "Whooohaaa!" she shouted. "Let it ride, baby!"

Seth laughed tentatively.

Miriam steered the car right and then left. She pressed the accelerator and sped up again.

"Easy . . ."

"I have it under control, dear. You just sit back and relax."

Listen to her. She was sounding like him. Dear? She grinned, pulled the car through another wide turn, and sped back out into the desert.

"Now you're talking," Seth said. His confidence was back. "Take it behind the rocks and out into the desert a bit. We need to get out of sight for a few minutes. Someone's coming down the highway."

His revelation alarmed her only because he seemed comfortable in depending on her to take them from danger. She guided the car around the boulders, weaving more than she would have liked. Perhaps her confidence was a little premature. But she did manage, and she had saved them from crashing into the boulders. Never mind that she had nearly crashed them into the boulders in the first place.

She drove for twenty minutes while he continued to give her pointers. They headed further out into the desert, weaving around boulders and sand patches. By the time she parked the car behind a large rock formation, they were a good distance from the road. But that was good. The traffic on the highway was hopeless for the next hour anyway, Seth said.

Miriam stepped from the car fairly floating with satisfaction.

"You are absolutely right, my dear," she said. "*This* feels like freedom!" She threw her arms around his neck impulsively. "Thank you."

He staggered backward, chuckling. "Whoa!" She caught herself and released him, suddenly self-conscious.

They sat on a rounded rock next to each other and shared another bag of chips with a bottle of water, and Miriam wasn't sure she had ever been so thrilled in all her life.

She looked at Seth as he tilted the bottled water to his lips and drank. His neck was strong and bronzed by the sun, rising to a perfectly sculpted jaw. His hair was loose, not unlike the Greek sculptures that graced her uncle's villa in Riyadh. Allah had sent her a Greek god to take her through the desert in a Cadillac.

She looked away from him. *Listen to you, Miriam. You're definitely having feelings for him. You're being taken by him.* She reached into the bag of chips and ate one.

Yes, of course, because the Greek god called Seth was a master at the art of love, equipped as he was with this foreknowledge of his. He had an unfair advantage! And she was untrained in the art. A hopeless woman raised in a black veil, easily picked off by the likes of him.

"Are you manipulating me, Seth?"

He turned his head, eyebrows arched. "Manip—please. What do you mean?"

"I mean, are you taking advantage of me?"

He looked shocked. "Do I act like I'm taking advantage of you?"

"Of my mind."

"What are you talking about? I can't take advantage of your mind."

She looked at the tall western peaks. He seemed genuinely surprised by her questions. How, if he had already seen the possibility of her asking it? Maybe he was losing his touch. He had missed the possibility of her driving into the rock earlier. Unless he was *pretending* to be shocked! The thought sent a chill over her skull.

She stood and dropped the bag of chips in his lap. "Please don't play with me. I know very well that you know what I'm going to say before I say it. I know you can simply choose the right words to evoke the right response from me. And now that you're pretending to be shocked by my question, I can't help but think that you are manipulating me."

"Your question *is* shocking. Okay, I might have seen the possibility that you would pursue this line of questioning, but you have to understand, it's only one possibility out of thousands wandering around in my mind. I never took it seriously. It appears I was wrong."

"Don't try to turn the tables on me! You still possess this crazy ability to make people do something by encouraging the future in which you see them doing it. I can't believe that you don't do that with me all the time. You're manipulating my feelings."

He hesitated. "Nonsense. I would never do such a thing. And just so we're clear, this *crazy ability,* as you so affectionately refer to it, is saving your life."

"Do you deny that you could make me feel things?"

"Of course I can't!"

"How do you expect me to handle this show of affection you've thrown at me?" *You're saying too much, Miriam.* "First you tell me that you have feelings for me, and then I begin to think that I may have feelings that—" She caught herself.

His eyes widened. What was she saying?

"You have feelings?" he asked.

Miriam pushed past the embarrassment that flushed her face. "Do you deny that you can at least make me do things?"

"Yes, I do deny it," he said. "I can't *make* you do things."

"But out of all the things that I might do, you can make me do those things you want me to do."

He hesitated. "No, not necessarily."

"Ha! I don't believe you."

"I can't make you do anything you don't want to do."

"Is that right? Please, let's not mind the technicalities. I saw what you did in the church yesterday. I think you can see an almost unlimited number of my responses to what you say or do, and then you can do whatever results in the one you want."

He spoke quietly. "It's not exactly like that."

"Then show me what it is like. The least you can do is be forthright with me. Let me test you. See if you can make me do something."

"Please, Miriam. We shouldn't do this," he said. He was afraid, wasn't he? She felt a sketch of empathy for him. And then she immediately wondered if he hadn't expected that by the phrasing of his words. *Please, Miriam, we shouldn't do this.* He knew that if he said that she would respond with sympathy! She decided then that she had to know.

"I insist." She paused. "Make me do something. Make me kiss you."

His pallor reddened. How could he fake that? His lips twitched to an embarrassed grin. "You're presuming that's something I *want* you to do?"

"Oh, please. Okay then, let's *pretend* that you want me to kiss you. And I suspect that most red-blooded males would like to kiss me. Deep inside, where you are brutally honest with yourself, I don't think you would mind either. That's close enough, isn't it? So then make me kiss you, Mr. California Stud."

He chuckled nervously. "Mr. California Stud. That's good. That's real good."

"I'm waiting."

"Don't be ridiculous. I can't *make* you kiss me."

"Do you *want* me to kiss you?"

"Right now?"

The way he said it betrayed him. Surprisingly, she was pleased by the fact. And then conflicted. *Be careful, Miriam.*

"Sure, why not," she said. "The desire had obviously crossed your mind. Just pretend it has resurfaced this morning here, in this hot desert so far from the nearest living soul." She couldn't suppress a small grin.

For his part, Seth was now thoroughly embarrassed. He just looked off in the direction of the road and shook his head.

"You're saying that at this moment, you see no possible futures in which I kiss you in the next few minutes?" she asked.

"That's not fair," he said softly.

"You don't want to be forthcoming with me? You want to hide the truth from me? You have the gift and so you are permitted to see what I might or might not do, but I am a lowly woman and so—"

"Stop it!" His tone surprised her. She had pushed him, as much to see him squirm as to know the truth. What did he really feel for her? And what if he actually made her kiss him? She would never do it! This was the power of a woman.

The thought was comforting. "Then tell me," she said.

"Okay, if you really must know, there *is* a future in which you kiss me in the next—"

"That's impossible!" she said. How could he say that—she would never kiss him!

"So now I tell you the truth and really you don't want to hear the truth after all," he said. "I'm sorry, dear, but it is indeed true."

Miriam stared at him, shocked by his claim. *You are losing your soul, Miriam! No, he is mad. Disgusting and sick. I am a woman made for Samir, and I've told him that and now he is taunting me, saying that he could make me kiss him!*

He was avoiding her eyes.

"Then make me do it," she challenged, suddenly furious.

"I can't."

"Do it! Don't you dare tell me that I will kiss you without giving me the opportunity to prove you wrong."

"Okay. Roses are red, violets are blue; I'll kiss a toad, but I won't kiss you."

She blinked at him. "What is that supposed to mean? This is your way of enticing a woman?"

"You're right." A sly smile spread across his mouth. "Roses are red, violets are blue; you are without doubt the most beautiful woman I have ever seen."

She paused. "That's better but it doesn't rhyme. And as you see, my lips are still not on yours. I don't feel the slightest impulse to walk over there and kiss you. You can do better. Don't toy with me."

Perhaps a very small part of her did want him to kiss her. *Stop it! Stop it, Miriam!*

He cleared his throat, thinking. He suddenly jumped to his feet on top of the rock. He ripped open his shirt, pulled it off his shoulders, and put one hand behind his head and the other on his waist, cocking his hips in a pose, so that his stomach muscles rippled. "Hey, baby, you like what you see?" he said, winking.

She stared at him, astounded at his gall. A giggle rose from her belly. He grinned and relaxed his pose. "No?"

She swallowed her laughter, but could do nothing about the grin on her face. "You're impossible. I still haven't run into your arms."

He jumped down from the rock. "That's because I can't *make* you do anything. And I never would, even if the thought of kissing you did cross my mind in a mad moment of *brutal honesty,* as you put it. And for the record, the future in which I saw you kissing me involved a kiss on the forehead. Just so you know."

Miriam just looked at him. *In another life, I'm not sure I wouldn't have kissed you, Seth Border.* She walked up to him, put her hands on his shoulders, and kissed him on the forehead.

"There you go. Now I've fulfilled your prophecy," she said, satisfied by his blush. She picked up the bag of chips and walked away.

"Would you like to test the truth in *your* heart?" Seth said behind her.

She turned. "I thought we just did."

"I was thinking about God," he said. "We don't see eye to eye on the issue, and it's occurred to me that I may have a way to test which one of us is right. A tangible test, no arguments."

"Isn't it okay that we disagree? I don't see the problem. You've already done enough to plant seeds of doubt in my mind. I don't see how doing more would help either of us."

"Actually, there is a problem. According to your faith, I'm an infidel. Your godsend—that would be me—is headed for eternal torment. How can you be okay with that?"

"I'm not sure there's anything I can do about it. I'm not even sure how true it is anymore."

"That's a start. But trust me, according to the teaching of Mohammed, I am definitely headed straight for the pit. I just thought you might care enough about me to know whether that's true."

He was cornering her again, she thought. But this time she didn't mind. She'd seen that he cared for her, not only by saving her with this gift of his, but by the way he had reacted to her as a woman. Other than Samir, Seth was the only man she'd met who respected her and honored her as an equal. She trusted him for that more than for any other reason.

"Why do you hate Mohammed?" she asked.

"I don't hate him. And I don't hate the men who've killed in the name of Christianity either. Although I do think there was a vastly significant difference between Jesus and Mohammed. Jesus, although misguided by the delusion that he was God, followed his own teaching in an extraordinary way. To the death. He may not have been God, but I can understand why some might believe that he was."

"And Mohammed was not sinless," Miriam said for him. "You've already said—"

"Mohammed was not only riddled with sin, he was a charlatan, Miriam. Please, I'm not bashing him. He was no worse than you or me, but any careful study into his life reveals a man who made up a religion to serve his own purposes, much of it on the fly. His version of Islam—which has admittedly changed in many parts of the world over the centuries—was part Christian, part Jewish, and part pagan, created piecemeal from dozens of desert religions of his day. His so-called visions hardly contain an original thought. When he married his seventh wife, Raihana, who was a Jewess, parts of Judaism sprung up in his revelations. The same with his first and eighth wives, who were Christian. But he couldn't even get his wives' stories straight—he mixed up a slew of facts in retelling the history of Abraham. Even his recounting of history was undoubtedly taken from hearsay, not from mystical revelations in the cave as claimed."

She listened to him, mildly interested, but not angry. Surprisingly, she believed him when he said he wasn't trying to discredit the prophet. He was simply relaying the facts as he knew them. And he seemed to know more than she. Either way, his opinion had little bearing on her faith.

"Even the teachers of Islam say Mohammed was not perfect," she said.

"And I'm saying that's a gross understatement. This is a man who preached peace when he had no army, but as soon as he had enough men to wage war, he emerged from the cave with a revelation that Muslims should slay all unbelievers unless they repented—that's sura al-Taubah 9:5, if you're interested. And as you know, Mohammed claimed that if any of his revelations contradicted any of his earlier revelations, the earlier ones were no longer valid. A convenient device, if you ask me. This and a handful of other suras annulled 124 earlier, more tolerant verses and allowed Mohammed to subsequently lead 66 battles, and encourage countless others executed by his generals. This is a man who received a revelation to change the direction of prayers from Mecca to Jerusalem in order to appease the Jews he was trying to convert, but then seventeen months later, having failed, received another revelation to change the direction *back* to Mecca. This is a man who beheaded all the male Jews at Quraiza, one by one, and forced the women and children to convert."

Seth took a deep breath. "But none of that's the point. I could go on for hours, revealing what is little known to Muslims about their founder. But—"

"Christian Nazis killed the Jews. The crusaders killed Muslims," she said.

"Hitler was as much a devout Christian as I am a toad. The same for the crusaders, for that matter. Militants like Bin Laden, on the other hand, are indeed very good followers of Mohammed. They are doing what he not only commanded but essentially did himself."

Miriam had heard some of this before. He was sounding like the fundamentalists in Saudi Arabia. Hearing it from Seth, she saw that they had a point.

"Either way, I'm not that interested in the *followers* of the prophets, but the prophets themselves," Seth said. "More to the point, the God of the prophets."

"There is only one God."

"And Allah means God in Arabic, to both Christians and Muslims. I know. But what if the God that Jesus prayed to wasn't the same as the God Mohammed prayed to? What if one of them wasn't really God at all? Or even more likely, what if whoever Mohammed heard from in his cave wasn't the same being Jesus listened to in the garden of Gethsemane?"

Miriam looked at him standing there with his shirt unbuttoned from his little show on the rock. A modern-day prophet of entirely new dimensions. One who saw into the future but did not believe beyond what he saw. He knew too much for his own good. If he were to say what he just said in the streets of Riyadh, he would be dead already.

"And you have a way to prove which God is real, do you?" she asked.

A twinkle came to his eyes. "I might."

"Please, don't let me stop you," she said.

"You suggested testing my integrity through my ability to see the future," Seth said, pacing past her. He whirled around, wearing a crooked smile. "Why don't we do the same with God?"

"You can't test God."

"So they say. Maybe I can."

Seth bounded over to a group of small boulders and scooped up an armful of medium-sized rocks. He ran to a bare patch of ground and set them in a circle. Miriam watched him curiously, afraid to ask.

He returned to the pile and grabbed up more stones. "Ever hear of Elijah and Mount Carmel?" he asked, dumping the stones into a second pile, ten feet from the first.

"No," she said.

"It was a battle between the prophets of Baal and the prophet Elijah. They prepared altars and called on their respective deities to respond with fire. Elijah's God won." He finished the second circle and stood back. "Here we have two altars. This one"—he indicated the one on his left—"is an altar to the God Mohammed heard from. We'll call him Allah so we don't get confused, even though Allah does mean God. And this one is an altar to Yahweh, the God Jesus heard from. The God of Mohammed, and the God of Jesus. We will see if either of them responds."

He seemed delighted with his idea, but Miriam was still unclear about his intentions. "You want Allah to descend in fire?" she said. "This won't prove a thing."

"No, not fire. But if I pray to each God to do something—anything in the immediate future—I will be able to see if even the *possibilities* of the immediate future change."

It was unorthodox to be sure, perhaps foolish even, but she didn't see the harm. There were no mutawa around to see his mockery, and he could hardly do more damage to the reputation of Mohammed than he already had.

"Don't you see?" he said. "It's like having a giant stethoscope up to the heavens. If there's a God, and if that God actually responds in any way that even has the possibility of affecting life here on earth as a result of my prayer, I'll know it! For all we know, this is the first time in history such a thing has even been possible."

"But *I* won't know that anything has changed," she said.

"True. You'll have to take my word for it." He looked at the altars. "It's been a while since I said prayers. Maybe you should do the honors."

"I'll have no part in this."

"Fair enough. But surely I don't have to bow toward Mecca to get Allah's attention, do I?"

"I wouldn't think so."

"Still, better to be sure."

He faced the east before the altar he'd declared was for Allah, his back to her. He dropped to his knees and bowed. The desert fell silent.

Miriam glanced around, awkward in the absurdity of it. She was embarrassed for him, bowing like an idiot before this pile of stones.

"Seth . . ."

He held up his finger and motioned silence. Miriam crossed her arms, feeling stupid.

Seth stood and turned around, eyes closed.

"What are you doing now?"

"I'm searching the future." His eyes sprang open. "As I expected. Nothing. Nothing has changed. I prayed to Allah to either reveal himself in any way or to clear our way once we hit the state line. I haven't told you, but I haven't seen a way through yet."

She lowered her arms. "You're serious? Why didn't you say something!"

"If I told you every time the future looks bleak, you'd be a mess. Don't worry; it'll come to me. Always does. That's why we're out here in the desert learning to drive and discovering our passions and arguing about God. I'm waiting for a future to open up that will get us across the state border without getting nailed. That means caught."

He turned to face the other altar and sighed. "Strike one. Now the other." He fidgeted with his hands for a moment, considering how to proceed. Then he lifted his face and arms to the sky. His lips moved in silent prayer.

This was truly insane. Miriam's mind went to his confession about not being able to see a way beyond the state line. How often had that happened without her knowing? And yet he withheld it from her, determined not to concern her. Her Greek god, who was at this moment standing ten meters off, with his arms lifted like an idiot, determined to prove something she didn't care about in the first place. She believed in Allah because she believed, not because he had proven anything to her. Her confidence was a matter of faith.

Seth lowered his hands and turned around. Once again, his eyes were closed. After a moment they flickered open and he smiled.

"Well?" she asked.

"Nothing." He stepped toward her. "Absolutely nothing, *nada,* zip. It would appear that, at the very least, neither God is terribly interested in us at the moment. We'll have to depend on good old—"

Seth suddenly froze midstride, eyes wide.

"What?"

His mouth parted. For a fleeting moment she thought he'd had a heart attack or something similar.

"Seth!"

He blinked. "Oh . . . my . . . God!" He swallowed and turned around, dazed.

"What happened?" she demanded. "What's going on?"

"How's that . . . That's impossible!"

"Seth!"

He spun to her, face white. "It happened!"

"What?"

Seth collected himself. "Nothing. Let's roll." He walked past her.

She hurried for her door, evidently on the passenger's side, considering he had his hand on the driver's door already.

"Don't say *nothing*. I know you saw something. What did you see?"

"I don't know," he said. "I saw that we have to roll."

26

THEY APPROACHED THE NEVADA BORDER on Highway 178 and stopped five miles from the crossing. Seth had remained quiet about the altar episode. He said he was still trying to figure it out but refused to explain what *it* was. The future had changed; the fact that they were making a run for the state line was evidence enough. He had prayed and the future had changed, and Seth was not at all at ease with the fact.

Slowly Seth came to himself. He stared at the blacktop ahead, hands on the wheel. A mischievous grin grew on his face.

"Okay, the way I see it, we have three ways to do this." He looked at her. "One way would be violent and bloody, one would be crafty and quite brilliant, and one would be very bold and silly. Which is your pleasure?"

She thought through the choices. Violence was acceptable to neither of them. What could he mean by silly? Either way they would succeed, wouldn't they? Although he had made some errors lately.

"Bold and silly," she said.

"You sure?"

"Maybe not."

"No, I think it's a splendid choice," he said. "Let's do it."

"Okay."

Seth slapped the steering wheel. "Excellent!"

He climbed out, ran to the front of the car, yanked off the Cadillac hood ornament, and hurled it into the desert. Miriam got out, amused by his antics.

"What is this?"

"This is our disguise, madam." He ran to the trunk, popped it up, and returned with a large knife. Without warning he bent and slashed the right front tire. With a terrible hiss, the air bled out. The sound struck her as maniacal.

"I cannot imagine this is a clever idea," she said.

He ran to the rear wheel and slashed it as well. "You chose bold and silly, remember?"

"Yes, but I didn't choose stupid."

Seth laughed and jumped around to the other side where he repeated the slashing. All four tires were as flat as millet cakes.

"Let's roll," he said.

"You can drive on these tires?"

"For a few miles. That's the point."

They started down the road, and within a hundred meters the thumping began. Within another hundred the racket was so loud that Miriam was sure the wheels would fall off.

"This is ridiculous!"

"Ha! You think *this* is ridiculous?"

Now she began to worry in earnest. He had never failed them, but this madness was a new thing. Perhaps he had actually *lost* his gift back at the altar.

A loud bang suddenly sounded from the engine and Miriam started. Steam began to seep from the hood. Now what? The engine was going to blow up!

"Seth! Shouldn't you stop?"

"No!" He was delighted. "This is it!"

"I'm not sure that this is a good idea! What on earth are we doing?"

"I need you to do me a favor," he said. "I need you to mess up your hair and put some of that white sunblock on your face. Could you be a darling and do that for me?"

She looked at him in horror. "Stop talking to me with your darlings and dears! Just tell me what we are doing. For heaven's sake, this is madness!"

"I'm sorry. We're putting on a disguise. Just enough so that he won't recognize you for a few seconds. That's all we need. I thought white sunblock would be better than grease."

"Who is 'he'?"

The smile left his face. "I'm sorry, but we're starting to run out of time. We're committed, and honestly, if I tell you too much, this won't work. I swear I'll make anything you find less than hilarious up to you later, but now we don't have time. Now you have to make yourself look non-Arabic."

Smoke was now streaming out of the hood. A tremendous *thump* sounded under them.

"We lost a tire," he said, grinning again.

She stared at him for one last moment, and then scrambled for the back where a small bag held their toiletries. "I don't like this," she said, pulling out the tube of white cream. She smeared the paste over her face. "I don't like this at all."

"You look like a ghost."

She grabbed the visor and looked at her image in the mirror. A streaked white face stared back. The car suddenly stopped in a cloud of smoke.

"Perfect," Seth said. "The crossing is just around that corner. Just drive nice and easy and stop before you get to the police cruiser."

She spun to him. "Drive? I can't drive!"

"Sure you can. You have to. It's the only way. I told you it would come in handy, didn't I?"

Captain John Rogers had just put out his last Lucky Strike and was thinking he'd much rather be back in Shoshone, having a cold brew at Bill's Bar, than watching a deserted road, when he saw the cloud of smoke rolling his way from around the bend.

His first thought was that someone had ignited a smoke bomb, but he discarded the thought when he saw the grill. It was an overheated car, limping slowly as if running on the last cylinder. Banana peckers, that thing was barely crawling. Didn't the fool driver realize he was frying the engine?

He couldn't make out the car because it was crawling under a mask of steam, but by the square grill he pegged it as an old sedan. These here were tourists from New York or Vermont, come to take a picnic in Death Valley without knowing the first thing about the harsh realities of the place. John had seen it a hundred times.

He grunted and leaned back on his hood. "Banana peckers," he said. He didn't know how the fool could see past the windshield. It was wobbling too. In fact, if he wasn't mistaken . . .

Good night, the thing had burned its wheels off! Was that even possible? The situation had just gone from New Yorker stupid to hardly imaginable imbecile. In his eleven years patrolling these parts, he couldn't remember seeing anything quite like this.

He stood up and put his hands on his hips. "Double banana peckers," he said. "Wait'll the boys get a load of this."

The car sounded like a limo pulling strings of empty cans after a wedding. It clanked up to a steaming halt ten yards off.

John rested his right hand on his gun. Never could be too careful. A man stupid enough to drive this deathtrap was stupid enough to do anything.

The engine died. Hissing smoke boiled skyward. All four tires were gone. Now how in the world was that possible?

The door suddenly flew open and someone stumbled out, coughing and gagging on the smoke.

"Hold it there!" John yelled. "Just hold it right there!"

The person straightened, frantic. It was a woman and her face was white. Either sunblock or makeup. Her hair flew every which way and she reminded him of Gene Simmons wearing that Kiss makeup. The sight made him blink.

She gripped her hair and turned in a slow circle, moaning.

A faint breeze cleared the smoke for a moment. The car was empty. He edged forward and peered through the haze.

"You must help me," the woman moaned.

"You alone, miss?"

She suddenly began to jump up and down, screaming at the top of her lungs. "The arks are after me! The arks are after me! Help me, the arks are after me!"

Startled, he followed her terrified look back down the road. "Okay, just go easy, miss. I don't know what you're on, but everything is fine now. There are no arks after you."

"The arks! You don't understand, I have the ring and the arks are after me!"

He eased toward her. The woman was either high and hallucinating, or plain lunatic. Not terrible actually; she would be his ticket off this post. He held out a reassuring hand.

"Please, miss. I've been here all day and I can assure you, there are no arks in these parts. Now if you'll just calm down."

It suddenly dawned on him what she was trying to say. He stopped four feet from her and waved a hand through the smoke. "Do you mean the Orcs are after you? Like the Orcs from *Lord of the Rings*?"

She stopped and looked at him, surprised but no longer frantic, as if a light had just gone on in her head.

A door slammed behind him and he spun back. The cruiser!

"Hey!"

A hand slapped at his waist, and he twisted back to see the woman hurl his revolver over the guardrail. He grabbed at her but she was past him, running for the cruiser. He took a step in the direction she'd thrown the gun and immediately realized he would never retrieve it before they took off. He whirled to run after the woman.

"Stop!" He knew then that these were the two they had been looking for. "Stop!"

The car fired and the woman piled in. With a squeal of tires his cruiser shot backward, peeled through a U-turn, and then roared off, leaving him straddling the yellow lines on the road.

He glanced down at his waist. No radio. He could get the gun, of course, but . . .

John turned around and looked at the steaming car they'd abandoned. The tireless wheels were mangled. It was going nowhere. The trunk was open. The man had come from the trunk and snuck around, using the smoke for cover while the lady went on about the Arks. Orcs.

Banana peckers! This was not good. Not good at all.

27

THEY DEPOSITED THE POLICE CRUISER in a small town called Pahrump and took a bus into Las Vegas. Miriam made it abundantly clear to Seth that his notion of "bold and silly" was far better characterized as "crazy and ridiculous," and then only in generous terms—although she had done her share of laughing as they sped away from the stranded cop at the state line. The fact that she had raved on about an "ark" when she should have said "Orc" was the worst of it. He insisted he'd said Orc, not ark. But she finally decided to forgive him. He had, after all, only done it knowing the outcome, and the outcome was in their favor. The whole incident seemed to have endeared her to him, even more so than before.

Still, despite his outward pleasure with her performance, he maintained the same introspective nature he'd found after his experiment with the altars. His ability to see forward in time hadn't stretched beyond three hours, but he seemed to see more futures in that time. His sight was broadening, if she wasn't mistaken, and at some times more than others. His headaches had increased with his vision, judging by the number of Advil he kept taking.

Las Vegas was a city of true wonder, surpassing her wildest imaginations with all its lights and colors. Seth referred to the huge casinos as hotels, but in her mind they were nothing less than enclosed cities.

They took adjoining rooms in Caesars Palace, both deluxe rooms in the Forum Towers. Miriam wasn't unaccustomed to luxury, of course, but nothing she'd experienced compared to the magical aura that surrounded them in this magnificent palace.

The rooms were lined with gold and mirrors and ancient symbols of Greeks—pillars and horses and, yes, Greek gods, like her own.

"It's a waste of resources," Seth said as she swept through the room, delighted.

She stopped at the window high above the city and looked out at a dizzying ocean of colors, red and blue and orange and green, moving and flashing with more glitter and glamour than she thought she could endure.

She let the sights go and faced him. "A waste on whom? I'm not worth this?"

He looked at her, blushing, and she knew his mind was scrambling. "No. That's not what I meant. For you, this is hardly acceptable."

For a moment they searched each other's eyes. His were soft and lost, and looking into them, she felt suddenly sad. *In another time, in another place, I could love you, Seth. But not here. Never.*

Seth cleared his throat and turned to the window. "Hilal is here," he said. "But he's not what I expected."

"And what did you expect?" Miriam asked.

"I expected Clive to have the police out in force, searching the hotels and streets for any sign of us. But the Las Vegas police aren't even aware of us. I can see numerous incidents in which we could walk by the authorities without being noticed, much less shipped off to prison. Hilal must be here on his own."

"Are we safe or are we not?"

He paused. "Safe."

"Then let's go shopping," she said.

"Let's."

They wandered through the shops in the forum, engulfed by a sea of people who meandered about in a daze, much like she. The prices seemed high, by Seth's counting, but price was one thing she had learned to ignore. Being a princess did have one or two advantages.

In addition to the costumes they bought for the coming day, Miriam could not resist purchasing suitable clothing. A simple yet elegant emerald dress for her and a pair of black slacks with a beige shirt for Seth. And new shoes for both.

They dined at the Terrazza restaurant, on lobster and crayfish, a favorite of Seth's. She insisted and he agreed. It wouldn't have mattered what they ate; Seth was clearly more interested in her than in the food. She decided then, for the first time, not to discourage him. Women were created to be beautiful for a reason. Their faces were not meant to be hidden away by black veils for their husbands alone. Why should she submit herself to the torment that had badgered her over the last five days? She was in Las Vegas, for heaven's sake! She was free! Seth liked her, maybe even loved her. She liked him very much as well. She would make nothing more or less of the matter.

Miriam sat across from Seth and laughed with him, truly unencumbered by the shackles of her past for the first time. They drank wine and they drank freedom, and Miriam could not have imagined either tasting so delicious.

They retired early and she, at least, slept like a baby, properly pampered and refreshed for the adventure before them. It was ten o'clock in the morning before Seth knocked on the door that separated her suite from his.

"Come."

Seth opened the door, grinning. "The gentleman has arrived."

She stood back and looked at him, stunned by the transformation. His hair was neatly slicked back above his ears. His face was clean shaven and smooth except for a mustache he'd attached to his upper lip. Dressed in the black slacks and beige shirt, he looked every bit the dashing man.

"My, you do clean up, don't you?"

"And you, my princess," he returned, eyeing her. "You are absolutely stunning."

"Yes?" She cocked both hands and touched her wig. "You like it?"

"But of course. I think I would find you beautiful in a gunnysack, but you are quite ravishing in this dress."

"Thank you."

The brown wig was straight and hung just below the ears, masking her own long black hair. The disguises were Seth's idea, and despite the apparent lack of danger, he had insisted they carry through. They would be at the gambling tables for some time, perfectly framed by a dozen cameras. No need to advertise.

Seth pulled his shirt straight and walked in, upright. "Your future awaits us. Are you ready?"

"I'm breathless with anticipation," she said, stretching out her hand for him.

He took it, kissed it lightly, and then spun her around in a dance. She smiled and twirled so that her dress rose to a bell.

"My, aren't you the queen of dancers," he said. He bowed, put one hand on his hip, and marched across the room with her, in a kind of dance she was positive he was faking from watching others. When they reached the window, he spun around and marched her back.

"This is the way we dance in California," he said in a British accent.

Miriam saw that one end of his mustache had detached itself and hung awkwardly. She couldn't hold back a giggle.

"What?" he demanded, still in proper British character.

"It seems that the gentleman's mustache is objecting."

Seth felt his upper lip. "What? This?" He ripped off the mustache. "Nonsense! This isn't a mustache at all. It's a morsel left over from dinner last evening. I've been saving it for now." He stuffed the strip of hair into his mouth, jerked his head back as if swallowing, and then promptly spit it out.

"Whew! Terribly stale, what!"

Miriam put both hands to her face and howled. It was something a barbarian might do in her country, but in Seth she found it hilarious.

He smiled, suddenly embarrassed. She walked up to him. "You've ruined your disguise. Although I will say, with your hair combed you look quite different."

Someday she would either be forced back to Saudi Arabia or delivered safely to Samir by this man. Her heart surged for him. She would miss his company terribly. Miriam looked into his eyes and placed a hand on his cheek. "I owe you my life, Seth. I want you to know that. There is nothing I can ever do to repay what you've done for me."

She stood on her tiptoes and kissed his cheek.

Seth turned beet red. She could grow accustomed to the power that a woman held in this country, she thought.

"Well, then. Let's go win us some money," he said. "This should be like taking candy from a baby."

He turned for the door, took two steps, and pulled up, dead in his tracks. He stared at the door. A bolt of heat rode down Miriam's spine. Now what?

"Seth? What is it?"

He gazed ahead, frozen.

"Seth?"

He blinked once. Twice. Then he swallowed and cleared his throat.

"Nothing. It's nothing," he said.

"I've seen 'nothing' with you, and 'nothing' is always something. What's going on?"

He forced a grin and faced her. "Really, it's nothing. Nothing."

"I won't accept that!"

He suddenly stepped forward and kissed her on the forehead. She stiffened. But he was only kissing her on the forehead, and it was a gentle kiss.

He pulled back and blinked. "That's in case I don't see you after today."

"What do you mean?"

"You'll understand later."

He faced forward and just like that shed the fear that had overcome him. "Ready? Let's go," he said and walked for the door.

Clive Masters waited patiently in the Lear jet as it taxied for the Las Vegas Airport terminal. Now that he'd arrived he couldn't waste any time. Assuming his gamble worked at all.

He picked up his telephone and dialed the Las Vegas chief of police's private number. Benson answered on the second ring.

"Send the car."

Benson spoke off the phone and then returned. "It's on the way."

"Good. Now I need you to do me a favor—"

"Listen, Masters, NSA or not I need to know what you're trying to prove here. I'm not accustomed to working blind. You asked me to have a car ready for you without offering any explanation—"

"I'm trying to explain. Forgive me, but I honestly didn't know myself until just a few minutes ago. I need you to pull every string you have to launch crash surveillance on the casinos. In particular the larger ones with high-stakes tables. I can't tell you whom we're looking for, or what they look like. Just check for anything unusual."

"Do you know who you're looking for?"

Clive hesitated. "Yes. But I can't tell you. Trust me. And I don't want them apprehended, just reported. Can you do that?"

The phone was silent for a moment. "I suppose. Why no word until now?"

"You wouldn't believe me if I told you. Just go with me on this. I need eyes. I'll wager my pension you'll find something, and if I'm right, we have only two or three hours."

"Can't you tell me anything?"

"No."

"I'll see what I can do."

"Another thing. I know this goes against every rule you've ever been taught, but you can't use any regular law enforcement. No police, no nothing. This needs to come strictly from camera operators at the casinos."

"Now you're over my head, friend. That's not the way we find people in this town."

"It is today. Just do it. I'll explain when I get there."

He hung up and sat back. The terminal building rose to his left.

The whole idea was quite simple, really. Everyone was in the dark. Clive was little more than a blind fool chasing a man who could see clearly in this world of futures. He could not see into the future himself, so he would blind Seth by taking the futures away. At least those futures that involved a pursuit.

Convincing the teams to pull *back* from Las Vegas, rather than smother the city with every available law enforcement officer from Los Angeles to Salt Lake City had been a war he barely won.

If what Seth had told him in the alley was true, then Seth's gift was characterized by two critical elements. One, he was seeing *potential* futures. Two, he was only seeing futures a brief time out. He was whipping them on the street because he knew their next move before they did to the tune of two or three hours.

So then they wouldn't give Seth their next move.

The only way not to give Seth their next move was to remove their next move from the universe of his futures. And the only way to remove their next move from any futures in Seth's world was to remove those futures from their own worlds. Confusing, but true. Maybe.

In words that the politicians could understand, it went like this: If Clive didn't know what he was going to do next—if he deliberately removed any plans for chasing Seth from his agenda—then his own future would be removed from any of Seth's futures. Seth would suspect nothing until Clive had formed a specific plan to apprehend him. And in fact, Clive had no plan to apprehend Seth. At least to the best of his knowledge. Neither did Benson. Benson was just looking without knowing what for or why.

At least that was the theory. A few mind-boggling possibilities turned Seth into an invincible foe, but Clive refused to accept any of them.

Thinking about it now, the whole plan—or lack thereof—was a bit shaky. First, Clive had removed from Las Vegas anyone with any notion that there even *was* a hunt on for Seth. Second, he specifically did *not* decide to go to Las Vegas. He simply planned to make a decision at some point to fly into the city and set up immediate surveillance. If all went well, he would intercept Seth before any of their futures crossed.

The single greatest gamble was timing, of course. His "unplanned" decision to go had to correspond with Seth's presence at the casinos. This was pure guesswork, and he'd guessed that Seth was not only going to Las Vegas, but that he would take two days to arrive.

The chase was now one big, brilliant mind game, and Clive had most definitely met his match.

It took them fifteen minutes to reach the station. Clive had virtually crushed his walnut during the drive. Every second counted; every passing moment created a slew of new possible futures; at any time one of those futures could cross one of Seth's and he would know Clive was in town.

Another five minutes passed before he found himself in Benson's office, and by the time he closed the door he had convinced himself he had failed already. This whole plan would never work. They were way too slow.

"Well, well," Benson said, dropping the phone in the cradle, "you wouldn't believe your fortune. That was security at Caesars Palace. They have a man and a woman running hot on the roulette tables as we speak."

A chill washed down Clive's back. "Pictures?"

The fax began to hum. "On the way now."

Clive stepped over to the machine and wiped sweat from his eyebrows. *Settle down, boy. You're gonna have a heart attack on this man's floor.* He was as keyed up as he could remember being. He took a calming breath and ripped the first page from the fax machine.

A fuzzy black and white of a man and a woman sitting at a roulette table stared up at him, with a note scrawled along the bottom.

$32,000 in thirty minutes.

The man wore a mustache, and his hair was slicked back. The woman, short dark hair. Wrong.

"Not them," Clive said. "Keep looking."

Every second's another thousand futures, Clive. One of them is going to tip him off. He grunted, crumpled up the sheet, and tossed it in the waste bin.

"That's a lot of money," the chief said. He picked up the phone and dialed. "Not them, Sam. Keep your eye peeled."

"Ask him how often someone wins like that," Clive said.

Benson glanced at him. "How often does someone win like that?" he asked. He nodded. "He says never. First time he's seen it."

Clive blinked. He dipped into the wastebasket, pulled the crumpled fax out, and smoothed it flat.

It's a mind game, Clive. Forget the hard evidence; go for the mind.

"How long will it take us to get to the casino?"

"To the casino, twenty minutes. To the tables, another ten."

The fact was, Clive had no idea if this was Seth and Miriam. If they went in and it wasn't, they could be tipping off the world of futures to the hunt. If they sat and waited, they could give the world of futures time to work.

On the other hand, winning thirty-two thousand dollars in half an hour at the roulette wheel would be like sleeping for a man like Seth.

Clive spun and walked for the door. "We go. Three cars, six men. Now."

"Security can pick them up."

He stopped and turned. "No. There's a chance he doesn't know yet. If he's the one, the minute security makes a move, he'll be gone." He paused. "Tell them to seal the exits."

"And he won't be gone if you go?"

"I've got a shot; they don't."

"Oh? And why would that be?"

"Because I'm smarter, Benson."

28

BLACK TWENTY-FOUR," Seth said, pointing to the spot on the roulette table. He stared into her eyes and casually stroked the mustache he'd reapplied in the elevator. "What do you think, honey? Twenty-four feel like a lucky number to you?"

"I don't know. Is twenty-four in any of our birthdays or phone numbers?"

"No. But if you divide 327,115.2 by 13,629.8, you get exactly 24. I say we go 24."

Miriam bit back a smile. The poor dealer had long ago given up his cute comebacks to Seth's ramblings. He stared at them, dumbly.

"How much?" Miriam asked.

"All of it," Seth said.

"I told you, there's a thousand-dollar limit," the dealer said. He tucked the steel ball under the lip of the wheel and sent it hurling around.

"That's right, Junior. I forgot. I'm not especially good with numbers. Ten thousand is a pretty big number." Seth looked at her, eyes sparkling. He had purposefully lost many bets, as planned, but the pile of chips was growing steadily.

Seth raised an eyebrow. "A thousand?"

"That means that if the ball lands on the black twenty-four we will win how much?" she asked, knowing full well.

"Thirty-five, I think."

"Let's do it." She slid a thousand-dollar chip out on the space and winked at Seth.

A crowd of seven or eight onlookers gathered behind them, peering over their shoulders as the ball slowed to a crawl, dropped into the wheel, bounced around like a pogo stick, and then rattled into the small square that read . . . twenty-four.

Someone gasped behind them.

"We won!" Miriam exclaimed, throwing her hands up. She wrapped her arms around his neck and planted a kiss on his cheek.

"Yes, will you look at that. We did win. I'll be a toad on a stool at the bottom of a pool." He reached out and pulled back a tall stack of black chips, each etched in gold, *$1,000.* Seth tossed the dealer one of them. "That's for you, Junior. It's our lucky day."

Chips were as good as cash in Vegas. The thin dealer blinked, looked over at the pit boss, and palmed the tip. "Thanks."

Seth dipped his head and smiled coyly. "Which number, honey?"

Miriam had never felt so bold and thrilled in all her life. Pretending to be his starry-eyed lover, staring into his bright green eyes—it was all delightful! They were sitting under the cameras Seth said were planted in all the black domes above them, winning at their will and doing so without breaking a single rule. They could win millions and millions if they placed the right bets. A man like Seth could never be poor.

This game of roulette was all child's play, of course. Seth had another plan up his sleeve. Initially he'd calculated that they would need over a million dollars, but that had changed. He'd told her in the elevator that they now needed less. Something had changed, but he refused to tell her what. It would be a surprise.

"I don't know," she said with a sigh, feigning reluctance. "Perhaps we should stop while we're ahead."

"We're on a roll," he said. "I say we go again."

"Okay then. Again."

"I say eleven," he said.

"Is eleven part of our birthdays?"

"No. But if you divide 24, which was a pretty lucky number, by 2.18181818 ad infinitum, you get 11."

She paused. His way with numbers was not a part of his ability to see into the future, she knew. He simply had that kind of mind. "Then eleven it should be."

He reached for the chips, and his hand stopped just short of them. It trembled.

Miriam glanced up and saw the look of alarm on his face. She was growing accustomed to his responses, and this time she took it in stride. "No? Maybe eleven is not the best choice."

"No. I think our luck has just run out."

Seth scooped up the thousand-dollar chips—over fifty of them—and stood from the table. "The rest are yours, Junior." He turned to Miriam. "Let's go."

They walked from the table, leaving a stunned group of watchers in silence.

"What is it?" Miriam asked as nonchalantly as possible.

"Clive has arrived."

"Clive?" Her heart bolted. "Then we have to go! You didn't see him coming?"

"No. No, it seems Clive has pulled a fast one." A grin crept onto his face. "Pretty smart."

"Then where will we go? We have to get out! I can't be taken into—"

"We *can't* leave. Not yet. Besides, the exits have been blocked for over ten minutes now."

"But you see a way out."

"Yes and no."

"What is that supposed to mean, yes and no? You are making me very nervous. We should leave immediately!"

"We can't. Not yet. What we can do is finish what we started here. It's time to rock and roll."

❦

Omar had taken a room in the Tropicana because that's where Hilal had taken his room. Three doors down the hall, in fact. Like clockwork Hilal had made his calls to the general in Saudi Arabia, growing more frustrated by the hour. He still received updates from Clive, but they were filled with meaningless drivel. Hilal was sure that Clive was withholding information, and he was just as sure the agent's reticence had to do with this clairvoyance Seth evidently possessed.

Either way, everybody was coming to Las Vegas; Hilal had staked his reputation on it.

Omar knew Hilal's every move, of course. Which meant he knew Clive's moves and at least what they knew of Seth's moves. The wait in this box high above the strip had been maddening, but that all changed an hour ago, when Clive landed.

"I don't like this," Assir said.

Omar leaned back in his chair, one hand on the scanner that sat on the table. They'd been listening to police traffic for two days. The city was a sewer filled with lowlifes and prostitutes. One day, under better circumstances, he would have to return.

So far, Hilal had lived because Omar needed his information. But the chase was dragging out too long; he couldn't risk Hilal's interference any longer. His life would probably be easier if Clive just took the girl into custody. Without Hilal to whisk her back to Saudi Arabia, the State Department would have to make other arrangements. The delay would give Omar needed time. If he had to, he would kill Clive and take her then. Either way, Omar was where he wanted to be.

"Sit down, Assir," he said calmly.

Assir ignored him and walked into the kitchen.

The radio crackled with the endless police jargon. Americans were bent on crime—a few good laws could change that. Islam could change . . .

"Roger. We have Clive Masters with the . . ." Omar glanced at the radio. " . . . NSA now. ETA Caesars Palace, fifteen minutes. We got a man and a woman who may be on the run. I'll call back in twenty. Out."

Omar blinked. Assir ran in from the kitchen. "It's them!"

"Yes." Omar stood. "It's them." He grabbed his bag and walked briskly for the door. "Hilal first." Caesars Palace lay only one block to the north, but getting in and out of these monstrous hotels quickly was the challenge.

Assir ran past him and eased out of the room into the empty hall, silenced pistol cocked in his hand. They walked for Hilal's room, but the door flew open before they reached it.

Hilal had only just stepped into the hall when Assir's first slug took him in the head and knocked him back into the doorpost. He stared wide for a brief moment, then slid slowly to the ground, dead.

Without speaking, Sa'id and Assir pulled the dead body back into the hotel room, quickly wiped the blood from the doorframe, and closed the door.

"Caesars Palace," Omar said. "We have to hurry."

They practically ran through the tables, dodging the gamblers as if running an obstacle course. Miriam lost her sense of direction, but Seth seemed to know exactly where he was headed.

They burst into a room where about twenty gamblers, mostly gentlemen, sat or stood around several tables. Two men hovered in the corners, arms folded, overseeing the action. A waitress served drinks to a large man dressed in a tuxedo. These were not your typical gamblers.

Seth pulled up inside the doors and scanned the room. To a man the gamblers turned to face the intrusion. Silence settled in the room.

"I would like a wager," Seth said loudly.

No one responded. The man from the right corner, a bearded man who looked like he might have the power to break Seth's neck with a single swipe, dropped his arms and walked toward them.

"One bet," Seth said. "And then I will leave you to your small games."

The fat man chuckled.

"I'm sorry, sir," the guard said. "This room is reserved for invited guests only. You'll have to leave."

Seth ignored him. "I have fifty thousand dollars in chips." He held up his full hands for all to see. "I'm willing to put these down on any wager that anyone here will make me."

"You'll have to leave now, sir."

A thin man with white hair and large ears spoke from Miriam's right. "Hold on, John. Let's not be so hasty." He approached and held out a hand. "Name's Garland."

"Hello, Garland. This would be easier if I had fewer chips."

The man eyed him with a smile and then nodded to one of the dealers, who picked up five golden chips. "Fifty?"

"Count them."

"Oh, I will." This got a few chuckles. The dealer took Seth's fifty chips and gave him the five golden chips.

"What kind of bet do you have in mind?" the fat man said.

"An interesting bet. I now have five chips worth ten thousand dollars each, and I need to walk out of here with fifty of them. Any bet that will allow me to do that in under five minutes. I'm afraid that's all the time I have today."

Despite the urgency in Seth's voice, Miriam could not help a smile. The fat man humphed and turned away, dismissing them. Others followed his lead. They weren't taking him seriously.

"Well, now. I've never turned down a donation," the thin man with big ears said. "*Any* bet?"

"Any bet that requires me to beat the odds." Seth walked over to a table and set down his chips. "I'll wager these five chips against a pool of fifty from five brave souls, that I can guess any number any of you writes down in five consecutive turns. I can do it blindfolded, and I can tell you the name of every man who writes a number."

The skinny man turned slowly to the others and raised an eyebrow. "Is that so? Any number or all the numbers?"

"All. But we're running out of time."

"That's the stupidest thing I've ever heard," the fat man said. "We're here to gamble, not to watch a magic show."

"Please remain quiet, sir. You're not going to play anyway. I see that. But Garland here is and so are you, you, you, and you." He quickly pointed out five men. "You're going to play because a hundred thousand isn't that much money to you, and no one has ever placed such an absurd bet for so much money in all your life, and you can't just let it pass by without taking him up on it. So let's do this. Who's got the blindfold?"

Garland was enjoying this immensely by the smile on his face. He slowly pulled off his tie and handed it to Seth, who took it, wrapped it around his head, and turned around so that his back faced them.

"Each of you put your ten chips on the table and take a card. Write a number on the card. Then put your name on the card and give it to Mr. Garland here. Can I trust you, Garland?"

"I suppose we'll find out, won't we?"

"I'll take that as a yes. Are you writing?"

They each did what he said, although not quickly and not without exchanging looks of raised brows.

"I have the cards," Garland finally said.

"Good, Tommy." Garland's eyes jerked up. "Now mix them up." He did so.

"Now the rest of you children gather around Tommy for a look-see. The first card is a jack of spades, and Peter has written the number 890.34 on it. He was trying to be tricky with the decimals, but that's okay."

Three of the gamblers immediately glanced around the room, looking for mirrors. "My God," one of them said. "How did you do that?"

"God may or may not have anything to do with it," Seth said. "Ask me in a week. The second card is an ace of diamonds and Don has written a 5 on it."

Seth went down the list, reciting as though reading. He whipped around, pulled off the tie, and grinned at the stunned onlookers around the cards, ten now.

"Thank you, gentlemen. And by the way, the fat man is about to hit a winning streak, although now that I've told you, he will not win as much as he would have. Never turn down a sure thing. Good day."

He swept up the stacks of chips and marched from the room, Miriam smiling beside him.

"Now that is what I call sweeping the board."

"We have to hurry." Seth was frantic. "We only have a few minutes."

"But we will—"

"Samir's here, Miriam."

She stopped. "What?"

"Samir. Your great lover. Remember? He's here and he's looking for you. We have a five-minute window. If we miss it, we miss him."

"Where is he? How is he here?" She knew it! He had come! A tremble shook her bones.

"I don't know. But I knew while we were in your room that he'd be here."

The kiss!

"At the moment he's hurrying this way, searching the casino for you. I can only guess that he knows what Clive knows."

Miriam craned for sight of him. People crowded the floor, blocking her view. "I don't see him."

He sighed. "You will, dear. You will." It struck her that Seth was not thrilled about this development. *But, Seth, don't you realize, this is what I want! You are so dear to me, but Samir . . . Samir is my love!*

For a moment she wanted to say that, but she knew as soon as she thought the words that they would only hurt him.

And then another thought filled her mind. The thought that she was about to leave Seth. Panic swept over her. She couldn't leave Seth!

Of course you can. And you must. He is your savior, not your lover! She took a deep settling breath.

They rounded a tall bank of slot machines and there, not ten feet away, stood Samir, neck stretched, looking the opposite way. Familiarity flooded her bones at the sight of him. This was the man she loved. The man who had loved her and been with her nearly every day of her adult life.

"Samir."

He whirled around, saw her, and softened. They stared at each other, as if caught in a trance. Moisture flooded his eyes and he smiled.

"Miriam."

She walked up to him and he swept her up in strong arms. Like a tide, relief swallowed her. Seth would be okay. He would take one look at Samir and know she was happy with him. That would please him.

"I knew you would come, Samir! I knew it!" She stepped back, unable to stop the tingles that swept over her skin.

Samir saw Seth and for a moment his face darkened. "We have to hurry," he said. "The authorities have sealed off the building."

"Actually you have a couple of minutes to spare," Seth said, studying Samir. "Where are you going to take her?"

Samir glanced at Miriam and then back. "And who are you?"

"He is my savior," Miriam said. "Without him I would be dead."

"I see. Then you have my country's gratitude," Samir said.

"Where are you going to take her?" Seth repeated.

Samir searched Seth's face. "There is a hall that leads to the—"

"I mean after you escape."

"To . . . to Madrid. I'm not sure it's any of your business."

Seth frowned. She'd never seen him so serious. "The hall to the kitchen is a mistake," he said. "There's only one way out. Instead of taking the door to the kitchen, take the next one. It will lead you to a window with a fire escape. Take the ladder down to the back alley and head for your car. You'll be safe for at least the next three hours."

Samir blinked in confusion.

"Samir, we must listen to him."

Seth picked up a white bucket and dumped the chips into it. "Here's five hundred thousand dollars. I doubt you'll need it, but it's Miriam's. I would hide out for a while and then return to cash it in. Not all at once."

Miriam saw that he was finding this difficult. She walked over to him and looked into his eyes. Her back was to Samir. "Thank you." He had said good-bye with his kiss already, the way an American said good-bye. Had she known, she might have returned it. No, she *would* have. Yes, she would have. Now she couldn't.

Instead, she winked. "Thank you so very much."

Samir stepped forward and took her hand. "We must go."

"Good-bye, Seth."

"You should know something, Miriam." Seth swallowed. "God changed our futures yesterday. There's no other explanation for what happened. And it wasn't the first God. If you ever need help, you might want to try the second God."

She stared at him, stunned by his sudden revelation.

Samir pulled her, and then they were hurrying around the slot machines, running for the exit. They had just entered the hall that Seth had pointed them to when she heard the yell over the cacophony behind her.

"Police, freeze!"

She spun. Others stared at the spot where she'd left Seth, and she knew he'd been caught. He'd allowed them to apprehend him.

Samir pulled her arm. "Hurry!"

They ran.

Omar watched with five hundred other onlookers as the police handcuffed Seth. He'd found them a minute too late and seriously considered shooting the blond-headed American right out from under them. This, after all, was the man who'd taken his wife and surely violated her.

He wasn't foolish enough to risk the purpose of his mission for the sake of revenge, however. He'd come for Miriam, not Seth. And Miriam was gone. She wasn't with Hilal for obvious reasons, and she wasn't with Clive or Seth. Which meant she was either alone, hidden by Seth, or . . .

Omar worked his way closer to Clive and Seth, careful to avoid any eye contact.

"Where is she?" he heard Clive ask under his breath.

"She's gone." Seth seemed at ease, not in the least bit concerned.

"Is she still in the building?"

"No."

It occurred to Omar that Clive asked such matter-of-fact questions because he knew Seth would answer truthfully.

"Alone?"

Seth looked up into the detective's eyes. "She's gone, Clive. She's in good hands and she's no longer a concern to the State Department. It's me you want now. You have me. Let's go."

Clive hesitated and then nodded at the four policemen who had drawn guns. "Put them away. Let's go."

They led him out under the gaze of the crowd.

She's in good hands and she's no longer a concern to the State. It could only mean one thing. Omar could not help the smile that tugged at his mouth. Khalid had told him that he suspected the sheik had sent his own man. Samir. So now Miriam was with Samir. Headed back to Saudi Arabia with her lover.

My, my, what a surprise she was in for.

Omar turned and walked for the rear exit. It was time to go home.

29

FEW KNEW OF THE ROOM deep in the bowels of Cheyenne Mountain, down the hall from the command center and the JFT, one of the only computing rooms in NORAD's massive digital complex that hosted only one desk. On the desk were mounted four active-matrix monitors, two on top of two others. Opposite the desk, a ten-by-ten screen virtually exploded with the contents of the four moni-tors—strings of numbers and symbols that made Clive's head spin.

Clive peered into the space from an observation room above and behind the desk. Two technicians, Peter Smaley, and four-star general Harold Smites watched with him. But it was Seth Border, the man who sat behind the two keyboards now manipulating those numbers, who held most of Clive's attention.

Seth had insisted on working alone, without the distraction of propeller heads leaning over his shoulder. Their breathing bothered him. Three days had passed since Seth's apprehension. Testing him had been Clive's idea; testing him in the war room had been Smaley's.

But testing a man's mind required his participation, and Seth had already proven that he was not the cooperative type. Their compromise had been simple. The government would drop all of its charges against Seth in exchange for his cooperation. Clive had explained the consequences of aiding and abetting a known fugitive on the way to the Las Vegas Airport, and then had presented their deal. Seth had looked out the window, silent, and finally nodded.

Smaley had already arranged for the tests at NORAD and actually arrived in Colorado Springs before Clive and Seth—the deputy secretary had developed a fascination for the case. It had taken a day to modify the scenario programs with Seth's help, during which time he had remained quiet and introspective.

Clive had spent four hours debriefing him on the chase while the computer geeks set up the computers with Seth's specifications. Apart from engaging him on a string of fascinating though rather trivial facts, Clive had come away with three significant conclusions.

One, Seth might have actually *saved* Saudi Arabia from a coup by breaking the law and aiding Miriam.

Two, with or without his clairvoyance, Seth's pure cognitive powers surpassed Clive's greatest expectations of the man. Destroying a mind like Seth's would indeed have been like killing an Einstein or a Sir Isaac Newton before their great discoveries.

And three, Seth's clairvoyance was changing dramatically. What had started out as a gradually increasing ability to see possible futures was now fluctuating between massive breadths of sight and a loss of that sight altogether, like a pendulum swinging back and forth. Seth could see beyond himself and clearly beyond Miriam, but only part of the time.

"This is incredible," General Smites said, breaking the silence. He crossed his arms and rocked back. "If I wasn't watching it with my own eyes, I wouldn't buy it for a second. How many of these battle simulations has he completed?"

"Sixteen in the last two days," one of the techs, Garton, said.

"And he's won every one?"

Garton nodded. "The first battles were simple ones—simulations of single sea battles in which he commanded a single destroyer against a slightly superior force. We moved him up to tank battles with odds stacked in the enemy's favor and then on to full-scale invasions."

"So he just sees what's going to happen and counters it?"

"Not exactly," Garton said, tapping his pencil on the window. Seth spun around, eyes darting. Garton held up his hands in apology, and Seth dove back into the simulation in front of him.

He wasn't unlike an overgrown kid playing the world's most complex simulation games, battling the likes of IBM's ASCI White, a computer that ran at a speed of 7,226 gigaflops. One gigaflop was equal to a billion mathematical operations per second. Even for a man with Seth's capabilities, the task was daunting and he hated distractions.

"Strung pretty tight," Smaley said.

"Wouldn't you be?" Clive said. "He's holding countless bits of information in his mind, tracking each from one moment to the next and adjusting for countless variations. I get a headache just thinking about it."

Garton smiled. "And that's only half of it." He looked down the windowpane to the general. "He's not seeing *the* future, but *possible* futures. There's a big difference. If he were just seeing what's *going* to happen, that would be easy enough. But evidently the future doesn't work that way. He's living proof. What's going to happen one minute from now hasn't been decided yet. If a tank is standing on the battlefield facing ten enemy tanks, there may be a thousand possible outcomes, depending on decisions the commander makes. Seth has to see them all and choose those in which his tank kills the other ten tanks and escapes unscathed. It may be a half-hour battle with a long string of decisions chosen from a million possible decisions."

He chuckled and faced Seth again. "Now try that with a thousand tanks, each facing ten tanks, and try commanding all thousand tanks at once. If you can imagine that, you have an idea what he was doing yesterday."

A few moments drifted by. Clive couldn't imagine it, not really; none of them could. It was beyond the ordinary mind.

"And what's he doing today?" the general asked.

Garton took a deep breath. "Today he's directing a zero-casualty campaign."

General Smites's eyes skipped to the techs and then back.

"It was actually his idea," Garton said. "Took us most of the night to set it up."

"A battle in which he incurs zero casualties?"

"Sort of. That was his idea, but we took it further. It's not a battle; it's a war, and he's trying to win it without any casualties on his side."

The general blinked and stared at Seth, who worked madly below them, hunkered over the desk, hands flying nonstop over the keyboards.

"This boy's invaluable."

"Actually, it's more than just a war," Garton said. "It's a nuclear offensive. Question: How do you win a worldwide nuclear offensive without sustaining a single casualty?"

"That's possible?" It was Smaley this time.

The tech they called J. P. answered. "Winning is possible, yes. This morning, at 0843 our time, Seth could see two different futures in which the United States could launch a full-scale attack, including the use of nukes on China, parts of the former Soviet bloc, several Arab states, and a dozen smaller targets, and walk away pretty much having a lock on world power."

"You're telling us Seth knows how to take over the world?"

"Not necessarily. I'm telling you that he saw two very specific and unique futures in which that would have happened if the United States had done very specific things beginning at 0843 this morning. Our time. It's now 1315. Those futures don't necessarily exist anymore. The premier of China might have eaten a bad steak for lunch, gotten indigestion, and as a result might now react differently to the news of incoming nukes than he would have if they were launched before he ate the steak. Seth's seeing a ton of stuff, but he can still only see three hours out."

"But you could go down there now and ask him for a scenario in which we could take over the world, so to speak, and you're saying he could give you one?" the general asked.

J. P. frowned and nodded. "*If* there was a way now. And *if* he wanted to give it to us."

"That's not the point! The point is he actually *has* that capability?"

"That's what we're saying, yes. The notion of taking over the world sounds a bit James-Bondy, but I'm sure he could just as easily tell us how to shift power in the Middle East, say, or neutralize China, at least in the next three hours."

The general was beginning to understand what they had here, Clive thought.

"As I was saying," Garton said, "the simulation he's on now is infinitely more difficult. The two scenarios Seth saw this morning returned hundreds of thousands of American casualties. He's trying to figure out how to conduct a similar campaign that returns zero casualties, using mostly conventional weapons. That means he's directing hundreds of battle groups, feeding each one orders that return both successful missions and zero casualties. It's tantamount to giving every field commander specific directions and then telling every soldier on the battlefield when to duck and when to fire."

The room fell silent again. Clive knew men like the general well enough to realize that Smites was already thinking about both sides of this equation.

"So basically we're looking at the most powerful man in the world," Smaley said.

"And the most dangerous," Smites said.

Yes, indeed, *and* the most dangerous.

The general shook his head, still staring through the glass at Seth. "This is unbelievable. You're absolutely sure all this is possible?"

"Two days ago I would have said no," Garton said. "But hard data doesn't lie."

"Has anybody ever shown this kind of clairvoyance before?"

"Well . . . there's always the prophets, if you buy them. Isaiah. Nostradamus. Saint John."

"The prophets foretold what *would* happen, not what *might* happen," Clive said.

"Some of their predictions, yes. But most were of events that *might* happen if Israel didn't do such and such. Unless they were talking about something that wasn't a real possibility, they were talking of possible futures. Isn't that essentially the same as we have here, on a different scale?"

It was, Clive saw.

"But to answer your question directly, General, no. I'm quite sure this kind of ability to see into many futures all at once and to see them only for a short time out has at least never been recorded. This is a first."

"Phenomenal."

Clive decided it was time to throw the wet blanket on their fire.

"There *is* a slight problem. At least some might consider it a problem. His clairvoyance is . . . changing. It's become cyclic."

"It comes and goes," J. P. said, as if the others needed the clarification.

"It started four days ago, while he was still with Miriam," Clive said. "His ability to see began to expand beyond their immediate concerns, but it also became intermittent. Every few hours he slips into a regression that returns him to normalcy."

"Meaning what?"

"Meaning he's becoming blind to the future. When he sees, he sees a whole lot, but his sight is limited to a few hours. It's almost like his batteries wear out and he needs a few hours of rest to recharge them. At first the periods of blindness were short—he says he made some mistakes out in the desert. But with each passing day it seems to be getting worse."

"How long do we have?" Smaley asked.

Clive forced a grin. "It's not like we can go to the local library and check a book out on how to sustain clairvoyance, Peter. It could last his entire life, or it could be gone tomorrow. We don't have a clue how this works. Ask him and he'll tell you it's on the way out."

"Based on what?"

"Based on the fact that Miriam is now safe. He believes his gift was tied to her."

"Either way, we should proceed as though he will lose the ability at anytime," J. P. said.

"You're recording what he's doing?" Smites asked.

"Yes."

"Then we could create models from his work, right? They would at least give us scenarios to study. Like creating histories that we can learn from."

"Yes."

"Or we could actually use Seth now," Smaley said. "Feed him a scenario that we actually use without telling him. Feed his directives to the battlefield as he enters them and execute them in real time."

"He would see what we're doing," Clive said. "Now that you've mentioned it, he probably already sees it as a possible future, lingering somewhere in his mind."

The general shook his head and grunted. "I have to make some calls, gentlemen. Keep me informed." He walked out, leaving them to watch.

Clive's thoughts returned to a lingering problem. One he wasn't of a mind to share with them. The problem was Seth. Seth was no ordinary man, with or without this sight of his. He had a mind of his own, and Clive was sure it was occupied with more than how the United States might take over the world.

30

TO SETH THE BARRAGE OF FUTURES felt like a sustained explosion of images and ideas that far outstripped his capacity to single out any specific one. Still his mind handled it without conscious effort. At least most of his mind.

The other part was consumed with Miriam.

The part playing these games they had given him was in an autopilot of sorts, albeit an excruciatingly intense autopilot. He supposed the process was not unlike the way the mind controlled so many involuntary body functions. His fingers seemed to follow their own will, striking the keyboard with commands that would implement his choices from the myriad of futures available.

The part consumed with Miriam slogged through an abyss of pain. Her face had parked itself in his mind's eye and refused to budge, no matter what tricks he threw its way. He had known long before they reached Las Vegas that he was falling for her, but he'd assumed that once she was safely out of his life, his good sense would make quick work of her. He was an intelligent man, after all, not given to emotional responses. It seemed his mind had betrayed him.

Love. Yes, he was in love with her. Not just love, as in dear-me-I-think-I'm-in-love love, but *Love,* as in pass-the-poison-I-must-die-without-you love. This new beast his mind had to wrestle with presented a more difficult challenge than any he'd ever encountered.

He had thrown himself at the games for the challenge of them. But perhaps more for the distraction they provided. From her face. From her long black hair, swirling gently in the desert heat. From her lips kissing him in return, and her eyes winking at him across the roulette table, and her throaty laugh as he spun through an absurd dance in her hotel room. From Miriam, the bronzed goddess who had swept into his life on the winds of—

Seth slammed both fists on the keyboards. *Stop it!* He looked at the lower right monitor. A box in the upper right-hand corner. Casualties sustained = *0.*

And there was as well this gnawing awareness of his gift's source that wouldn't let him go. This madness about God.

Seth lifted both hands and rubbed his temples. The seeing had sustained itself for four hours already. Soon it would release him for a reprieve before returning again in all of its fury.

The door opened behind him. "You okay?"

He closed his eyes, and then opened them. The casualty box had changed. *3. You see, you lose your concentration for a few seconds and see what happens? You're killing people.*

"I'm fine," he lied.

Clive stopped behind him. The casualty numbers started climbing rapidly. *100. 300. 700.*

"Take a break," Clive said.

Why not? He'd blown the simulation anyway. Seth nodded.

Clive led him to a break room near the back of the complex.

"Coffee?"

"Advil," Seth said.

Clive tossed him the bottle from the counter and poured himself a cup of coffee.

"I don't know how long I can go like this," Seth said, dropping into a chair. "I'm not sure which hurts more, my mind or my fingers."

Clive ignored the complaint. "Any changes?"

"Yeah. About three seconds ago. I found my sanity again."

Clive looked at him curiously. "So right now you can't see—"

"Right now I'm as blind as a bat. Futuristically speaking, that is. And if I could take a drug that would keep me here, in the land of the blind bats, I would take it intravenously."

Clive sat back and sipped at his coffee. "I'm not sure I blame you."

He paused. "The Saudis are having a fit about Hilal's death. The State Department passed on your theory that Miriam was supposed to marry Omar as a part of a deal with Sheik Al-Asamm."

Seth glanced at the NSA operative. "They're just hearing that *now?* That's not a theory—it's Miriam's testimony. Do they know where she is?"

"Evidently not. And in their eyes the testimony of a woman doesn't hold water against the word of a prince." Clive shrugged. "Besides, it's a moot point now. Miriam's been saved by Samir. Remember? Even if there was a planned marriage, it's obviously off now." Clive grinned deliberately.

"So why are the Saudis having a fit?"

"They're accusing us. Fahd's hold on power is tentative enough without rumors of a coup floating around." He coughed. "In honesty, I think they're still undecided. But they can't just arrest a prince and kill a sheik because a woman told you to tell us to tell them that it was Khalid and his nasty son Omar. Doesn't work that way with the House of Saud."

"I'm not sure it is a moot point," Seth said, looking down at his fingers. They were red. He touched the tips. Maybe bruised.

"And why not?" Clive said. "Miriam's gone, right? You turned her over to Samir. No one knows where they are, but wherever it is, it isn't Saudi Arabia. He'd be a fool to take her there. They're probably holed up in Spain under false names about now."

"Seems sensible. But there's only one problem." Seth wasn't sure how to say this. Wasn't even sure he believed it.

"And that would be?"

"That would be . . ." He frowned. "I can't get her out of my mind."

Clive sat back and sighed. "The curse that follows beautiful women—"

"It's more than that!" Seth caught himself and looked away. "I can't get her out of my mind. What does that tell you?"

"That you're in love with her?"

"Or maybe it means that whoever put her in my mind hasn't taken her out. Maybe for a reason."

Clive arched both brows. He held a walnut in his right hand, polishing it with his thumb. "Really? And who might that be?"

Seth stood at that most awkward juncture sometimes referred to as the moment of truth. He had been here many times, of course. It came with having a mind like his. The road forked before him. One road, the beaten path, required that he explain himself only in terms familiar to Clive, excusing him from taking the man out to a cliff where they could glimpse a breathtaking vista of new ideas. The other road, the one that led to said cliff, required that he actually try to make Clive understand.

For the most part, he'd always found the latter to be a painful experience. Perhaps similar to a woman's pain during childbirth. Considering the subject, he found nothing to suggest this time might somehow be different.

On the other hand, Clive was a clever fellow. And the idea was begging to be birthed.

"You're pretty sharp, Clive. Do you believe in God?"

Clive smiled. "I don't know, should I?"

"Actually, approaching the matter from a purely logical perspective, yes. All the evidence points to the existence of a creator. The single *greatest* body of evidence is the dismal failure of man's desperate attempts to come up with a reasonable alternative, beginning with evolution. I've always looked at the universe and seen a creator as plainly as most people who look at the ocean see water. That's not really my question, though. The real question is whether there's a purposeful God who interacts with us."

"I would have to say no. And forgive me for pointing it out, but it would seem that you, with your ability to see many futures, have already cast doubt on the existence of an all-knowing God. At least the kind of God preached from pulpits. How is it possible to change what God already knows will happen?"

"That was my first thought when I began to see multiple futures. I thought I'd lost my belief in God. But it seems I was wrong. Out in the desert, I talked to God on a whim without even believing he existed. I asked him to change the future. If he existed and actually changed my future, I knew I'd be able to see it." Seth could see the wheels turning in Clive's eyes.

"Makes sense. And did he?"

"Yes."

A gentle smile crossed Clive's face. "How do you know it was God?"

"Because I also saw that nothing man did changed that future. Normally when the future changes, it's because someone makes a choice to do something different, which creates a new thread of possibilities. But when I prayed, one of those threads changed midstream without the help of man. One second I saw the car driving for the state line with no chance of escape, and the next I saw the engine blowing just before we reached it. This allowed us to escape."

"Engines blow up sometimes. How can you attribute that to God?"

"Because I had already seen the futures. It takes some doing to search hundreds of thousands of possible futures, but we had some time and I was sure I'd searched all possible futures. The engine didn't blow up in any of them, and we weren't able to cross into Nevada in any of them. But then I prayed and the future changed. Sorry, my friend. *Deus ex machina.*"

"God from the machine," Clive said. "Like in those old plays where the god just reaches down and fixes things." He looked at the Coke machine, lost in thought.

"But you're right," Seth said. "How could this sort of God not know *the* future, the actual future that is to happen? That knowledge would fly in the face of many possible futures. When the prophet Jeremiah told the people of Israel that they would go into exile if they didn't change their ways, did God already know their choice? And if he did, could they have done anything different? Could they have tricked God by doing something different than what he already knew they would do?"

"A conundrum," Clive said.

"I think I have an idea. Actually it's not entirely mine. An English professor, C. S. Lewis, suggested something similar once in his book *The*

Great Divorce. I rejected it at the time as misguided—too convenient for solid logic—but since you guys have me caged up here I've had more time to think about it. Expand on it in light of my experience."

Clive just looked at him, rolling that walnut in his right hand.

"Time," Seth said. He sat up.

"Time," Clive said.

"Time. Time and the natures of God. God had to have created time. By definition that would put him outside time. So the future, which is an element of time, doesn't work for him like it does for us. That nature of him that is with us in time doesn't necessarily know *the* future. But that nature of him that is in the future, so to speak, knows it as a matter of history. He's already been there."

Clive's eyes flickered. "So you're saying that God doesn't know the future?"

"No, he does. He must. By definition, by my own experience. Omniscient."

"But you're saying that there's a *nature* of God that doesn't know the future. And that nature of him that doesn't know the future can change. He can change his mind in the present—"

"Without it being some silly foregone conclusion," Seth finished. He took a deep breath. "It's just a theory, of course. Trying to figure out God is a bit difficult for us mortals. I'm no theologian, but from what I've read, C. S. Lewis was well respected."

Clive chuckled. "I don't know. Sounds a bit like the Trinitarian argument. Three but one."

"Or like the claims of Christ. Fully God, yet fully man," Seth said. "An impossibility in this dimension. But what if they're right?"

"The theologians?"

"Yes. I know it sounds silly. How could a pack of right-wing fanatics have uncovered the most elusive reality known to man? It's tantamount to a preschooler discovering the theory of relativity. But maybe a preschooler is really like a nuclear physicist in spiritual dimensions."

Clive shifted in his chair, uncomfortable.

Seth eyed him. "Did Jesus Christ know the future as a child? Could he walk up to a marble game at age seven and know precisely how to win? And yet he was fully God."

"According to some theologians."

"And I'm saying that I think they may be onto something. It's the only explanation that makes sense to me."

"I don't know, Seth . . ."

"I know a few things. I know that everything we do changes the future. I know that God changed my future in the desert. As far as I can see, the only reality that can accommodate both of those is at least similar to the one I'm suggesting. Do you realize the implications of this, Clive?"

"Tell me."

"Prayer may just be the most powerful tool mankind has."

Seth sat back. His own words sounded absurd to him. Imagine the Berkeley faculty's reaction to that. *Our brightest student has just lost his mind.*

"Either way, there's a whole other dimension out there, and I feel like I'm drowning in it. I'm convinced I was given this ability as a gift. From God. I know that sounds as stupid as everything else I've said, but it's the only thing that makes sense. And if that's true, then we might have a problem."

Clive set the walnut on the table. "Yes. The problem is you're losing that gift."

"No. My gift is changing, but I still have it. Which means that I still need it."

Clive sat still, eyeing him. "Don't let your infatuation with a girl—"

"That's not it. I'm beginning to think Miriam may still be in trouble. And that, my friend, is not merely about my love for a woman. It's about the stability of Saudi Arabia and the Middle East. It's about the future of America, far beyond what I can see with this gift of mine."

31

MIRIAM SAT IN A BEACH CHAIR beside the villa's pool, overlooking the beautiful Madrid skyline, drawing delicately on a tall banana daiquiri, feeling as vacant as a dry lake bed.

Samir had brought her here, to this wonderful city in which they had first spent time alone. To her surprise, no one interfered with their trip. Although he had false identification for her, she expected his own name to raise questions at the borders. But they had cleared customs without the slightest delay.

The reunion had been wonderful in so many ways—she was once again with the guardian of her youth. The man who represented freedom and love. That alone was enough.

Samir had understandably treated her with a measure of aloofness during the trip—he was, after all, a Saudi citizen traveling in the open with a woman. But she'd been confident that as soon as they arrived at their final destination, which she assumed to be Madrid, the flowers of love would once again bloom.

They had been in this grand villa for two days now, and Samir was gone, "tending to their future," he'd said. Miriam wondered what that meant.

Seth would know.

A soft grin drifted across her face. Her mind had flitted to Seth a hundred times since leaving him in the casino. She'd become a different person in his company. He was like a fragrant aroma that had swept into her life and resuscitated dying tissue. Delightful and intoxicating.

The smile faded. When she allowed herself to listen to the quiet voices of her heart, they told her that she'd been sick to leave him.

Yes, sick—the kind of sickness that comes from having a hole in your heart.

But that was nonsense, because Samir would fill that hole. Who was Seth but a conflicted American who'd stumbled into her life?

His last words haunted her. *If you ever need help, you might want to try the second God.* This from an agnostic. To say that her week with Seth had completely shaken her firm faith in Islam would not be an understatement.

"Would you like another drink, madam?"

She looked up at the servant who'd approached from her right. "No, but thank you." Even her voice sounded vacant, she thought.

The servant dipped his head and walked away. Miriam glanced back at the courtyard for Samir. A friend owned the villa. They were here for her protection. That's all Samir would tell her. Not that it mattered; she was here in his care and she trusted him. He'd been mostly gone since their arrival, returning only for dinner, because he was arranging a secret future to which they could flee together. Perhaps an island, or a city in southeast Asia.

There was no sign of Samir now, and she settled back into her chair.

Seth wouldn't have left her alone by the pool, would he? He would have taken her with him to choose their future together. *Please, Miriam, you cannot compare Seth and Samir. You're comparing a rose to a Mercedes. They're not comparable.*

For most of the trip she'd successfully buried the images that kept trying to resurrect themselves. But here by the pool with hours to waste, she found herself powerless to resist them. Memories of Seth hauling her into the toilet, and dropping from the vent over her bed, and praying with arms raised before his hasty altar, and leaning over the roulette wheel, pretending to be a fool. If anyone else had done these things, she *would* think him a fool. But Seth had been her rose in the desert. Her savior.

Perhaps one day, if Samir would agree, they would go to the United States and find him. They both were in his debt. Miriam for her very life and Samir for his bride-to-be.

Miriam rolled to one side, heart aching. *Think of the future, Miriam. Think of the freedom that lays before you.*

But sadness swept over her instead, and she could not stop the tears that swelled in her eyes. How could these memories bring her so much pain? Why couldn't she just wipe him from her mind and indulge in her new freedom?

Seth, Seth. My dear Seth, what have I done?

"Miriam."

She jerked up. Samir approached, dressed in a blue suit and dark glasses. She quickly dabbed her eyes.

"We have to leave. Your clothes are waiting in your bedroom. Our flight leaves in one hour. Please hurry."

Miriam stood to her feet, alarmed. "Our flight? To where?"

He hesitated. "To your father."

"I'm going to see my father? How? I thought—"

"You can't be married without your father's blessing," he said, smiling.

Married? Yes, of course, but how could her father suddenly change his mind and bless this marriage? That couldn't be right! "My father's future depends upon my marriage to Omar! Now he's agreed to our marriage?"

"You think your father is so heartless?"

"But, I thought . . ." She didn't know what to think.

"Hurry, Miriam. The plane is waiting." Samir walked away.

His blessing! And why not? She watched Samir—the suit looked good on him. He was not himself, she thought. *He's about to be married; what do you expect?*

Miriam flew to her bathroom, thoughts of Seth vanquished by this sudden turn of events. She showered quickly, strung with nervous energy. It was Egypt to be sure. The sheik had gone ahead to Cairo and made the preparations. She was to be married to Samir in Egypt!

She ran to the bedroom. Married! Her suitcase lay open, already packed. And Samir had laid a black gown over the pillows for her to wear. He was thinking of his bride already. She took two steps toward the bed and froze.

It was an abaaya!

And a veil.

Ice seeped through her veins. An abaaya! The sight of the black prison made her head spin. What was Samir thinking? Surely he knew that she would never—*could* never—wear such a thing. Never again!

Trembling, she pulled on a dress from the suitcase and ran from the room. She found him standing at the large picture frame window, hands in pockets, staring out at the pool.

"Samir! There is—"

"You must wear it, Miriam." He turned and she saw that his jaw was firm. It softened. "Please, we are going to meet your father. Surely you know that he must approve. Are you thinking to throw out all of Islam and chase after the American way? This is what that man has done to you?"

For the first time since his rescue, she heard anger in his voice, and it terrified her. He was talking about Seth. Did he suspect anything? He was wounded.

"No." She took a step toward him. "No, Samir. But I can't wear the abaaya. Please, you have no idea what this means to me. This is not Saudi Arabia."

"But your father is a Saudi. And I am a Muslim. Put it on."

"I can't!" Tears welled in her eyes. "Don't you see it? It's a prison! It makes me nothing!"

"It's who you are!" he said. "It's who your father is! And it's your only way to receive your father's blessing, which I, for one, insist on. It's just a piece of cloth. Put it on."

She blinked at him. Perhaps he was right. One last time out of respect for her father. And it was just a piece of cloth. They faced each other for several long seconds. *He is only trying to do what is best. Because he loves me. This is no easier for him than for me.*

Miriam turned, his chastisement burning in her ears. *Be a good, obedient woman, Miriam. You cannot just throw out all of the past and pretend you are someone you are not.*

She entered the room and stared at the black cloth. How could she possibly put it on? But what choice did she have? Refusing would only drive a wedge between her and Samir. He was her only hope now.

Miriam closed her eyes and picked up the abaaya. Working blind with her breath held, she pulled the robe on.

It is nothing. It is only a piece of cloth.

She slipped the veil over her head without looking. Ten days had passed since she last wore the veil, and to her it felt like a lifetime. The span between life and death.

She opened her eyes. The world was gray.

She would not look down; she would not look in a mirror; she would pretend she wore gray sunglasses. After all she'd been through, was this so impossible?

Driving to the airport Samir sat in the limousine's front seat and ignored her entirely. She had truly become a nonperson again. One black sack among a million—walking coffins, bought and paid for, destined to wash and clean and make babies.

She walked through the airport behind him, her mind buzzing with inhuman thoughts. Rage and despondency rolled into one bitter pill that spread poison through her chest. She saw nothing—refused to see. She stood in the corner, arms crossed, and let Samir make the flight arrangements. He collected her after some time and she followed him again, toward a private jet ramp.

Just a few hours, Miriam. When you see Father, you will tear this sack off. Many Arabs did not require their women to wear the cloth. Most in fact. Islam was hardly about what you wore.

But she was a Saudi princess, of the Wahhabi sect. She—

Miriam stopped. They were entering the Jetway. She'd been so distracted and humbled by the dress that she hadn't paid any attention to her surroundings. Now she saw the pilot, and she was sure she recognized him. She glanced out the window to her left. Too dark. She lifted the veil and saw the jet. It had Saudi markings!

A man angrily motioned to her to lower her veil. She dropped it and ran to catch Samir.

"Where are we going?"

"I told you—to your father."

"But where! *Where* is he?"

Samir took her elbow firmly and pulled her forward. "Please, Miriam. You can't make a scene. There are those who will do anything to stop us!"

She hurried down the causeway with him. "Then tell me where," she whispered harshly. They entered the jet, which she immediately saw was empty except for a dozen men seated near the rear. They stared at her as one.

"We are going to your father in Riyadh," Samir said. "Sit here." He pointed to a seat in first class.

Miriam's legs went numb. She wasn't sure she was breathing. She sat without realizing that she was doing so. Riyadh! Why? Wasn't that where Khalid and his son Omar were? Wasn't Riyadh the city she'd fled?

Samir sat in the rear of the plane with the other men, and Miriam felt certain something had gone terribly wrong. She could understand the possible necessity of everything else that had happened, but not this. Not Samir choosing to sit with men in the back when he had the choice to sit with his bride in first class.

Unless he was simply following the Saudi way. That would be it, of course. Saudi men were not expected to even know their brides, much less sit with them. He was only protecting their marriage by being discreet.

But why Riyadh?

Miriam hated every minute of the short flight. She spent the time carefully constructing scenarios in which all this made perfect sense. Samir was doing only what must be done for their future. She could not expect to walk into paradise without paying a price. The sheik wanted a Saudi wedding in Saudi Arabia.

But why not in Jiddah or Dhahran, his hometown?

They landed, and for a few brief minutes Miriam was thankful to be hidden from prying eyes beneath the veil. Then they were in a limousine once again, speeding for the countryside. Still Samir refused to talk to her. Of course. The driver.

The limousine came to a stop before a tent—the same one she'd met the sheik in less than two weeks ago—but this time a dozen smaller tents stood nearby, and at least a dozen vehicles. In her eagerness, she stepped past Samir and ran into the tent. She pulled off her veil.

"Miriam!"

She spun to the sheik's voice. He hurried to her, arms wide, smiling. "It is so good to see you, my dear daughter. You have had me so worried!"

She walked in, confused and suddenly hopeful. He kissed her and invited her to the same table she had eaten at before. Two men stood to her left—guards.

She walked forward. "Father, you must know how much danger coming here—"

"Life is full of danger, Miriam."

"But if I am to marry Samir, why couldn't we have the wedding in Cairo or at the very least in Dhahran?"

"Please. Sit, Miriam." His smile softened and he glanced over her shoulder.

She followed the glance. Samir stood just inside the tent, looking at her with glassy eyes. He was crying? She faced her father, terrified.

"I *am* marrying Samir, right?" Her voice was tiny.

"You will marry Omar," the sheik said. "I have given my word for the kingdom and for God. Sit!"

Blood flooded her head and the tent spun crazily. "Omar?" She turned around and stared into Samir's eyes. "Omar?"

"We cannot put our desires ahead of God's, Miriam," Samir said, eyes begging. "What we do now must be for the love of God. The kingdom is at stake. You have been chosen by God to deliver us. I am only glad to have loved a woman so chosen."

"This is absurd!" she cried. They really meant to do this, didn't they? "What kind of God would force me into marriage with a beast?"

"Watch your tongue, woman!" the sheik said.

Miriam lost her mind to panic. She glared at Samir. "Your love will *kill* me! You know that, don't you? Omar will kill me or keep me in a living death! And you will allow this?"

"He will not kill you!" Samir said. "Your death would sever ties with your father. Please, Miriam—"

"No!" Rage swept through her. She hated them. She hated them all! Suddenly she was flying at Samir, screaming. She landed on him, fists flying, beating at his face as he warded off her blows.

"Miriam! Please, I beg you!" He was desperate and she didn't care. No human could do this to her and claim to love her.

"I hate you!" she screamed and landed a blow on his cheek.

Hands grabbed her from behind and pulled her back. Something hit her back.

"Don't bruise her," her father said. "She is to be married tomorrow night. The groom will not want her bruised."

In that single moment, with those words, all of the life Miriam had found with Seth drained from her body. She relaxed. The horror she always feared had found her. Sita was not the only one to die.

Now it was her turn to know death.

32

THE DEEP SLEEP had brought this new and improved clairvoyance on, Seth thought, and he thought it even as he slept.

He had gone to bed without the burden of clairvoyance and sunk into the first REM sleep he'd had since that last night in Las Vegas. Close as he could figure—in the way one figures things while dead to the world—the new and improved sight had hit him while he was still in REM sleep, spared from the barrage of concerns that pummeled him during the day. As a result, he could see with a degree of clarity that he never guessed was possible.

He was in the future; he knew that. But it wasn't like the future he'd seen before, focused on the events that might transpire in his life or in the computer models in the next few minutes. He was in a future that did not extend beyond one second, a future that didn't really have time to result in any event at all. He was in the next millionth of a second of a thousand possibilities.

He was in the very fabric of the future.

That's the only way he could think of it. If he had seen a computer chip before, he now saw the very circuitry of that chip, not as an event but in its state of being.

And what he saw made him groan.

Not because he didn't like what he saw, but because he had not seen it earlier, without this unique perspective.

Light roiled around him, like a measureless sea of fireflies. Each pinpoint of light was a possibility, and each was fueled by the same force that had brought them to life. Without this power of life, there could be no future, he realized. But it was the source of that power that turned his stomach. He groaned again, furious with himself.

He reached out his hand and brushed through the pinpoints of light. In the blink of an eye a thousand blipped to blackness and another thousand sprang to life. It was how the future changed, in the blink of an eye, fueled by the creative force of the universe itself, yet so easily changed by the move of his hand.

One of the tiny lights caught his eye, and he focused on it. It expanded in his mind's eye, and suddenly he was looking at a future the way he had become accustomed to seeing it.

He was about to turn away when the details of this particular future stormed his mind. Miriam.

Seth jerked up in bed, fully alert and breathing hard. The sheets were soaked in his sweat.

It was Miriam! The first time he'd seen her in the futures since Las Vegas. His pulse thumped through his veins. It wasn't just Miriam; it was Miriam and Omar. He knew that because he'd found a picture of the Saudi prince on the Internet two days earlier. But the man he saw in the future no longer smiled royally as he had in the picture.

"Oh, God!" he said. The words came out breathy and scratchy.

He threw his covers off and tore for the door. "Oh, God, please!"

Seth had cleared the door to his room before he remembered that he wore only his underwear. He slid to a stop, confused for a moment, and then raced back for his pants. That was enough for now. He ran down the hall toward the quarters that housed the other guests.

He crashed into Clive's room without knocking.

"Clive!"

He hit the light switch and an overhead fluorescent blinked to life. The agent bolted up in bed and instinctively clawed under his pillow for a nonexistent gun they'd taken at the front gates.

Clive gawked at him. "What are you doing?"

"I just saw the future, Clive." Seth paced past the bed and then back, grasping for words. He spun to the man. "I mean, I saw it like I've never seen it before."

"You come crashing into my room"—he glanced at the bedside clock—"at three in the morning, to tell me—"

"I saw Miriam."

"Miriam? You dreamed of a beautiful woman and you—"

"Stop it! Miriam's in trouble. She's marrying Omar. There's going to be a coup."

Clive swung his legs to the floor. "How can you know that? You saw further out than three hours?"

"No. But I know the intentions. Her life's in danger."

"How's that possible? I thought she was with Samir."

"He must have betrayed her." Seth closed his eyes. Why hadn't he seen anything in Samir at the casino? Because Samir really did love her. He was sure of it. And yet . . .

He rubbed his temples. When he opened his eyes, Clive was pulling on his slacks. "When do you think this will happen?"

"I don't know. But I have to go, Clive."

"Forget it. You're staying here. We can tell the State Department to warn King Fahd."

"No. That won't work!" Seth was desperate. "Warn them, yes, but I have to go! The State Department can't help her! You know that."

"You can't go. They'll *never* let you go. And even if they did, you couldn't even get into Saudi Arabia. You can't just hop on board the next United flight and sail into Riyadh. It's a closed country."

"So was the Nevada border. I managed then."

Clive paused. "That was before your clairvoyance became intermittent. Can you see now?"

"No. But I was seeing just a few minutes ago and I'll see again." He had to find a way to make Clive understand. They were locked away in the world's most secure fortress; without Clive's help he was going nowhere. And Miriam needed him. If she ever needed him, it was now.

Assuming you can help her now. You're blind, boy!

Seth walked to the wall and spun around. "I'm going. In a few hours, I'll be able to see again and I'll walk out. You know there's no way you can stop me."

"Maybe."

"No. Really. But I don't have a few hours! I was given this gift for her protection, Clive. You have to see that!"

"Given by God," Clive said.

"Yes!" Seth yelled. "Given by God!"

"Like it or not, you're the single most valuable asset this country has in its possession right now," Clive said. "You're also the most potentially dangerous. They'd kill me if I let you walk."

"You'll be sentencing Miriam to death and the United States to a major political crisis if you don't!"

Seth slapped his back pocket. Still there. He pulled out a disk and held it up.

Clive lifted an eyebrow.

"Something I did on my own. It's a scenario I ran while the techs were going over this morning's battle results. This is the only copy."

"So."

"So, it's a look at what will happen if Khalid were to take power away from King Fahd. It isn't pretty."

Clive looked at him skeptically. "How can you see what might happen in the Middle East without looking past three hours?"

"By stringing together consecutive three-hour segments."

"How . . . You did that?"

"I did. Only on the computer. I went out three months, and trust me, a lot of people will die if Khalid takes control of Saudi Arabia. If I'd known it was important, I would've told you earlier. Now it is important." He tossed the disk to Clive, who caught it.

"And how does this help you?"

"It helps me because I don't think there's any way to stop a coup without my help. You may think that I'm valuable in here, playing your games, but I may just be the only option you have out there, where it really counts."

"There's no guarantee that you could even reach Saudi Arabia, much less stop a coup. The State Department—"

"The State Department will fail," Seth said.

"You know that?"

Seth took a deep breath. "No. But what if I'm right? What if the only way to stop this whole mess is through me? What if this gift of mine has been given for that purpose? If you don't let me leave, your decision will go down in history as the greatest act of criminal negligence ever willfully exercised. I'll make sure of it."

Clive stared at him for a few moments. "Do you have any idea what you're asking?"

"Yes."

"Do you even know what you would do?"

"No."

"This is ridiculous. You want me to let you walk out of here because God has handpicked you to save the world. And you expect me to explain that to the generals, three of whom are on their way here as we speak for a meeting with the secretary of state tomorrow."

"Pretty much, yes. Show them the disk and tell them that if I'm wrong, I promise I'll come back and let them pry through my mind. Keep me here and I'm dumb. Your dog and pony show tomorrow morning will be a terrible embarrassment. In fact, I may just feed them with miscues. You'll wish you'd never found me."

Clive chuckled nervously, but with one look at Seth, he stopped. He stood and walked across the room, hands on hips. "I can't believe I'm actually considering this."

"You'd be an idiot not to," Seth said.

"This is really about Miriam, isn't it?"

"Maybe. But where Miriam goes, Saudi Arabia goes."

Clive looked at Seth for a long time. A frown settled on his face. "You have me in a box, don't you?" Seth nodded and grabbed a shirt off the chair.

"Okay. You win. But if you're going to try this, whatever *this* is, let me at least help you get the papers you'll need to enter the country. Follow me."

33

THE MORNING CAME AND WENT in a vague cloud that barely registered in Miriam's consciousness. She resolved to show no emotion. None at all.

The afternoon crawled by, bustling with activity, but distant—an impossible nightmare to which she had resigned herself.

Because of the secretive nature of the marriage, the usual party of familiar relatives was absent. Instead, the sheik's wives and servants made the preparations to Miriam. They brought in an elaborate peach-colored silk gown, one Samir had purchased in Cairo, they told her. Miriam stood on numb legs while they pulled it over her head for a hasty fitting. The dress felt loose, and one of the wives ordered a maid to take it in at the waist. Miriam decided that peach was a ghastly color.

She lay obediently for the halawa ceremony, performed by the wives. A sweet-smelling mixture of lemon juice, sugar, and rose water that had been boiled to form a glue was spread over her entire body and allowed to dry. When they peeled it away, her body hair came out with it. Under any other circumstances, she might have protested the pain, but it felt like no more than an absurd abstraction. Were they stupid enough to think that cleaning her outer body would in any way present a purer package to the beast they intended to feed her to? In a strange way, she welcomed the pain.

The wives rinsed Miriam's hair with henna to make it shine and painted her nails a rose red—preparing their whore for this ungodly union. Two weeks earlier she had watched Sita endure the preparations, encouraged her to make the best of her new reality. Sita had just stared at her with glassy-eyed dread. Her friend had sentenced herself to death, and now the notion grew on Miriam. She could not fathom the idea of Omar touching her. She would die first.

But Omar would not kill her. Doing so would break his family's ties with her father. No, instead he would keep her in a living hell, bound and gagged in a dungeon, maybe. Whipped and bleeding for his own pleasure, perhaps. The thought of physical death appealed to her as an escape. If she could only find a way to die without killing herself. Allah would not smile upon suicide.

And where *was* Allah? *Who* was Allah? God in name, of course, but who? How could God allow this horror to be done in his name? The Jews had suffered horror, but their suffering had come *because* of their beliefs, not as part of them. Followers of Jesus had been martyred, but at the hands of their enemies, not at the will of their own people. She was being sacrificed by her own people, because of their beliefs, because Allah had commanded it, because they believed that a woman was a possession to be sacrificed for the pleasure of a man. Surely there were many good Muslims in Saudi Arabia who would be horrified by what she was about to face. Surely this could not be the fault of Islam, but of evil men.

Seth had told her to call for help from the second God. The God of Jesus. Muslim teachers called Jesus the greatest prophet, but was his God different from her God? Was Allah not the God of Jesus? Who was this God of the Christians? And how should she pray to him?

As night approached and the prayer calls crooned from the minarets, Miriam whispered a helpless, hopeless prayer under her breath. *Help me, God of Jesus.* It was scarcely more than a halfhearted attempt to mock her own God. He offered her no help.

Unable to maintain her resolve to show no emotion, Miriam began to cry. The gnawing horror that she'd ignored all day rose through her chest like a black dragon. The horror of her leaving Seth showed its true colors now, and it was nothing less than the most sickening kind of horror. She had willingly left the one man who truly did love her. Her savior, her love, who would be stealing her away to fields of flowers now instead of turning her over to slaughter in the name of Islam!

She cried long and she cried hard, alarming the two wives who watched over her. She cried for Seth. She didn't care that she distorted her picture of his love into more than it was. She needed someone to love her now, and now there was only Seth.

A religious sheik came at dusk and asked Miriam's father for his consent of marriage. They signed documents, and then the sheik left to repeat the process with Omar. Her father's will was sealed. In exchange for his daughter, he would receive the agreed upon bride price, in this case loyalty and power rather than money.

One of the wives gave her a pill to swallow—a drug to calm her nerves, she said. Miriam thought of Sita, drugged before the drowning, but she took the pill anyway. They led her into a limousine at dark. She sat in the back with her father and one of his wives. A train of cars followed.

For the first time since accepting her fate, Miriam felt the cords of panic wind around her heart. The limousine remained deathly quiet as they rode for Omar's palace. *I am their sacrificial lamb.* She thought of jumping from the moving vehicle. She eased her hand onto the handle. The doors were locked. She could feel the drug start to take hold. Sweat lined her palms.

"Father?" Her voice was high and squeaky.

The sheik turned his head, smiling as she imagined a proud father might smile before giving his daughter to the man she loved. "You are a beautiful bride, Miriam. You will make a wonderful wife."

"I don't want to do this, Father."

The sheik looked away. "Your fear will pass. You can't always think only of yourself. You are a woman now, and you must begin to think of your husband."

"I don't think he will make a good husband."

He faced her with glaring eyes. "He is whom I have chosen! Do not question my authority!" And then, "Don't worry, he will earn your love over time. I have demanded it of him."

She sank back into the seat, begging it to swallow her whole. Nausea swept through her stomach. She closed her eyes, but the swaying of the car made her dizzy, so she opened them again. There was no escape, was there?

They came to a large palace and Miriam was led into a study with one of Father's wives. Drums beat to laughter on the other side of the walls. She wondered how many guests had been summoned. Whether they knew the truth behind her marriage to Omar hardly mattered. The women in attendance were guilty by their very acceptance of their *own* captivities in their own marriages.

A knock sounded on the door and Father's wife stood. She smiled sympathetically. "It is time. Be strong, Miriam. For your father's sake, be strong. There is nothing we can do."

Miriam just looked at her.

"Come."

She held out her hand and Miriam stood. The woman lowered Miriam's veil and led her out to a large hall with towering pillars. Several dozen women stood, watching them walk to the front of the assembly. Miriam heard her shoes echoing on the marble floor with each step. There was no sign of Omar.

She was left at the front and stood alone, facing the women. She couldn't bear to look at them, now standing without veils and colorfully dressed, as was customary at weddings. The ceremony intended to show the true woman in all her splendor, but to Miriam it was a terrible farce, a mockery that made them foolish for believing—

A door sprang open to her right. Her father stepped out. Behind him another man she recognized as Khalid bin Mishal. And then another man, dressed in black, smiling wryly. Omar.

A tremble shook Miriam's body. It was the first time she'd seen Omar. He walked across the floor with the other two men, hard shoes clacking on the marble.

She looked away, terrified to catch his eyes. Their walk seemed to stretch forever. Their clacking in the hollow hall. From her left the religious man who'd met with her father earlier stepped through another door and approached. The drug she'd taken an hour earlier seemed to slow everything down. Perhaps it really was all just a nightmare after all.

The footsteps stopped. She could hear breathing to her right. Omar's breathing. Her face flushed with heat. *God of Jesus, help me, I beg you.*

The religious man stepped out in front of them and began to talk, to her father and then to the others. He did not address her. The transaction was between her father and Omar.

A low, gravelly voice spoke, and she immediately knew it belonged to Omar. She didn't dare turn to face . . .

Suddenly he was there, in front of her, lifting her veil. She held her breath. The face she saw through watered eyes was bearded black with dark eyes. A soft, knowing smirk bent his wet lips. His eyes drifted down her body and then returned to her eyes. He grinned and winked at her.

If not for the dulling effects of the drug, she might have run right then. Instead, she began to cry softly. They ignored her and said a few more words to complete the ceremony.

Omar walked past her and headed for a side door. The room broke out in the ululating cries of the women, like a flock of crows warning her. Miriam stood frozen, head spinning.

The religious man stepped forward and told her to follow Omar. She turned and walked, hardly aware that she was doing so. Omar entered the same study in which she had waited, held the door for her, and then closed it behind them. She stood with her back to him, terrified.

His hand touched the top of her veil. He ripped it off and slowly stepped around her. "You are more beautiful than I imagined," he said.

She would not look at him. She would never give him the satisfaction of looking into his eyes.

"Are you afraid of me?"

She didn't answer.

Omar lifted a flask from the desk and poured himself a drink. The clinking of the glass sounded obscenely loud. He took a drink and set the glass down.

"I think you are. And I want you to know I prefer that. Fear has a way of transforming a woman into a thing of terrible beauty. Did you know that? There is nothing worse than a submissive woman."

Miriam stared across the room. She was nothing more than a helpless maggot here in his presence.

He approached her and walked around her, drawing his finger over her shoulders. He leaned in close and she could smell his liquored breath wafting over her cheek.

"But you aren't only afraid; you are angry, yes? I'm not sure I've ever had a woman who is both afraid and angry. I think it will be a great pleasure."

"I will never . . ." Miriam stopped, surprised that she had spoken.

"Yes? Go on."

Her voice was soft and scratchy. "I will never give you pleasure."

He laughed, a deep throaty laugh. "Yes, I think you actually believe that. That's very nice. There will be consequences, of course, but this, too, could be part of the game."

He squeezed her cheeks with a powerful hand and wrenched her head to face him. She looked into black eyes. Her lips were squeezed like a fish's.

"You are my wife now, Miriam. That is what you are. Nothing more, nothing less. You will please me, and if you are fortunate, you will bear me a son. That is all you will do. Do you understand?"

The room swam through fresh tears. She closed her eyes.

"I have something very special planned for you, Miriam. A very special chamber. Something so delicious must not be rushed. You will take a night to prepare yourself for me. Fear is good, my sweet. Let the drugs wear off and let your fear take hold. When you are fully tenderized, I will take you. It will be delightful, you will see."

Omar leaned forward and kissed her on the lips. She felt as though she might throw up before he pulled away.

Then he released her. She swayed on her feet, nauseous again. When she opened her eyes, he no longer stood in front of her. After a moment she looked around cautiously. The room was empty.

Miriam stepped carefully to the sofa, sat gingerly, and began to weep.

"This stinks!" Peter Smaley said. "Running from a manhunt in California is one thing. Waltzing into Saudi Arabia on a half-brained rescue attempt isn't remotely similar. What were you thinking?"

"You don't exactly control a guy like Seth," Clive said. "When he's on, he's unstoppable."

"When he's on."

They sat in the same conference room they had planned on using to debrief Seth: the two generals, a colonel, the secretary of state, and the deputy, Smaley. Clive had told them about Seth's ultimatum and escape; he was holding back the disk as his ace.

"Either way, you allowed him to leave," General Smites said. "That's not unlike giving them the keys to this mountain."

"Overstated," Clive said. "It's a mistake to assume that he intends to do anything in Saudi Arabia but help Miriam, if she's there. His actions will benefit our interests as much as Fahd's. And like I said, he was going, whether we agreed or not. I couldn't have stopped him."

"You put a guy in a locked cell and he's not going anywhere; I don't care what he can see."

"That's not necessarily true," Clive said. "And he wasn't here as a prisoner." It wasn't altogether true, but it was the best he could come up with at the moment. They looked at him, and honestly he wasn't sure if they would end up giving him a medal or ripping his head off.

"I realize how significant a man with Seth's abilities is to the military," Secretary Gray said after a long period of silence. "But frankly I'm more concerned with the stability of Saudi Arabia. I don't need to educate you on the pains we've taken to keep militants from power in the Middle East. If there's validity to what you're saying about Sheik Al-Asamm carrying through with this marriage, we could have a real problem on our hands. It wouldn't be the first time the balance of power shifted on the Arabian Peninsula as the result of a marriage."

Clive cleared his throat. "Then you may want to take a look at something Seth left with us." He rolled his chair over to a computer and slid the disk into the drive. "This is the scenario he ran yesterday afternoon while we were occupied. He found a way to string consecutive episodes together. It starts with a future in which Khalid succeeds in taking power from Fahd and extends out three months."

"How's that possible?" Smaley asked. "I wasn't aware he could extend beyond three hours."

"Neither was I. He found a way. I showed this to Garton; he checked the algorithms Seth used. He's convinced it works."

He tapped a few keys. The monitor blinked and then filled with numbers, seemingly random across the screen. Streams of text rolled up the picture at a rate too fast to read. Several hundred lines passed by in a blur, and then a single page popped up. *Key Indicators of the Kingdom of Saudi Arabia and Region—Plus Three Months.*

Clive rolled the monitor stand toward them. "Not a pretty sight."

They read Seth's conclusions.

The secretary looked up at Clive. "What are the chances that this might be accurate?"

"If Khalid takes control, pretty good. Short of having another scenario contrary to this, we'd better assume that what we see is at least probable."

For a moment no one spoke. Gray pushed his chair back. "Where is Seth now?"

"If he makes all the flights, he'll be in Riyadh"—he glanced at his watch—"in seven hours."

"Do you have any confidence that he might upset this wedding?"

Clive shook his head. "Your guess is as good as mine. When he left, his clairvoyance was cycling, a few hours on, a few hours off. Without it, he's a sitting duck over there. He can read Arabic, maybe even speak a bit, but there's no way he'll pass for an Arab. And there's the distinct possibility that his periods of remission might lengthen. It's a crapshoot at best."

"The king doesn't know?"

"No, sir," Smaley said. "We don't have any corroborating intel—"

"This is good enough for me," the secretary said. "We tell him that we suspect Miriam has been returned to Saudi Arabia and is being given in marriage to Omar bin Khalid in an agreement with Sheik Al-Asamm. And we urge him to arrest Khalid bin Mishal immediately. At the very least, we strongly suggest he be prepared."

"He won't have the political will to arrest Khalid without concrete evidence," Smaley said. "That's not the way they work over there."

"I know, Peter. I know. That's his choice." The secretary stood. "I'll make the call myself." He looked at Clive. "No offense, but I pray you're wrong. God help them if you're not."

"No offense taken. And you might find it interesting that one of the conclusions Seth came to in his state of heightened awareness was that prayer works."

They stared dumbly at him.

"Excuse me, gentlemen," the secretary said. He turned and walked from the room.

34

King Khalid International Airport sat thirty-five kilometers north of Riyadh, a city covering roughly six hundred square kilometers of ground, occupied by over three million inhabitants. Seth knew without a shred of doubt that negotiating his way past immigration and into the city would be impossible without his clairvoyance.

The travel documents that Clive had drummed up took him to London and then on to Beirut, where he'd caught a four-hour flight into Riyadh. All good.

There were only two problems. One, immigration would reject his visa—he'd seen that in every possible future. Clive's masterpiece was no masterpiece at all. And two, his clairvoyance was about to run out. He couldn't see exactly when—he couldn't ever look into the future and see how his clairvoyance would act; it was like a double indemnity that effectively canceled itself out. But he'd been seeing plainly for about two hours now, and by his last calculations, two hours was now his limit. The duration of his clairvoyance was shrinking steadily. Worse, the time between episodes was expanding by nearly an hour each time. When his seeing faded this time, it would not return for at least six hours.

Even worse still, he not only saw for shorter durations with longer gaps of blindness, he saw less each time the clairvoyance returned. Gone was the expansive sight that reached beyond his immediate surroundings. His gift was simply fizzling out.

Seth deplaned and walked for immigration, sweating bullets. He was still seeing. The trick was to thread his way past their eyes. It was the only way. He had to go only when and where he would not be seen. Effectively walk right past them without their knowing.

Even if he did get past them, he would still be no closer to finding Miriam. Fear sat like lead in his gut.

Concentrate!

His mind's eye showed him precisely who would look where and when. At least as a sea of possibilities. He would have to isolate a particular thread in which none of the immigration authorities would be looking at a particular spot at a particular time. He would have to be in that spot then, and string together a few dozen unseen spots to get past the authorities without being seen.

Three lines wound into immigration stations where officers examined and stamped passports before allowing the passengers past. Two stations to his left were unmanned, closed off with red rope. He could slide under the rope easily enough.

Problem was, he couldn't actually see any futures in which he was unseen. The likelihood of all the guards diverting their attention long enough for him to slip through was, in and of itself, very small. Very, very small. He discovered a number of futures in which the left of the hall went unseen for a period of several seconds, and a few futures in which the right went unseen for brief moments, but none with enough time for him to walk through unseen.

He stepped behind a large pillar and did his best to look relaxed. It wouldn't help his case to be seen dripping in sweat and shaking like a leaf. Unless something came to him soon, he would not be able to avoid either appearance.

Maybe he should go back to the plane, pretend he'd left something on board. That would buy him time. But no, he had to make his move while the immigration stalls were still busy and distracted with other passengers.

This is it, Seth. You're finished. The gas chamber awaits dead ahead, and the Nazis have their machine guns aimed at your gut.

They wouldn't kill him, would they? No, he was an American. Unless a coup changed loyalties. The thought did nothing to ease his perspiration.

A mother, cloaked in black with two daughters clenching fistfuls of her abaaya, passed by. Seth forced a smile and stepped out. The immigration line was just ahead.

This was crazy! He felt like he was walking for a cliff with the full intention of stepping off. Willfully going back in history to step into the shower, knowing full well that deadly gas, not water, would come out of the showerheads. He couldn't do this!

A picture of Miriam filled his mind. She was sitting across from him at the table, cracking a crab leg with her teeth, smiling over the candlelight at him.

Seth stopped and bent to tie his shoe to buy more time. The problem with the future was that it depended on others' decisions as well as his. In this case, the authorities'. He saw that he could actually get up to the gate without being spotted, using a string of unseen spots, but there at the gate, a guard who now stood behind the stations would spot him in every future he saw.

A drop of sweat ran down his temple, tickling. *This is insane! What were you thinking! Think! Think, think . . .*

He blinked.

No, don't think. Step beyond your mind.

Seth's heart thumped in his ears. He stood slowly, still staring at the floor. Step beyond your mind.

God . . . change the future, he prayed.

He swallowed. It sounded silly. *God, change the future?* What kind of prayer was that?

God of Abraham, Moses, and Jesus, change the future. Open up a new possibility that will allow me to pass through . . .

He caught his breath. His mind had snagged a new thread, and he knew it had come from beyond him.

He stood there stunned, staring ahead like an idiot.

Walk! Now! Walk!

Seth wiped his slippery palms on his corduroys, walked forward three steps, and turned to his left. He took two steps, counted to four, and then turned right. It was lunacy.

No one yelled. No one shouted out, "Stop that, idiot!"

Trust it, Seth. You can't stop now.

He hurried ten paces to the right.

If any of the authorities had seen him, they would have undoubtedly stared in amusement. The American in the black corduroys who was walking ten paces to the right, stopping, taking three steps backward, and then crossing at a slight angle to the other side of the hall. A lunatic marching around the terminal as if he were in a play with a dozen other unseen characters.

In reality he was stepping precisely where their view of him was blocked by a head or an arm, or when this one or that one was looking down. One small boy watched Seth the whole way, for all five minutes it took him to reach the gate. But the boy's only response was to stare at him as he jerked his way about the hall.

The future that had changed required that he stand at the gate, face the far wall, and clear his throat. The sound bounced off in such a way to pull a distant guard's attention away just long enough for Seth to walk past.

And then he was through. Trembling and nauseated with dread, but through. He walked away from the immigration posts on numb legs.

"Thank you," he whispered. "Thank you." He'd read of Christians walking through guard posts, smuggling Bibles, but he'd never imagined it would be so strenuous. Christ had walked through a crowd unseen once, just before his crucifixion. Was this God's way of blinding?

He was still seeing. That would end at any minute, and then he would be blind.

Seth quickly located the bathrooms and hurried for them. An abaaya hung in the ladies' room—he needed that abaaya. Thank goodness he had seen at least that much.

He slipped into the rest room unseen, hands quivering from the exhilaration of his success. If he could just . . .

The world suddenly blinked to black. The clairvoyance was gone!

Panic swelled in his chest. He spun around, saw the black abaaya, and grabbed it off the hook. He fumbled for an opening. Found one.

Top or bottom, he didn't know—he'd never touched an abaaya, much less worn one.

He threw it over his head and pulled it down. There were no arms as such and he quickly gathered it around him in a fashion that matched the pictures he'd seen. His leather shoes poked out the bottom—that might be a problem. He snatched up the veil and pulled it over his head. Ha! Perfect!

The door suddenly opened and another woman entered.

Another?

She looked at him as if something were wrong. For a moment neither moved. Then she stepped over and straightened his head covering, mumbling something he couldn't understand. Seth nodded his thanks and walked out.

He stood for a moment, gathering his senses. He was blind to the future. Did women in Saudi Arabia ever wear leather tennis shoes? He desperately hoped so; he sincerely doubted so. He couldn't very well slip on a pair of pumps though, could he? He'd be tripping in every crack.

He'd seen enough of the future to know what he should attempt now, but he hadn't seen whether he would succeed. He could get to the city riding a shuttle bus. But the specifics of that future had faded. Not the general future, but the tiny things that made a difference. When to say what, which seat to sit in—those sorts of things.

He struck for the sign that indicated buses. There was no going back now. This was Miriam's homeland. The thought brought her rushing to his mind. She was here; he could feel that in his bones. *Where* was another matter entirely.

The bus ride involved little more than suffering through an hour of humiliation. Several men glared at him, focusing first on his hairy hands, which he quickly hid, and then on his shoes, which he could not. Whether their distaste of him came from his choice of shoes or from not having a man traveling with him, he couldn't guess. It took some effort to resist the temptation to slap the one male who evidently saw it as his duty to scowl at him, but otherwise he survived his first hour in Saudi Arabia like a regular champ.

He stepped off the bus in downtown Riyadh near midnight. He walked away from the others as quickly as possible, painfully aware of several continuing glares.

The city was virtually deserted at this hour. If he had his sight, he might be able to begin his search now, but he was still blind. And he would remain blind for another five hours. There was nothing to do but wait. And hide.

Seth found a deserted alley and settled to his haunches behind a large garbage bin. The night hid him well. He *was* the night. A black blob in a dark alley in the dead of night.

He hadn't felt so deserted and lonely since his father had kicked him out of the house for spilling his Coke on the kitchen table at his fourth birthday party.

There was screaming and there was hitting and Seth awoke.

"Get up, get up, you filthy woman!" someone screamed in Arabic. A stick hit his head, snapping him to full awareness. He jerked up. A man stood over him—the wielder of the baton. A mutawa by the looks of his dress.

Seth scrambled to his feet. The mutawa drew back to strike another blow, and Seth did the only thing that came to his mind. He ran.

Curses rang down the alley after him. The abaaya flapped around his ankles and he pulled it up to give himself room to make the getaway. Something about the sight silenced the mutawa. His shoes, maybe. Or his long stride.

He couldn't take any chances now. If the man suspected that Seth was something other than a woman, he would go on the prowl. Cross-dressing wasn't exactly encouraged in Saudi Arabia.

Seth hurried down the street and cut up another alley. He snuck around the shops in the Souq for ten minutes, satisfied the mutawa was no longer a threat. The abaaya made a perfect disguise among other women, so long as there were other women. At this dawn hour they weren't out.

The day's first prayer call warbled through the cool morning air. That would bring some men—those devout enough to brave the early rising—but he would have to wait to start his search until enough women could give him cover.

His plan was simple: He would find lots of people and search their conversations with his sight into the future. Someone somewhere had to know something about Omar. If he could find Omar, he was sure he would find Miriam.

The absurdity of his situation hit him as he walked through the market, trying desperately to look as if he belonged. But the fact was, he didn't belong. He imagined Miriam walking this same market before her flight to America. In so many ways, she belonged.

Where could she be now? If she were with him now, he would belong; without her he was lost. And without his clairvoyance, he might as well be in a tomb. The thoughts brought a lump to his throat.

Miriam, my dear. Where are you? He was here to find her, still powerless to begin.

An air-raid alarm suddenly wailed across the city. The sound of automatic weapons fire, like popping corn. His heart bolted. The air fell silent. What could that mean? Trouble. But this wasn't the local authorities chasing him down. This was something that crossed the city.

Seth hurried for a large structure that stood against the horizon, half a mile ahead. He needed his clairvoyance now. He needed it badly.

And if it didn't return?

It did return, two hours later. Seven hours after it had left him. Seven hours! And it would be gone in under two.

The cause for sirens suddenly roared through his head. Someone in a passing car was about to tell someone else on a cell phone and Seth saw it as a future.

"What I'm saying, Faisal, is that we can't just pretend that nothing is happening. The Royal Palace is under siege, you imbecile." The connection faded as the car raced out of range. Seth spun around, terrified.

So, the coup *was* underway! Which meant Miriam *had* married Omar. Seth felt ill.

He madly searched the futures for something beyond this small square. Nothing came. His gift had started like this—revealing only what was in his proximity—and it had expanded to encompass whatever he put his mind to, as with the war games in Cheyenne Mountain. But now the gift was reverting. If it was truly a gift from God, he had either failed or the game was coming to an end. Or both.

If militants had put the palace under siege, they were keeping it well concealed—it hadn't upset daily life in any obvious way here at the city's heart. A few police cars screamed by followed by lumbering army trucks, but the streets were filling with pedestrians, seemingly unconcerned.

Okay, boy. One step at a time.

Seth hurried out onto a crosswalk that overlooked a large courtyard before the Al Faisaliah Mall. The structure towered high above the skyline, a narrow pyramid shape, oddly modern among its peers. Seth's attention turned to the people crowding at its base.

He could walk up to any one of the thousands that passed by and ask if he or she knew who Omar bin Khalid was and, if so, where he lived. That created possible futures. He could see those, and he could see all the possible answers. His task was to look into those futures and find the one who knew the answer to both questions.

Seth stood over the people. He was a woman frozen on the walkway, unusual only because she was alone. The futures spun through his mind, fruitless for ten minutes. And then twenty. And then forty.

A hundred thousand people must have passed in the crowd below and not one of them knew Omar? Actually, he saw that eight of them would have responded positively to his first question, but as to where Omar lived, they possessed no more information than he. If he could just find *one* who knew, he could probably trick them out of the answer.

What if the coup had already succeeded? If Miriam was actually married to Omar, what could he, an American citizen with no diplomatic status, possibly do? Kidnap her again? The questions made him sick.

A girl to his right suddenly caught his attention. She was hardly more than a child, still unveiled, and he knew immediately that she was the one. She spoke English and his conversation with her would have gone like this:

"Excuse me. Is this man Omar one you could know?"

She looked at him, amused. "You are English?" she asked in English.

"Yes! Yes, I am."

"Then speak English. Do I look like a fool? And why are you dressed like a woman?"

"You look positively brilliant. And I am dressed like a woman because I am from the theater."

"We don't have theaters."

"There is one and it's a secret. Do you know of Omar bin Khalid?"

"I don't believe you. There are no theaters that I know of. Yes, I do know Bin Khalid."

"You do? That's wonderful. And where does he live? I must speak to him about the theater as soon as possible."

She looked at him for a few moments and then smiled softly. "I still don't believe you. Omar has many villas, but his newest is the Villa Amour, in the wealthy district on the west. It is well known."

"It is? That's wonderful! And do you know, was there a wedding there recently? In the past few days?"

Her eyes widened. "I could never tell you that. You are a man," she would have said.

And indeed, she never would tell him. But she just had, hadn't she? The conversation could have become quite interesting, but he had what he needed.

Seth whirled from the railing. He had to find a way to the Villa Amour. He had less than an hour before the clairvoyance ended. Maybe a lot less.

35

KING FAHD stormed into his office, furious at the incompetence that surrounded him. He felt naked without his security chief, who lay dead in a box somewhere on its way back to Saudi Arabia. Hilal would have ended this madness already if he hadn't gotten himself killed. For that he blamed the Americans.

"How many men do they have?" he asked, sliding behind his desk.

General Mustafa crossed his legs. "The sheik claims to have ten thousand just beyond the city to the west."

Fahd eyed the general. This man had persuaded him not to act after receiving the call from the American secretary of state. With the crown prince in Indonesia, Fahd had weighed this man's advice. Not that he wouldn't have agreed anyway, but now that Khalid had actually taken control of the palace perimeter, Fahd wondered whether General Mustafa was not divided himself.

"Where is the crown prince?"

"His plane has been turned back to Jakarta," Mustafa said. "Khalid has taken control of the airport as well."

The airport! "Ali is with Khalid?"

"It would seem so."

"How many other ministers?"

"At least twelve that we know of. Khalid has planned this for a long time to have such a broad base of support."

Fahd stared out the window. The sky was blue. A pigeon soared by. It wasn't the first time a prince had tried to remove him from power—the threat was constant. But this time, this one seemed to have some momentum. "You are speaking about my death, General. Not a political rally."

"No, Your Highness. They've made no such threats. They've given you twelve hours to evacuate the government. If they planned on storming the palace, they would have done it already, when they had the advantage of surprise."

"Don't be a fool. They've given me twelve hours purely for political reasons—to appease the half of the city that supports me. They have no intention of allowing me to walk out of here alive. I've always been a threat to the militants."

The general waited before answering. "Perhaps they have other ways to contain that threat."

"I have no intention of rotting in a cell. How many men does Khalid have outside now?"

"It's not how many, sir. It's where he has them. They control all of the security outside the palace itself. And they control most of the ministries."

"No change in the military?"

"No. Both the air force and the army are standing down. They aren't necessarily with Khalid, but they aren't against him either."

"So in the end, Khalid's real force consists of the sheik's men?"

"Yes. And the sheik has another twenty thousand standing by."

Fahd closed his eyes and thought about the events that had led up to this moment. His father had always found a way to prevail, using both cunning and brute force. In reality Khalid was probably more like Aziz than he. But the world had changed since his father's death. It was smaller. They could not build their private kingdom in defiance to the West forever. As the Americans had shown with Iraq and Al Qaeda, they would only tolerate so much before they reacted. And when they reacted, it was always with overpowering force.

"We still have communications?" he asked.

"No telephones," General Mustafa said.

"Then get a message out with a courier. You can do that, can't you, General?"

"Perhaps. Yes, I think so."

Fahd opened his eyes. "Good. I want you to let the city know what's happening here. We will create as much confusion in the streets as we can. Tell them that the Shi'i have besieged the palace. That should get a reaction. Sheik Al-Asamm is the key. Perhaps we could do what Khalid has done. Perhaps we could dislodge his loyalty to Khalid."

The general was silent.

"What do you think, General? Can the sheik's allegiance be shaken?"

"I don't know. If it is, Khalid will fail. But Al-Asamm is bound by marriage, and he's a very traditional man."

"Yet he broke his bond with me."

"Only because the religious leaders agreed that he could, under the circumstances."

"And what about you, General? Where do your loyalties lie?"

"With the king."

"And if the king were to be Khalid?"

"The king will be whomever Allah has willed. But I believe that he has willed you, Your Highness."

"I see. And is Khalid following God's will?"

The general didn't have an answer. Conviction had split the country in two between fundamentalists, who took the Qur'an at face value, and more moderate Muslims, who recognized that Islam must change if it was to survive. But like many, Mustafa himself was probably double-minded. Fatalism was indeed convenient at times.

"If I don't hear rioting within the hour, I will assume you haven't spread the word, General. That is all."

"The coup is six hours old from what we can gather, but we have no direct contact with the House of Saud so we can't be sure," Smaley said. "You're still in Colorado Springs?"

So Seth had been right! Clive shifted the cell phone to his right hand. "I'm on my way to the airport now. You're saying that Khalid bin Mishal has actually succeeded?"

"We don't know yet. Too soon."

"So Seth was right. Then he may be our only hope."

"He obviously failed to disrupt the wedding—we're seeing evidence of that now. We haven't heard a thing from him. As far as I'm concerned, he's dead in the water. You, on the other hand, may be able to help us out." Smaley paused. "Look, you were right on this one, and you have my apologies. Meanwhile, we have a serious situation on our hands, and the department's powerless. Khalid has sealed off our embassy in Riyadh and both consulates in Dhahran and Jiddah. We have no idea how Jordan and his staff are doing; communications are down. It's a mess."

"Miriam's alive?" Clive asked.

"We don't know. But we do know that Sheik Al-Asamm has gathered a pretty decent force east of the city. We can only assume that means he's cooperating. Which is why we want you back in the lab with that last scenario Seth ran. Was the sheik part of the coup attempt he ran?"

Clive quickly used his free hand to maneuver the car into a 7-Eleven. "Not that I can remember, but I didn't spend much time with it. He must have been. In any real scenario the sheik would have to be dealt with in one way or another. You want me to analyze the actions of the sheik and Omar in Seth's scenario? Makes sense." He swung the car around.

"The techs are already doing it, but they don't have your sense of this thing. We think that our best hope may rest with the sheik. We need to know his weaknesses, his responses to real situations. If Seth's scenario was real, it could give us that, right?"

"Maybe. Maybe not. Do you have contact with the sheik?"

"Not yet, but we think we can get to his personal line. Either way we don't have a lot of time here."

Clive motored back onto the 24 bypass and headed for Cheyenne Mountain. "I'm on my way. So nothing from Seth, huh?"

"Not on this end. That may be a good thing. The last thing we need is for some maniac American to walk in and kidnap the sheik's daughter. We need Al-Asamm's cooperation, not his anger."

"You still don't get him, do you, Peter? It's a good thing he's beyond your reach now. At the very least, don't go out of your way to stop him."

"For all we know, he's dead," Smaley said. "You should've never let him go. Forget it, Clive. He's no longer a factor."

Clive wanted to object, but on the surface, the deputy secretary made sense. For all he knew, Seth had lost his gift altogether by now. And if Miriam was married . . .

Still, even without clairvoyance, Seth was no idiot.

"I'll call you if I get anything," Clive said. He turned the phone off.

36

TIME WAS EVERYTHING NOW. Seth had found a taxi driver who knew the location of the Villa Amour. Despite butchering a few words in Arabic using his best impression of a woman's voice, Seth convinced the driver to take him, as Seth knew he would. But the effort had wasted half an hour.

A tall wall ran around the villa and guards stood at the gates. Didn't matter—he saw no way past the gate anyway. The only way in without being noticed was over the wall at the south end. Thank the stars he was still seeing.

He ran as best he could in the abaaya without looking like a bat floating down the sidewalk. He jumped for the edge of the wall, caught it, and hauled himself over.

The villas were called palaces and he could see why at first glance. Tall Greek pillars framed a fifteen-foot entrance made of wood. But he had no intention of using the front door. It was the servants' housing near the back that interested him.

Not so long ago he would have been able to stand here and know precisely what was in the villa by scanning through possible futures. But at the moment he was capturing only glimpses, like at the start of this whole mess, when he'd first seen Miriam about to be attacked in the ladies' room at Berkeley.

Seth ran for the back, keeping to the bushes and palm trees that lined a huge fountain, spinning through the questions that had plagued him during the long cab ride. Why hadn't he seen Miriam in any future? This was Omar's newest villa; he knew at least that. And he knew that a wedding had been performed here recently. But he still did not know with certainty that Omar had married Miriam here or that she was still here if he had.

Seth grunted, aware of how thin his chances were. He placed his hope in the Filipino maid who would engage him in the servants' quarters. He didn't know how cooperative she'd be, but he had seen that she would talk to him. At least he had that.

One step at a time, boy. Just one step.

Seth paused at the door and glanced back. He couldn't take his seeing for granted anymore. He put his hand on the knob and turned. The door swung in.

A wood table, window coverings made of sheets, and an old wood stove furnished the dimly lit room. A dark-skinned woman, unveiled and dressed in a dirty tunic, turned from the stove, eyes wide.

Seth stepped in and closed the door. She would talk to him, in English. He knew that, but he also knew that he had to come off as a woman.

"Hello, could you help me, please?" he said, afraid his voice would crack. Sounded like a woman to him. The woman just stared at him.

"I am an American," he said. "I beg you for assistance."

"American?" She glanced at the window, obviously terrified. Filipino servants were common in Saudi Arabia—Muslims who'd come to the cradle of Islam in search of work—but their employers often badly mistreated them.

"Yes. I am willing to pay you." Seth slipped his hand under the abaaya, took a wad of U.S. dollars from his front pocket, and held it out to her. "Please."

She looked at the money for a moment, glanced one more time at the window, and then reached for the money eagerly. By the look in her eyes, it was probably more money than she'd seen in her whole life. Maybe a couple hundred dollars, Seth thought.

"I must speak to the woman who is here. Her name is Miriam." The servant still fixated on the bills. "She was married here, yes?"

The woman looked up, untrusting.

"Please, she is my friend. You must help me."

"No woman married here," the servant said.

Darkness dumped into Seth's mind. No! He was blind again!

He gasped. The woman took a step backward. He was standing in the middle of a guarded palace on the Arabian Peninsula with a coup raging about him, and he was blind.

Get ahold of yourself, boy. Dear God, help me!

"Please!"

"You're a man!" she said.

He cleared the frog from his throat and hitched his voice up an octave. "Please, I didn't mean to startle you. I have a pain in my stomach." That was ridiculous.

"No marriage," she said. "You cannot be here! If I am caught, they will beat!"

Seth reached out a reassuring hand, and then pulled it back when he saw that the hair on his arm showed, thoroughly unfeminine. "No, they will *not* catch you. I will go. But I must know. I will pay more."

He reached into his pocket and removed another bill. It was a hundred. "Here, take it."

She reached forward, but this time he pulled the money back. "Tell me. Where is the woman?"

She eyed him carefully and then looked at the money.

"Yes. There is a wedding," she said.

"When?"

"Last evening."

That was it! It had to be!

"Where is she?"

The woman held out her hand. "Give me money."

Seth gave it to her.

"I don't know," she said. "You go now. You go!" She picked up a broom and jabbed it at him. "You go now!"

Seth dispensed with his attempt at a woman's voice. "Tell me where she is!" he boomed.

The poor servant dropped her mouth in shock and then swung the broom. It hit him on the head, and he threw up an arm to ward off continuing blows. She began to squeal, and he knew that the ruckus would be the end of him.

"Okay! Hush! *Shh.*"

She continued beating at him, unfazed. Seth fled and slammed the door behind him. He ran five paces before thinking he must look like Darth Vader in a sprint. Anything but a graceful Saudi woman. He pulled up, heart pounding. But the grounds were still quiet.

Miriam was here. He knew that now. There was only one way to find her. For a blond-headed, green-eyed male racing through the palace, pulling open doors, an abaaya was a wonderful thing.

Seth breathed another prayer to the God of Jesus and hurried for the nearest door.

Miriam sat on the couch, suffocated by purple. The subterranean room had no windows, yet its decorator, presumably Omar, had lined the walls with heavy velvet curtains anyway. The red carpet reminded her of blood and it clashed badly with the drapes. The silk bedspread was black. The candles were violet and smelled of something similar to licorice. The room was nothing more than a lavish dungeon.

They'd brought her here an hour after the wedding and locked the door. Since then she'd seen or heard no one. The hours had crept by with mounting dread, and she had only managed to sleep for a couple, here on the couch.

Repeatedly she'd thought to kill herself rather than face Omar again, but suicide was not in her blood. She would rather be killed by him, and she intended to provoke him to it. The mutawa had said that Sita had done Hatam bodily harm; she wondered how her friend had injured him. Scratched his eyes out, maybe. Or smashed his nose. If Omar tried to kiss her again, she would bite him, and not gently.

She shook with the thought of biting down on his lip, hard enough to remove it. *If you want to play, I'll show you that I'm not your toy.* No, she was a woman. But in this man's hands she couldn't be a woman. He didn't even know women existed. To him they were merely flesh, possessions. Something to use up and throw away.

Her vision blurred with tears. *What have I done to deserve this?*

The phone rang and Miriam jerked.

The white porcelain receiver hung on a brass hook—she'd thought the device was only a decoration, but now it was ringing shrilly. She stood slowly. Should she answer it?

Miriam let it ring a dozen times before picking up the receiver and placing it to her ear.

"He is coming," a woman's voice said. "He has asked that his bride be ready."

A chill ran up Miriam's neck.

"Do you hear me?" the woman demanded.

"I will *never* be ready!" Miriam whispered.

Silence. A soft chuckle. "And that is what he wants, my dear. So then, you *are* ready. If you anger him, he will love you for it. If you submit to him, he will hate you. He has the blood of a king, and you are his queen."

The line went dead.

Miriam slammed the receiver down and screamed with rage. "Never!" She shook in rage. "Neveeer!"

She sobbed and crossed the carpet, still shaking like a twig in the wind.

There is only one way, Miriam. You must kill him. She closed her eyes. *You must distract him or hide from him, and when he isn't looking, sink the candlestick deep into his skull.*

A noise suddenly sounded at the door. Panicked, Miriam ran for the dresser and flattened herself in the shadows. She'd forgotten the candlestick! She reached out and snatched it off the dresser.

The door opened a crack. Miriam pressed into the darkness and held her breath.

The door swung open. A woman stood in the doorway, clothed in black. Veiled. Was this Omar's sick fantasy? To come dressed as a woman?

Revulsion swept through her gut, threatening to explode in a scream. She could do it. She would take his head off before he—

"Miriam?"

It *was* a man! Omar had come to her in an abaaya to mock her. If she let him come in and swung at him while he had his back turned, she might succeed.

"Miriam, are you in here?"

She blinked. The man was speaking in English. English! Did Omar speak English?

"Miriam. God, help me. Where have they put you?"

Her mind filled with his voice and one name screamed to the surface. The figure started to turn away. No. No! This could not be Seth! She was inventing a sick fantasy out of desperation. If she called out to him, she would give herself away.

The figure turned to leave.

Miriam could not stop herself. She stepped out of the shadows, candlestick held out like a weapon.

He spun back. "Miriam!"

Take off the veil, she tried to say, but she couldn't. Her throat was swollen shut.

He yanked the veil from his head.

It was Seth.

It was Seth! Miriam felt her knees weaken. How was this possible? Her face wrinkled in shame. She was crying. Why was she ashamed?

He was suddenly rushing her and she fell against him, unable to hold back deep sobs. She was saying things to him, telling him everything, but the words all came out like moans. Long earthy moans that sounded like death echoing around the chamber.

"Oh, Miriam, what have they done to you?" He did his best to hold her up, but she sagged against him and he sat heavily to the couch, embracing her tightly. "I'm going to kill . . ."

She could not stop the gushing of her heart. She knew Omar was coming at this very moment, and she knew that she had to warn Seth. But her body wasn't cooperating.

He rocked her. "You're safe now. You're safe with me. Do you hear me, Miriam? I'm here now."

"He's coming," she managed.

"Who? Omar?"

She struggled for composure. On impulse she grabbed his abaaya and kissed his face. "Thank you!" She kissed his hair, repeating herself through more tears. "Thank you, thank you. Thank you, Seth."

"Listen to me, Miriam. Where is Omar?"

Yes, he was coming, wasn't he? Miriam sat up, suddenly alarmed. She seemed to have lost herself. Omar was coming!

"He's coming!" Miriam said.

Seth looked at her, unsure. "Now?"

"Yes, now!" Panicked, she pushed off him and ran for the door. She stopped and spun around. "We have to leave now! Can you see anything?"

"No." He jumped to his feet and jerked the abaaya off. "Here, you wear this."

"No!"

Seth stopped at the anger in her voice.

"No," she said. "You wear the abaaya. Give me your clothes underneath. Hurry!"

He looked at her and then understood. It took them only a few seconds, fumbling madly with buttons and zippers, but in the end Seth was still hidden in a cloak of black, and Miriam wore his corduroys and a white shirt twice her size.

"My hair," she said.

He spun her around, frantic, and tied her hair in a knot behind her head. She felt for it. Horrible! She needed a ghutra. Anything to cover her head. She ran for the bed, pulled one of the pillows from its case, and tied the case over her head.

"You make a lousy man," Seth said.

"And you make a terrible woman," she said.

Seth reached for her hand. "Come on!"

They ran from the room and headed for the stairs. "Where's the garage?" he asked.

They had come through the garage yesterday, but she'd had other things on her mind. "I don't know. The back! Toward the back."

Together they burst onto the main floor. Seth seemed to know better than she where the back was, because he immediately pulled her into a hall and motioned to the end. They walked quickly now. A servant entered the hall and took two steps before turning back to them.

They walked on, a man and a woman: two strangers in the villa, oddly dressed perhaps, but nothing more. She hoped.

"May I help you?" the servant called after them.

"No," Seth said, and his Arabic was good enough, she thought. He said he'd lost his gift, which meant he was on his own. *They* were on their own.

Dear God, help us.

They found the garage at the back, beyond the study that Miriam had waited in yesterday. A row of cars lined the stalls. Mercedes, all of them. Shouts echoed back in the villa.

"Hurry!" Miriam tore for the first car, suddenly blinded by fury. She would never go back. Not alive. Never!

"I can't see a . . ." Seth ripped the veil from his face, vaulted the railing, and raced for the second car. Hers was locked. So was Seth's.

They tried all five cars. The one on the end ticked as it cooled. It was unlocked. She knew without a doubt that Omar had just arrived in this car.

Seth piled in the driver's side and stabbed the garage-door control.

"You can't drive! They'll stop you; you're a woman," Miriam said. "Women don't drive here." She glanced at the garage door that was rising at Seth's command. "I'll drive."

He hesitated and then pushed over to the passenger side.

Miriam slid behind the wheel and turned the keys. The black

Mercedes thundered to life. Movement from the side caught her attention. Omar stood in the door that led to the house.

You're too late, you filthy pig.

She faced forward, set her jaw, jammed the shifter down, and punched the accelerator. "Neveeerrrrr!" she screamed.

Seth ducked. "Watch it!" They plowed through a half-opened garage door with a wrenching of metal, but Miriam hardly noticed. She was breaking down the walls of prison.

"Go! Go, go, go!" Seth yelled.

She went. Straight for the front gate. But the gate was closed.

Seth grabbed the door handle. "Ram it!"

"Ram it?"

"Punch it!"

"Punch it?"

"Push the accelerator to the floor! It's a Mercedes; we'll make it. Just go hard!"

She had learned to trust him in the desert, and she had no reason to doubt him now. She pressed the gas pedal to the floor and they roared for the gates. They both ducked at the last moment. With a tremendous crash and a jolt that threw Miriam into the steering wheel, the car slammed through the gates. They dragged one of the gates for a few meters and then broke free.

Miriam spun the wheel to the right. The car swerved a few times before she straightened it out. Then they were flying through an intersection to the sound of honking cars.

"Slow down!"

She eased off the pedal. "We made it!"

He stared at her, wearing a sly grin. "For the moment. Do you know where we're going now?"

"Out of the city."

"Then where?"

"Then I don't know where. Do you?"

"No."

An army truck blazed past them and careened around a corner toward a mob of men gathered around a petrol station. So, the coup was underway.

Miriam didn't care. She looked at Seth, hardly able to comprehend his presence. "I can't believe this is happening," she said. "You came for me."

"Did you ever doubt me?"

She looked out her window, still dazed. "This is really happening, isn't it? We are free?"

"Not exactly. The palace is under siege," Seth said. "Looks like it's spreading. Let's hope we can get out of the city."

She only had to consider the matter briefly to know they would never make it out of Saudi Arabia. But they had escaped from Omar, and that was enough. The thought of going back to him made her shudder.

"I won't go back, Seth. I will never go back alive."

Seth didn't seem to have heard her. "What's this light?" he asked, tapping a black box beside the steering column.

"Did you hear me, Seth? Promise me that no matter what happens, you will never allow them to take me alive."

He looked into her eyes. He knew what she was asking. He said nothing.

"I would rather you kill me," she said.

"What's this device?" he asked again.

Her father's car had the same—it was common in a country with many rich and many poor. "It's an antitheft device. If the car is stolen, they can track it."

He looked up at her with round, blank eyes.

"They already know our every move. There's no way out of Saudi Arabia, Seth." Tears swelled again. She started to cry softly at the thought of being touched by Omar. She would far prefer death.

"Promise me, Seth. Not alive. Never alive."

His hand reached over and rested on her shoulder, awkwardly. "I'm not ready to give up yet." His voice was tight. He was fighting emotion as well. "You're free now. That's what matters, right?"

She sniffed. "Yes. And I owe you my life. Again. Thank you. Thank you with all my heart. But I cannot go back. That's all. As long as you understand that."

He looked at her and offered a forced but comforting smile.

"Drive, Miriam. Drive fast."

37

OMAR SPIT TO THE SIDE, furious. "What I'm telling you is that she's with another man!" he said into the phone.

His father's voice boomed in the receiver. "Then find him! And when you do, kill him! This woman makes you look like a fool. She escapes you once and now twice?"

Omar closed his eyes and gripped his hand tight. It was the American; he could feel it in his bones. Who else could have possibly found his way into the palace and then taken her? Who else even knew where he'd kept her? For that matter, he had no idea how even the American could have known.

"It won't be a problem," he said evenly. "You should concern yourself with the rioting. They're tearing the city apart."

"And we expected nothing less," Khalid said. "Let them riot! If the coup fails, it'll be because of the woman, not the protests in the streets. We must have the support of the sheik, and now that support could be threatened."

His father was right, of course. Fahd's supporters needed the opportunity to vent their objection, but in the end they would follow the new king. It was the way of the desert. But if Miriam came to harm, the sheik might become a problem. The old fool had actually ordered him to earn the love of his daughter! *I'll earn her love, old fool. With a whip!*

Khalid's voice eased. "Omar, we are very close. Everything has progressed exactly as I planned it. The borders are sealed; the ministries are sympathetic; the allegiance of the armed forces is split, and they've agreed to stand down. Fahd has until nightfall, and then we will crush him. But without the sheik, I will lose the support of several key ministers and the army. You know this. And you also know that the sheik is not a fool. He will turn on us as quickly as he turned on Fahd if we don't keep our end. Find your wife!"

Omar smiled. His father didn't often show desperation. "You worry too much. We are tracking the car now, headed south. It's low on fuel. I will have my wife before you have the city. And you forget that she is my wife. As long as she is alive, we have our bond with the sheik."

Khalid paused. "If this is the doing of the American, how do you propose to deal with him now where you failed before?"

"This time we are in *my* country. This time I know where they are. This time I will go after them with a great deal of force."

"Don't fail me again, Omar." His father cut the connection.

Omar ground his molars and strode for the driveway. Ten sedans lined the street, waiting. He walked to the first one and slid into the passenger seat. Beside him a simple tracking device showed the location of the stolen Mercedes. Saudi Arabians routinely used the devices; surely Miriam knew that much. But then, she could do little about it. She could exchange cars possibly, but finding a car to steal in this city would not prove as easy as it had been in America. And for that matter, tracking *any* car would be quite simple on these sparse roads. He would use the helicopter if he needed it. Miriam was on the run again, but this time the chase would be a short one.

"We have twenty men and are well armed," Assir said.

Omar nodded. "Go."

The train of cars moved out, a long black snake of Mercedes slithering through Riyadh's streets and then onto the highway, south toward Jiza.

Smoke from burning tires blackened the sky to the east. Scattered gunfire popped sporadically. The highway was nearly deserted, an uncommon sight for the noonhour. Change floated in the air. Surprising how easily and quickly it could come when all the pieces were in place. For twenty years, a rising tide among fundamental factions had threatened Fahd's power, and now someone would finally succeed. In reality, fundamentalists comprised more than half the country; the coup was nothing more than returning power to the majority. By day's end, the kingdom of Saudi Arabia would have a new face. His father's face, the face of Khalid bin Mishal; but ultimately, his own face.

His mind returned to Miriam. How ironic that a woman was proving to be the final stronghold. The next time he put his hand on her, he would not release her until she understood what it meant to be one of his women.

"Faster, Assir."

They tried stopping for fuel once, but the station was surrounded by a mob. Then they were south of the city. Turning back to find petrol would only increase the likelihood of running into the pursuit Omar had surely taken up. If Seth could have seen the futures . . .

But he wasn't seeing the futures. And if he was right, he wouldn't be seeing anything beyond his own eyes for a long time. At least five hours, if ever.

He'd tried to remove the small security box. He'd kicked at it in a frenzied attempt to disable it, to no avail. The tiny red light refused to stop blinking.

"We're running out of gas," Seth said. "This isn't good."

Miriam drove with both hands white on the steering wheel, her mind scrambling for sense. The desert sands drifted by on either side, strewn with sandstone and small shacks.

Seth lowered his head into his hands and groaned. He was as frightened as she had ever seen him.

"Please, Seth. You're frightening me."

"*I'm* frightening you? Or the fact that we're almost out of gas, with a maniac on our tail is frightening you?"

"*You're* frightening me! We can only do what we can do. We've made it this far—maybe there is a way. If not—"

"Don't say 'if not,'" he said. "How can you be so nonchalant about this?"

It was true—she did feel a certain peace that she hadn't felt before.

She'd been in the jaws of a living hell and she had escaped. It was enough to make a part of her giddy.

"I was dead in there, Seth. At least for now I'm alive."

"Well, I for one would like to keep you alive. I realize our situation looks hopeless, but I can't just give up, not after all we've been through. Doesn't make sense."

He had a point. Still, it looked hopeless.

"You say you won't see again for five hours. Maybe we can survive five hours."

"Maybe," he said, but he couldn't hide the dread on his face.

He took a deep breath and let it out slowly. "Okay. We have to find a place to hole up. If we run out of gas on the highway, we're toast. Do any of these side roads lead anywhere?" He indicated a dirt road that ran west from the highway.

"I don't know. They must go somewhere."

He turned and looked out the rear window.

"Any sign?" she asked.

"No. Take the next dirt road. We have to get off the main road."

"If they're close, they will see our dust."

"That's a chance we'll have to take. I'm sure they know where we are anyway."

Miriam slowed at the next exit, turned right, and motored up a packed dirt road that ran straight west. They were a good thirty kilometers south of the city now. Perhaps the riots had slowed Omar's pursuit. Maybe they were out of range for tracking.

"What's west of here?" Seth asked.

"The desert. Jiza."

They rode in silence for several minutes.

"Did I tell you that you look ridiculous in that abaaya?" she asked. "You look like a monk."

He faced her. "Yes." They shared a brief smile and Seth turned back to his window again.

"Did I tell you that I couldn't get you off my mind?" he asked.

"I was on your mind in America?" she asked. He, too, then.

"Like a plague."

"Is that a good thing?"

"Depends how infectious the plague is," Seth said.

"Now your American jargon is losing me."

"It depends on whether you have the same plague that I have," he said.

She thought about that. He was referring to his feelings for her, and he was asking if she shared them. If she loved him as he did her.

"How could I possibly not love you?" she said softly.

"Yes, of course. It's hard not to love your savior."

There was no sign of civilization this far out in the desert. They drove over a knoll and dipped into the vacant valley ahead. Dust was boiling behind them in clouds of brown. On the dashboard, the fuel indicator rested a millimeter below the E.

"I think we may die together out in this desert, Seth Border. If you could still see the futures, that would be the most likely future, wouldn't it?"

He thought a moment. "Maybe."

"Then before I die I should tell you that you've changed my life. I can't ever return to what I was before I met you. You've nearly ruined my faith in Allah. You've made it impossible for me to love any man who is not as gentle and understanding to a woman as you have been. You've shown me true freedom."

He smiled. "I'm terribly sorry."

"Don't be. I will die free. It's better than living in death."

Seth pointed to a shack that nestled at the base of a cliff to their right. "What's that?"

"Looks like an abandoned home. A squatter maybe."

"As good a place as any."

There was no driveway that she could see. The ground was rough and rocky. She swung the car off the road and gunned the motor. They bounced over the dirt.

"Just like Death Valley," Seth said.

She chuckled. Why not?

"Like Bonnie and Clyde," she said.

"Just don't run over the place. Park behind."

"Absolutely."

"Well, okay then." He smiled, but she knew he forced it.

Miriam slid the car to a stop between the rickety old structure and the cliff and turned off the ignition. Dust drifted past them. A faint ticking sounded from the engine, but otherwise it fell silent.

The shack was no more than twenty feet by twenty feet, constructed from mud bricks with a tin roof. A single grenade would tear it to pieces.

"Ready?" she asked.

"Now or never."

They climbed out and ran around the hut. A faint dust lingered over the road they'd come down, but as of yet they could see no pursuit from the direction of the highway.

"You think they missed us?" she asked hopefully.

"Maybe."

"You don't think so."

"We can always hope," he said.

The wooden door leaned dangerously to one side. Seth pulled it open, stepped through after her, and closed it as best he could behind them.

Light fell across a dirt floor from a boarded window beside the door. A rustic wooden table stood to the right, surrounded by two shelves and a couple of benches. A small bed made of planks sat in the shadows opposite the table.

Miriam crossed to the shelves and righted two large candles. Several pots and pans rested on the table next to an old dusty Qur'an.

"It's a common hut," she said. "Used by travelers on occasion." She picked up a box of matches and struck one. "They even left matches."

The candles lit the room enough to dispel the shadows. Miriam replaced the matches and turned around. Seth stood looking between the cracks of the window. He did look like a monk standing there, craning for a view, she thought. The monk who had been able to see many futures. Who was neither Christian nor Muslim, but who had suggested that she should pray to God. To the God of the perfect prophet, Jesus, a prophet to both religions.

She watched his Adam's apple move through a swallow and her heart swelled. She looked at his strained face and knew that despite his attempts to put on a good face, her monk was a desperate man at the moment. And for good reason. He had come to the end of his world.

Not an hour ago, she'd been as desperate, at her own end. But now she was seeing with different eyes. No ending could compare to the one from which she'd been rescued.

Seth turned from the window and walked to the bed, one hand on his hips, the other gripping his jaw, deep in thought. He stopped with his back to her, facing the dark corner.

Miriam walked slowly toward him. "Seth."

His shoulders rose and fell in a deep sigh.

"Seth." She stood behind him. "There is one more thing I must tell you." She put her hand on his shoulder, but he didn't turn.

She pulled him gently and he turned. His eyes swam in tears—one had broken down his cheek, leaving a trail that glistened in the candlelight.

"No, there are two things that I will tell you," she said quietly and wiped the tear from his face. "The first is that you have *not* failed me. You think you have and it's destroying you. But I am happy to die with you today."

He closed his eyes, fighting back more tears. She stepped into him and pulled his head down to her shoulder. She stroked the back of his head, fighting the knot in her own throat.

Suddenly he lifted his head, wiped his eyes, and sniffed once. "This is ridiculous. I don't know what my problem is." He turned away. "I've always been able to reason my way through this world. I've always been strong, you know." He walked to the window, glanced out, then turned and leaned back against the wall. "I really don't know what I was thinking, coming to Saudi Arabia."

She took a step toward him. "You came to give my life back to me," she said. "And you've done that."

He looked at her and his eyes misted again. She knew he couldn't understand how freeing her did anything but postpone the end.

"The other thing I must tell you is that I wasn't completely honest with you in the car," she said. "You've done more than change my life. You have stolen from me." She smiled. "Do you know what the punishment for theft is in this country? You're terribly guilty."

He just stared at her without understanding. She softened her smile.

"You have stolen my soul and my mind," she said. "You have stolen my heart. I am no longer complete without you."

The words sat between them, beautiful and elegant and demanding of silence.

She walked up to him and touched his face gently. "I am in love with you, Seth. I think I have been in love with you since we first met, in the bathroom."

She leaned forward, pushed herself to her tiptoes, and touched her lips against his. It was the first time she herself had kissed a man, and she felt as though a fire were sweeping over her mouth.

For a moment he did not respond. Then she felt his hands on her waist, and he kissed her in return, soft as a rose petal.

He suddenly pulled her to him and kissed her again, on her lips and then on her cheek. He wrapped his arms around her and held her tight. A soft sob broke from his chest and he caught himself.

"It's okay, my dear. We will be okay now," she said.

"I love you, Miriam. I missed you so much."

She was going to die—she knew that. But she felt safe and complete, and if she could arrange it, she would die in his arms.

38

CLIVE STUDIED THE PRINTOUT and drew his finger over the lines of print, nerves strung tight. Pencil marks covered the margins in a maze of arrows and notes. Three months of Seth's foresight had translated into seventy-three pages. He'd circled each event that mentioned the sheik, fifty at least—Abu Ali al-Asamm played heavily in a government run by Khalid. The question was what part of this future yielded any useful information that might be common to all futures, including the one they faced at the moment.

The coup was only nine hours old, and already the world was responding with something close to panic. A militant Islamic government in Saudi Arabia would play havoc in the Middle East, providing a safe haven for terrorists and dissidents bent on the destruction of a non-Islamic world. Those who followed the politics of the region knew that the destabilization in Saudi Arabia could easily spread to other Arab countries, as well as to other Muslim countries.

Fox News had been the first network to point out the fact that, at least in the understanding of many scholars, the prophet Mohammed had indeed ended his days teaching the destruction of Christians and Jews, rather than seeking peace with them as many Western Muslims claimed. Religious clerics had since pointed to Mohammed's earlier teachings that stressed peace, but in the prophet's own words, his later militant teachings superseded his earlier peaceful ones. And the fact that Mohammed had declared himself the *last* prophet sealed these later teachings as the final revelation of God. Bar none.

It was a simple reality, one that had been avoided for decades in the interest of political correctness. The only real solution for Islam was to admit that Mohammed had perhaps strayed in his final teachings. But only a few brave clerics were willing to walk that plank.

The military was already developing plans to take out a Saudi kingdom run by Khalid, but Clive held a printout of the future in his hands, and it wasn't reading as though an attempt to remove a militant king would be easy. In fact, according to Seth, they would fail, at least in the first three months.

He glanced at the clock. Time was running out. According to a call from within Saudi Arabia, Khalid would storm the palace in less than four hours.

"Come on, Seth," he muttered. "What am I looking for?"

An image of Seth bent over the computer, typing away madly, ran across his mind. What made a mind brilliant?

"You're still out there, aren't you, Seth? This isn't over, is it?"

Clive looked back at the printout. The secretary was right about one thing: A militant government would be dependent on the cooperation of the sheik and the Shi'i. A thin thread of an idea began to form, but it refused to gel into anything concrete. If Seth still had his gift, he would be able to tell Clive whether this mind-bending exercise would yield anything of value in the next few hours.

Forget Seth. Back to the printout.

❧

Sheik Abu Ali al-Asamm stood at the entrance to his tent, looking over the valley filled with his men. If Allah wills it, he thought. For twenty years, thirty years, Allah had not; today he had changed his mind.

Riyadh sat on the horizon, dirtied by a haze of smoke from a hundred tire fires. The afternoon prayer call was just now warbling over the city. *Yes, pray, my fellow Muslims. Pray, as Mohammed would have prayed.*

The House of Saud had grown softer with each passing decade—Aziz would roll in his grave if he could see Fahd today. They had left the fundamental teachings of the prophet for favor with the West. What would Mohammed say to that? Abu Ali grunted. So now those who clung to the prophet's teachings were called fundamentalists and regarded with distaste. How could anyone presume to follow the teachings of any prophet and not remain true to the fundamentals? Was religion a thing to change with cultural moods?

In the West, yes, evidently. They even called Christians who clung to the teachings of Jesus fundamentalists. Ha! Any devout man was a scandal in the whitewashed minds of the West. In the sheik's way of thinking, to stray from the fundamental teachings of either Jesus or Mohammed was scandalous!

Abdallah approached from behind. "We have received another message, Abu."

The sheik didn't remove his gaze from the city. "From whom?"

"It's the Americans," he said. "They are saying that, should the coup succeed, they will not sit by and allow fifty years of progress to slip into the sea."

Al-Asamm closed his eyes. Why the Americans insisted on putting their fingers into every jar, he would never understand.

"Go on."

"They say they are drawing up plans for the removal of Khalid already."

Al-Asamm smiled. They were a cunning lot; he would give them that. And it was true that his bloodline would only be fully established through the birth of a child. But they underestimated the value of both his mind and his word. *Everything* was negotiable in the American mind, whether it be their own religion or the writings of the prophet Mohammed or the word of his follower, Sheik Abu Ali al-Asamm.

"Tell them I am only doing what the prophet would himself insist. Tell them I am more interested in the will of Allah than in the will of men. Then remind them that they are merely men. Perhaps they would do well to listen to the voice of God. God spoke plainly through his prophet Mohammed and he said to destroy men like Fahd." The sheik paused. "On second thought, don't tell them that last part. It will only send them into a panic. Just tell them to mind their own business and stay on their own side of the ocean."

Abdallah dipped his head and walked to the room where they kept the telex machine. Abu Ali crossed his arms and walked to his mat. It was time to pray.

39

THEY SAT AT THE TABLE, her hands in his, sharing precious, impossibly mad minutes together. As they talked, Seth periodically stood and crossed to the window before returning.

Their predicament was hardly comprehensible. Miriam was a Muslim, at least as much as she could be one now, and Seth was a Christian, at least in heritage.

She was a Saudi princess, daughter to the great Sheik Abu Ali al-Asamm, and now she was married to a Saudi prince. He was . . . well, what was he? An American, surely destined to change the world by discovering light travel or a longer lasting light bulb, but an American, not a Saudi. And they were in love; this was a problem.

He told her briefly about his trip to Saudi Arabia. About how he'd awakened in Cheyenne Mountain after seeing her, and about how he passed through Saudi immigration. But he seemed oddly disconnected from it now. He'd had these powerful experiences so recently, but now he told her as if they were only distant dreams.

For Miriam they were not distant abstractions at all. Their implications burrowed through her mind in a terrible yet wonderful way. A particular truth resident in Seth's sight, something she hadn't named yet, contradicted what she had always known about God. Was it really possible?

Miriam stood and walked toward the candles. When the light was on in Seth's mind, he could see so clearly, but when it was off, he became blind. Yet the truth was still there, waiting to be lit by a candle, wasn't it? And what was that truth? Could she have been so wrong?

Seth sat in silence behind her. She lifted her hand and slowly ran it over the flame. So small and yet so real.

"Do you think it's possible that so many millions of Muslims could be wrong about Jesus?" she asked. She felt her pulse quicken even in speaking the question.

He was quiet.

"That he was only a prophet?" she said.

"They must be."

Miriam turned. "The implications are almost too much to bear."

"I know." He looked at the candle. "A week ago I would have laughed at anyone who suggested that he was . . ."

"God," she finished for him.

Seth nodded.

"And yet according to your gospels, he claimed to be," Miriam said.

"Yes, he did."

"Then why don't you believe it? I have my reasons, but after all that you have seen, you've still pushed it from your mind."

"I wouldn't say that. It's a bit of a shock to learn after twenty-six years that one of your basic presuppositions might be wrong."

"Might be?"

He looked at her. The candlelight flickered in his eyes. "Is," he said.

"And still you don't believe it. How do you expect me, who grew up a Muslim, to believe it?"

"I'm not asking you to believe it. And why do you say that I don't?"

"Because if you did, you would be asking him to change the futures again," she said.

"I'm not seeing the futures."

"Yes, I know. Every time you've seen God change the future, you've been able to see it with your gift. You see what happens when you depend on your mind?"

"What do you mean?"

"When you see things in your mind, they're easy to believe. All your life you've depended on this brilliance of yours. So now that these things—these futures you see—are no longer *in* your mind, you lose faith."

He stared at her. She could practically see the wheels spinning behind his eyes.

"See, even now you're dissecting what I've just said. You prayed and you saw God in the futures and you believed, enough to come to Saudi Arabia. But now that you can't see the results of your prayer, you lose faith. You have no faith in God."

"Faith?"

"Yes. Faith. Believing without seeing. You've never had faith, have you?"

"Hindus have faith in what they can't see just as much as Jews or Christians or Muslims. So do evolutionists. You can't convince any of them that they're wrong, because they ignore evidence in favor of what they want to see."

"And now your unbelief may cost us our lives," she said.

He stood, eyes wide.

"Think about it, Seth."

He turned and stared at the boarded-up window. He looked not unlike a stunned child who'd just seen a card trick.

"It's the only thing that makes sense," she said.

Seth spun back. "That's it! That's gotta be it!"

Miriam felt his excitement as if it were a drug passing between them. "If it was God who gave you your gift to see the futures, then should we assume that he's less powerful or less willing because neither of us can see him now?" she asked.

"Faith in whom?"

"In God."

"*Which* God?"

Yes indeed. This was the crux of the matter. "It does matter, doesn't it?"

"Yes. It does," he said. He crossed the room and straddled the bench. "If we're to believe, to have faith, then we have to put our faith in a reality, not in something that is, as a matter of fact, untrue. I can't just throw out what I *know* to be true, or I may end up putting my faith in a stone, right?"

"Yes." She knew what he was trying to say, and suddenly she wished he would just say it.

"In every instance, the future that I saw altered was altered by the God of Jesus."

It was precisely what she'd been thinking.

"Jesus," she said.

"Yes, Jesus."

They stared at each other. Miriam stood and crossed to the window. She crossed her arms and looked out. A small plume of dust rose on the horizon, but it was too far to tell its source. For Seth the issue was faith. For her it was the object of her faith.

"Then I suggest that we put our faith in him," she said.

"Believe without seeing," Seth said.

"Pray to Jesus," she said.

"Just like that?"

She turned. "Just like that."

40

OMAR HELD UP HIS HAND. "Stop."

Assir slowed the Mercedes to a halt. They'd crested a small knoll on the dirt road. The desert rolled out before them, silent, with outcroppings of rock, but otherwise unbroken except for this trail that divided north from south. A small shack rested at the base of a cliff, three hundred meters ahead and a hundred meters to the right. According to the tracking device, the car was there, perhaps behind the hut.

"The common hut." He pointed at the cliff. Assir eased the car forward and Omar picked up the radio. "They are in the common hut to our right. Do you see it?"

The radio crackled. "Yes."

"Weapons ready. Form a perimeter around the front. I don't want to leave an escape route. Don't underestimate them." He tossed the radio on the seat, pulled out his nine millimeter, and chambered a round.

The cars cut across the desert and approached the shack from multiple angles, raising ribbons of dust as they converged on the cliff. Assir followed a pair of fresh tire tracks and brought the car to a stop fifty meters from the shanty. Dust drifted by and then cleared. From here the hut looked abandoned.

The other Mercedeses stopped, one by one, in a great semicircle around the shack, cutting off any possible angle of escape.

"There's a car to the rear of the hut," Assir said.

Omar nodded. The Mercedes purred softly under him. Still there was no movement. For a full minute he waited, not expecting anything, just waiting. No one spoke over the radio; they would only follow his lead. It would be a menacing sight, this display of power, for Miriam to see through the cracks of the door. Ten black cars with tinted windshields poised ominously around the flimsy hiding place, waiting at his leisure for the final kill.

This is what it means to play with me, Miriam.

Omar opened his door. The afternoon heat immediately displaced the car's conditioned air, coaxing a sweat from his brow before he'd stood from the car. He looked down the line of cars over the roof of his own. One by one their doors opened and twenty men joined him, standing casually behind the cover of their doors.

Omar faced the shack. "I will give you to the count of ten to come out unharmed," he called. "Then we will open fire." He lifted his pistol and fired a round into the corner brick.

"One!"

"Don't be a stupid fool," Miriam's voice called out.

The strength of her voice surprised him. This in front of his men. He clenched his jaw.

"If you kill me, your father will take your head off," Miriam called out. "And if he fails, then I promise you my father will not! Put your silly toy away."

Silence. A hawk called from the cliff. She was right, of course. He hadn't expected to be able to call their bluff. But neither had he expected her to dismiss him as a fool. *Don't you know that I could easily walk in there, put a bullet in the American's head, and drag you out by the hair, you wench?* He clenched his teeth.

"And if you think you can come in here and kill Seth before dragging me out, you'd better reconsider," she called out. "Do you really believe that I would allow myself to be taken alive, only to be forced to look at your hideous face for the rest of my life?"

She was defying him in front of his men to draw out his anger. He knew it and was powerless to stop the chill that ripped through his bones. He decided then, staring through the heat at the shack, that Miriam would live only long enough to bear him a child. It was all he needed from her.

"You're making the noise of an animal," he said calmly. "I would like to speak to the man. To the American."

"Take a hike, Omar," a male voice called out. "She said she doesn't want to see you. *Capisce?*"

Perhaps for the first time in his adult life, Omar was speechless. Stunned and unfathoming.

"Okay, I'm sorry," Seth called out. "I take it back. But I'm afraid that Miriam has fallen hopelessly in love with me. We must allow love to—"

"You are talking about my wife!" Omar screamed. "My *wife!*"

His voice echoed off the cliff.

"Yes, well, that is a problem, I'll admit. But we've been praying to God in here and we think we have a solution to this mess. We've decided that it will be okay to share it with you. That is, if you're man enough to come in and join us."

The American was as naive as he was foolish. Omar glanced at his watch. In two hours the sheik would storm the palace. It was time to be done with this foolishness.

"Your wife has demanded that I kill her if you come in after her," the American called. "It will be like Romeo and Juliet. We'll both die, but we'll die in the embrace of true love. I'm unarmed, but there's a shard of glass in here that we think will do the trick."

Would he do such a thing? No.

On the other hand, the American had to know the situation was hopeless for him. And Miriam would probably prefer death over capture. The realization drove a small wedge of agitation into Omar's mind. He glanced down the line of cars. Seth stood to gain nothing by killing him. Twenty others here would storm the shack and take out their fury on him.

"I'm going in," Omar said to Assir.

"Sir—"

"He has nothing to gain by killing me. If anything happens, storm the place."

"And Miriam?"

Omar hesitated. "She stays alive."

He stepped past the car and walked for the common hut. Assir barked an order to the others behind him.

"The gun, Omar," Seth called. "Drop the gun."

He tossed the gun to the sand and walked on. The door came open with a gentle tug. He stepped into the dimly lit room.

"Close the door."

Omar turned to the corner where the American stood dressed in an abaaya, eyes flashing in the candlelight.

"Close the door!" Seth said.

Miriam stood beside him, wincing at the shard of glass he pressed against her neck. She was dressed like a man. They were both mad. Omar pulled the door closed and stood before them.

"Think I was kidding?" Seth asked. "Empty your pockets."

Omar hesitated and then pulled out some coins. He tossed them onto the table. "You do realize that there is no way out of here. We are surrounded by twenty heavily armed men."

Seth seemed not to have heard. "Pull up your pant legs."

The American was after his knife. How did he know? Omar pulled out a ten-inch Bowie knife from the sheath around his calf. He briefly considered rushing Seth then, but dismissed the idea with one look at the pressure of the glass against Miriam's skin. She could not be harmed. Not yet.

He dropped the weapon on the table.

Seth retrieved the knife, walked to the window, and slipped the glass shard through a crack. He waved the knife through the air and held his hand out to the table, inviting Omar to sit.

"Please. Have a seat."

Miriam backed to the corner, giving him a wide berth.

"We don't have time for this," Omar said. "You have nothing to gain by playing these games. You will give me my wife, or I will take her by force. It's that simple."

"Your wife. Yes. Actually, that's what I want to talk to you about. Indulge me. Like you say, you have twenty men outside."

Omar found something about the American compelling. This

man with the loose blond hair, clothed in this black dress, possessed one of the highest intellects of any living man, they said. It hardly seemed possible. What could the man possibly be thinking?

"You're in no position to order me around, you fool. This is—"

"Sit!" Seth spun behind Miriam and pressed the knife against her neck. "Sit, man! Sit, sit, sit!"

The American was crazed. For a moment they stared into each other's eyes. Seth wasn't as confident as he sounded. Omar had learned to recognize fear in another man, and he saw it now in the American's eyes. Still, he had the knife. If he were in the American's position, he would not hesitate to use it.

Omar walked to the end of the table and sat.

"Excellent." Seth pulled Miriam over to the opposite end. Now the table acted as a barrier between them. This man might not be a warrior, but Omar saw that he'd positioned himself well.

"You say that Miriam is your wife?" Seth asked.

He refused to dignify the question with an answer.

"But I don't think she is," Seth said. "Not really. And she doesn't think she is either."

"This is absurd."

"Shut up. You came; you should at least hear me out."

"Then say what you have to say quickly. The city is burning, or hadn't you noticed?"

"We don't think she's married because she hasn't married you, Omar. She was forced to go through a ceremony, true enough. But that's like saying I'm rich because I walk into a bank. You have to take possession of the money before you become rich. Miriam hasn't taken possession of you." He forced a grin. "But don't worry, we're not going to force the issue. We know that in both your eyes and her father's eyes, she is married and, unfortunately, married to you."

"Then get on with it."

"We want you to divorce her."

Omar stared at him, caught off guard. The man was not only mad; he was a brazen fool.

"That's our intent here. In your tradition, you can divorce her by simply telling her in front of witnesses that you divorce her. Easy come, easy go. If you divorce Miriam, then all our problems are solved. The coup will fail because her father will withdraw his support; you won't have to chase an unwilling bride around the world any longer; she will be free to pursue the love she has for me. It's a perfect plan."

Omar looked at him, unsure if he had actually heard this man correctly. Had he misplaced some of his English vocabulary?

"If you knew our ways, you would know that neither of you is a legal witness," Omar said. Rage spread down his neck. "Even if I wanted to, I couldn't divorce my wife here, you imbecile! You called me into this place with the expectation that I would divorce my wife? Simply because you ask me?"

"No. I'm asking you to divorce your wife because it's the best for Saudi Arabia and because she loves me. And because we think that God wants you to."

"I won't listen to this!"

Seth slammed the flat of his palm on the table. "You will listen!" He tapped his temple with his forefinger. "Think, man! Think!"

Omar squinted, unnerved by this presumptuous show.

"Okay, here's how it works," Seth said. "I evaded you and a thousand cops in the States. How? Because I could see into the future, right?"

He didn't respond.

"Right?"

"Perhaps."

"Not perhaps. That's what happened. I could see everything the police might do, and I knew what to do to encourage them to do what I wanted them to do. As long as it was a possibility, I could facilitate it." Seth and Miriam exchanged a look. "The future can be changed. We can change it; God can change it."

"Believe me when I say that there's no possibility that I will divorce my wife," Omar said. "So there's no way to facilitate that future. This is utter nonsense!"

"Ahhh. But we've both come to the conclusion that there *is* a possibility you will divorce Miriam," Seth said. "There's a possibility, not because I've seen it, but because we think God wills it. He gave me this gift to protect her from you, and to keep the Middle East from spinning out of control. So there must be a way it can be done. Whether any of us can see how or not."

"Then we will see Allah's will," Omar said. "And I can assure you that Allah's will is to sustain the marriage constituted in his name."

"Actually, we were thinking about the will of another God. The God of Jesus."

Omar felt a small twitch in his right eye.

"You *are* aware of Jesus," Seth said. "The perfect prophet. Are you willing to pray to the God of the perfect prophet and ask for his will?"

"I've already prayed to God and he's given me a wife. This is utter absurdity!" Omar stood to his feet, furious.

"Sit!" Seth slashed at the air with the blade. "You're refusing to pray to God?"

"Don't be a fool!"

"Sit!"

The American was out of control. He had the appearance of a man who would kill. Omar sat.

Seth took a deep breath. "Will you allow *us* to pray to God?"

"No!"

"Your whole society's based on the will of God. How could you not allow us to pray?"

"This society is waiting for me to execute God's will, in a city fifty miles north of here. We are returning Saudi Arabia to God!"

"What if Miriam agrees to go with you willingly if you allow us to pray?"

Omar clenched his fist to stop a tremble that had begun in his fingers. So this was their ploy—a game of prayer?

"If you allow us to pray and no future materializes in which you divorce Miriam, she will go with you without objection." Seth exchanged another glance with her. She looked nervous but didn't argue.

Never in his life could Omar have imagined a scenario as absurd as this. Fires were burning the city, and he was in a hut arguing about prayer with an American infidel and a woman who was his wife. He closed his eyes, desperate for control. Seth still held the knife.

What if he did play their game? Miriam would be forced by her word to come peacefully. He could then kill Seth and be done with it. If, on the other hand, he resorted to force now, Seth might kill Miriam.

"Your praying is a waste of time," he said and opened his eyes. "We do not have time for this. Please, be sensible."

"Be sensible? You do have time; you know you do. And if this prayer is a waste of time, it is your best weapon. You will have us! Surely you have enough above the neck to understand that much."

The man could hardly speak without insult. On the other hand, he was making sense in a childish sort of way.

"Then pray," Omar said.

"It would take us an hour to pray to him," Seth said.

"Nonsense!" Omar slammed his fist on the table. "A prayer takes only a few minutes, at the most."

"Not this prayer. We must have an hour! One hour, no more, no less."

"You're playing a game with me! You're only stalling!"

"Maybe. But isn't it better for you to stall for an hour than to risk killing the one woman on whom the future of this whole kingdom is staked? One hour."

However mad this notion of prayer, Omar could not refute the argument. He glanced at his watch, and then back at Seth. He stood and stormed for the door. "One hour."

"I'm sorry, but we need you to stay here for that hour. We want to pray with you."

Omar whirled around, furious. "This is the most absurd suggestion I've ever heard! I did not come here to pray for an hour with the man who has stolen my wife!"

"Still, in view of the agreement we've just offered, it makes a lot of sense. Something I would think royalty would weigh carefully."

Omar stared at Seth for a long time, scrambling for a reason to leave now and be done with this. None came to him. He finally pulled out his cell phone and called Assir.

"Yes?"

"I will be out in one hour. Wait for me."

He closed the phone before Assir had a chance to question him and walked to the table.

"You pray. I will wait."

"That will be fine," Seth said.

Miriam stood in the corner, doing her best to hide the quiver that worked its way through her body. Seth played his part very convincingly, she thought. It was a wonder he hadn't actually cut her.

Their predicament was as much her fault as Seth's. She'd lectured him on faith, and now he was going off the deep end with it. That was his way. Now they were committing their lives to faith. It was unnerving.

On the other hand, they were fresh out of options, as he put it. If she was right about faith, then the plan was foolproof, he insisted. It was like learning to fly an airplane during the day, and then trying it once at night. The principles of aerodynamics didn't change just because you couldn't see. The future could be changed through prayer, despite their inability to see it.

Faith.

Yes, but a fall from ten thousand feet was still a fall from ten thousand feet. They were flying blind, and she wasn't sure they weren't in a free fall. Looking at Seth now, some of the confidence seemed to have leaked out of even him.

"Yes, that'll be just fine," Seth repeated.

He waited for Omar to sit, and then he led Miriam toward the bed, winking once courageously. They stood facing Omar, who glared at them with dark eyes.

"You ready?" he whispered.

"Ready how? What do we do?"

"We pray."

"Pray. How do we pray?"

They held eyes.

"Do I lift my hands like you did in the desert, or do I kneel like I always do?" Miriam asked.

He thought about that. "I'm sure it doesn't matter. But I say we lift our hands together. We might as well give Omar a show. Think of it as Mount Carmel."

"Elijah," she said, remembering his explanation of the altars in the desert.

Sweat ran down Seth's temples. They both knew that unless God intervened, this was the end. Even if Seth's gift returned on the same cycle it had come and gone earlier, they would have to wait well over an hour. Omar would never delay beyond this hour. He was up against his own deadline—the future of Saudi Arabia hung in the balance. He'd agreed to the prayer only because, in his mind, he was assured of success. Omar would surely take his chances the next time. He would simply do his best to kill Seth without allowing him to harm Miriam.

They both knew that Omar's best was adequate, even if Seth did intend to kill Miriam, something Seth refused to discuss.

"Remember, this worked before," Seth said. "Twice. Like you said—faith." He forced a smile. "Okay?"

"Okay."

He lifted his hands toward the ceiling, knife pointed to the ceiling, eyes still on Omar. Seth was taking no chances. She glanced over and saw that Omar still eyed them, and then followed Seth's lead by raising her hands. She closed her eyes.

"O God," Seth said aloud. "Shaper of futures." He stopped. Miriam opened her eyes and he glanced down at her.

"What did you call him before?" she asked.

"God of Jesus."

She thought about that. Did it really matter what they called him? Seth wasn't accustomed to praying; she was.

"I'll pray," she said.

He nodded.

"God of Jesus, hear our prayer to you. Make a way for your will to find its end in us this day." She prayed quickly, in a low voice. "Jesus, who is God, save us, I pray. Save us from this evil man who claims to know you and who will kill in your name today. Have pity on your people, the Arabs in the kingdom of Saudi Arabia. Save them from this terrible man who will make war on other Arabs and use your created creature, the woman, as his footstool." A swell of emotion flooded Miriam's chest and clogged her throat. What if God himself actually heard this prayer and intended to answer?

"I beg you for my life and for Seth's life," she prayed in earnest now. "Do not let us die today. And do not allow this man to take possession of me as if I were his dog!"

She stopped. If the God of Jesus would answer that, he would have to move a mountain.

She swallowed. "You try it," she said.

Seth cleared his throat. "God of Jesus, and Jesus, who is God, change this future so that we can live. Do not allow Omar to destroy what you have created. Give us a way out. Ruin this man's plans. Amen."

Seth lowered his hands and she followed suit. She glanced at Omar and saw that he was still staring, eyes dark and angry.

"Should we ask for anything very specific?" Seth whispered.

"I think God's smarter than we are," she said. "I believe he heard us and will answer as he sees fit."

He nodded. "Now what?"

"Now we wait."

"Now you are finished," Omar said, making to stand. "You have failed. Now—"

"Sit!" Seth bellowed.

Omar seemed to flinch, if just barely.

"Now we wait," Seth said, calmly. "One hour. As you agreed."

41

CLIVE HAD READ AND REREAD THE PRINTOUTS three times when the idea dropped into his mind without warning. It wasn't the most unique thought—frankly, he wondered how he'd missed it earlier. He blinked and reconsidered. If Miriam were killed, the coup would fail, wouldn't it? Yes, everything was based on the bloodline Miriam would give the sheik. And if Seth was in the country . . .

Clive grabbed the cell phone and hit the last-call button.

"Smaley."

"I think I have something, Peter." Clive took a breath. "On the surface this may not seem like an obvious course of action, but trust me on this." He paused. Smaley would never buy this.

"Well?"

"Only the mixing of blood would guarantee the sheik royalty in his line. What would happen if we were to cut off the bloodline?"

"I'm not sure I follow."

"If anything were to happen that would *prevent* Miriam from bearing Omar a child, the sheik might reconsider his allegiance. He would have no guarantee of royalty in his bloodline without a son. Marriage alone doesn't cut it. The sheik needs a son out of this."

"I still don't see how—"

"If something were to happen to Miriam, she couldn't bear a son, could she?"

Smaley was quiet for a moment. "You're suggesting what? That we kill Miriam? We don't have a way to do that."

"No. I'm suggesting we *tell* the sheik that we will kill his daughter if the coup succeeds. We buy time."

"Buy time for what?"

"For Seth."

Smaley paused. "I thought we settled this. Even if we knew Seth was there and in play, he's not an assassin. I already made it clear; we don't involve him."

"I'm not suggesting that we use him as an assassin. He wouldn't kill Miriam anyway; he's in love with her, for heaven's sake. Telling the sheik is a bluff. Worst case, we buy time for another plan. This may be our last chance."

"You're saying that I tell the sheik we have an assassin in their country with Miriam in his sights, ready to pull the trigger and end her life the instant a coup goes through. If Seth *is* in play, we can't put him in that position. And if he isn't, I can't put us in a position of crying wolf. We'll erode our own credibility."

"We have to!" Clive wiped his forehead of sweat. Smaley was right, but Clive's gut was telling him that Seth was still out there and needed time. Time for what, he wasn't sure. Just time.

"I've been after Seth, remember?" Clive said. "They have to catch him to kill him. This buys us more time. This gives him a chance."

"This is crazy. We don't even know that he's in the country. What if the Saudis decide to take Seth out? Worse, what if they have already? Besides, the sheik makes one call to verify that his daughter's fine and the whole ploy falls flat. It buys us a few minutes and costs us credibility."

"Maybe. But it forces the sheik to make that call. And taking Seth isn't that easy. Look, don't ask me why this makes sense. Just do it. Please. The idea that we have a man in place ready to kill his daughter will get the sheik's attention. Guaranteed. And he'll realize that there's a possibility we could take her out after the coup, before she bears a child. Trust me, this will slow him down. He won't be able to rule out an assassin in a matter of minutes. It could take him hours."

"We're down to two hours," Smaley said. "Delaying them one more won't change a thing."

"Unless his daughter really *is* in danger. Unless Seth has actually made some progress. Don't count him out. This guy may still be able to see their moves before they can."

Another long silence. Smaley talked off line to someone and then returned.

"Okay, Clive. I'll see what I can do. That's all I can promise."

The sheik stormed into the tent. "That's impossible! How can they have an assassin in place already?"

"His name is Seth," Abdallah said. "The one who evaded Hilal and Omar in California."

Seth! The one who could presumably see into the future. The one who seemed to be able to walk through walls. He had come to kill Miriam?

"He was her protector in America. Now he will kill her? Do they think we have the minds of children?"

"They said his first objective is to take her out of the country, but if he is unable, he will kill her. They say he is in love with her."

So, if he could not have her, then he wouldn't allow another man the same privilege. This, Omar might do, but not an American.

"I urge you to consider this threat, Sheik Al-Asamm," Abdallah said. "It makes perfect sense to me."

"Why didn't they tell us this earlier?"

"Perhaps they weren't ready to show their hand. If they'd told us earlier, we would've had enough time to deal with the situation. Now, with just over an hour to go, we are forced to reconsider our plans. Frankly, it's good strategy on their part, bluff or not."

The sheik stepped out of the tent, alarmed, and breathed deeply. The sun was setting, a large orange ball in the horizon. He'd always taken comfort in Miriam's safety for the simple reason that she was too valuable to kill. But he'd never considered the idea that the Americans might kill her to force his hand. A shaft of fear seized him. Would they really do it?

And if Miriam were killed before she bore Omar a child, the sheik's agreement with Khalid would be worthless. His daughter and his dreams of royalty would be smashed in one blow! The Americans could be ruthless when they chose to be.

The sheik whirled around and strode into the tent.

"I must talk to Omar!" he said. "Tell Khalid that I will not move until I am assured my daughter is safe. And please hurry. We don't have much time."

Miriam and Seth sat on the bed, facing Omar. The minutes had ticked away in painful silence. Omar sat stone-faced at the table. The ten Mercedeses purred outside, waiting like tigers crouched to pounce at a word from their master. If not for the fact that Seth still had the knife, Miriam was sure Omar would have given the order already. But he couldn't risk the possibility that Seth might kill her.

The hour had wasted away, and Miriam still had no sense that they had accomplished anything but to delay the inevitable. For her own talk of faith, she felt none of its benefits.

They had remained mostly quiet, but now Miriam knew the end was coming. It hardly mattered what Omar heard. Nothing either of them could say would change these last few minutes. She decided it was time for Omar to hear the truth of the matter.

"Seth," she whispered softly. "No matter what happens I want you to know that I have loved you. Something profound has happened to me, and I believe it has been inspired by God."

"Profound? That's an understatement. Don't lose faith. This isn't over."

"We're running out of time."

Omar glared and she averted her eyes.

"I've been sitting here wondering what I would do if I could see the future," Seth said. He watched Omar like a hawk. But he'd obviously come to the same conclusion as she. They could say nothing that would affect Omar one way or the other.

"And?"

"For one thing, I wouldn't be sweating bullets. Assuming I saw a way out, which I know I would. Faith isn't easy on the mind."

"Very true."

"I'd probably be doing something. Or saying something. Each time God changed the future, I was still required to do something."

"Yes, but what this time?"

"We prayed. That's something."

"But God hasn't changed the future yet."

"We don't know that," Seth said, swallowing. "We don't see it."

She turned and spoke quietly so Omar would not hear. "How much time before you can see again?" she asked.

He wiped the sweat from his brow and whispered. "I don't know."

"We should try to delay—"

"Silence!" Omar said. He stood abruptly. "Your time is finished."

Seth stood and faced the man. They locked gazes for a few long seconds.

"I've played your game and now you will play mine," Omar said. His eyes shifted to Miriam and she immediately diverted her gaze. "You may come willingly as promised, or I will take you by force. The choice is yours."

Miriam stood with them, desperate. "If you take me by force, Seth will kill me!"

"I've decided that Seth is incapable of killing you," Omar said. "Say what you like, this game is now finished."

"Why am I incapable of killing her?" Seth asked.

"You don't have the backbone for killing her."

"You mean that I love her, don't you? You've been watching us for an hour and now you see that I have what you'll never have. Love."

Surprisingly, Omar didn't object. He just stared, eyes blank.

"But you're right," Seth said. He spun the knife in his hand and flipped it through the air. The blade embedded itself in the tabletop and quivered like a spring. "I couldn't bear to hurt any woman, much less the woman I love."

Omar only smiled. "And that is why you don't deserve this flower beside you," he said. "Today you will die."

"I will die only if God has decided that I should die. Neither of us knows that yet, do we?"

Omar reached over and plucked the knife from the wood. "Your hour of prayer is finished. God has not answered you. Now you stand unarmed, surrounded by twenty of my men and you're still foolish enough to continue with this nonsense? Without this gift of yours you're nothing but a clumsy fool."

"No. Without my gift I'm relegated to believing in the unseen. But my lack of sight doesn't make the future any less real. If I *could* see all of the potential futures right now, I would surely see one out of a thousand in which both Miriam and I survive. Just because I don't see that future now doesn't mean God isn't opening the door to it as we speak."

Omar shook his head in disbelief.

Seth was stalling. It was all he could do now. Omar was right, the game had come to an end. A lump rose into Miriam's throat. She stared at the knife in Omar's hands, suddenly furious at Seth for giving it up. He might not have the stomach to kill her, but she didn't have the stomach to return with Omar.

What if she made a break for it now? She might be able to reach the door and run into the desert before Omar could stop her. But they would come after her. She would have to kill herself. Jump off a cliff, perhaps. Could she really bring herself to commit suicide? Maybe not. No! How could she kill herself?

Desperation crowded her mind. Her sight blurred with tears. *Dear God, I beg you. I beg you!*

Omar flipped open his phone and calmly pushed two keys. He lifted the receiver to his ear and locked his gaze on Miriam. "We are coming out," he said. "If the American makes a move, tell Mudah to shoot him in the head. Under no circumstances is the woman to be harmed. And don't be fooled, the American is in a black abaaya, and she is wearing Western clothing." He snapped the phone shut.

He motioned to the door. "Go."

Miriam's heart felt like a giant piston. She could not move. Seth wasn't moving either.

"Are you deaf?"

"No, we're not deaf," Seth said. "We're just not good at marching to our deaths."

"We will not talk any longer," Omar said, reddening in the face. "We are finished!"

"But it doesn't feel finished."

"Out!" Omar boomed. His cell phone suddenly chirped in his hand. He ignored it.

"If you don't move, I'll have you shot in here."

Seth still made no move.

Omar spit to one side and strode for the door. His cell chirped loudly and he snatched it to his ear. "I'm coming, you fool!"

Omar took one more step and then froze, stunned. He listened for a moment, motionless, and then spun back.

"Forgive me, Abu al-Asamm. I thought you were one of my men."

Her father!

"No, of course your daughter is alive." Omar spoke quickly, momentarily distracted by this intrusion. He took a step toward the window and glanced out, listening now.

Miriam caught Seth's look. His eyes were wide, stricken with a look she hadn't seen in them before. A terrible desperation. He had decided something.

"No sir, you don't understand. I *have* your assassin!" Omar paused. "Yes, that's what I'm saying. I have the assassin and I have your daughter here. They are both in my control."

Seth suddenly leapt up to Omar, snatched the knife from his right hand, and jumped back before Omar could react. Seth spun behind Miriam, threw his left arm around her shoulders, and jerked the knife to her throat.

Omar whirled, dumbfounded.

"It's okay," Seth whispered in her ear. "Scream!"

She understood immediately.

"Father!" she screamed. "There is a knife at my throat! Fatherrr!"

The phone was still pressed to Omar's ear.

A fist pounded on the door.

"Tell them to leave or I will kill her!" Seth shouted. "I will kill the sheik's daughter!"

Omar blinked several times. The fist pounded again, accompanied by a muffled yell this time. "Sir?"

Omar finally came to himself. "Leave us!" he yelled to the man outside. "Get in the car and wait for my call!"

A garbled electronic voice squawked over the phone from across the room. Her father, loud now.

"No, Abu al-Asamm," Omar spoke into the receiver. "I assure you that there's no danger to your daughter. My men have this place surrounded! I have the situation under control."

"Scream," Seth whispered into her ear again.

"Fatherrrrr!" She put her full emotions into it now, wailing with the pent-up horror of facing Omar alone again. "Faaatherrr!" Agony and terror rolled into one cry.

Omar's eyes widened in disbelief.

It occurred to Miriam that Seth's ploy, however daring, probably still only delayed the inevitable. Seth would not kill her, and once his empty threats played themselves out, her father would understand that. Once the sheik satisfied himself that she was indeed safe, Omar would simply kill Seth and take her captive.

Miriam put the dread of this realization into her next wail. She sounded like a wounded jackal.

"Shut up!" Omar screamed.

Miriam took some small comfort in his momentary desperation.

"I assure you, Abu al-Asamm, there is no . . . Yes, he is here, but he's bluffing! Your daughter's screaming because she is *with* him! Speaking to her will prove nothing!"

The sheik was yelling at him through the receiver.

Omar pulled the cell phone from his ear and glared at Miriam, lips flat and trembling.

"You will prove nothing by this!" he spit. Then in a low hissing voice. "You will both pay before you die." He shoved the phone toward them. "Your father wishes to speak to you."

"No!" Seth said.

That stopped him.

"What do you mean no? She will not speak to her own father?"

Seth was still stalling.

"No," Miriam said softly. "I will not."

Omar lifted the phone. "She will not speak to you."

"Fatherrr!" Miriam cried. "I am dying!"

"She is *not* dying!" Omar said. "They are playing with us!"

"Fatherrrr!"

The sense of it had come to Seth as clearly as any algebraic equation. He'd seen enough of how futures worked to know that such an unlikely event as the sheik calling as he had, in the nick of time, was not random or without purpose.

They had prayed and the sheik had called. The call did nothing but stall Omar; Seth knew that, of course. But if there was a future in which he and Miriam survived, and if he could facilitate that future by stalling Omar, he decided it would be a good idea to stall him some more. But stalling meant getting the knife back, a prospect that filled him with dread. Fortunately his boldness had paid off.

He still didn't know how they were going to survive, but he did believe that they were *meant* to survive and that was enough.

"Fatherrrr!"

And then suddenly Seth did know how they were going to survive, because suddenly his mind opened up, as if the roof above their heads had been blown off.

He gasped.

Miriam gasped. "Ouch."

It occurred to Seth that he'd inadvertently jerked the knife against her throat, but it still took a moment for him to clear his mind of the streaming images and relax his grip.

The sudden immersion in potential futures felt like diving into a clear, cool pool after being left to die in the desert. Seth lowered his arms slowly. Now the stalling made perfect sense. Something had caused the sheik to call. Something beyond them. Nothing anyone would think of as spectacular or out of the ordinary. At any other time, in different circumstances, he would never have guessed that the hand of God had been remotely involved.

Now it was obvious to him. How often did that happen in daily life? He thought all of this as he faced Omar.

Miriam turned to him, no longer concerned with screaming to her father. One look at his face and her eyes widened.

"Of course, she will talk to you. Please, please calm down!" Omar said. He had no clue that anything had changed.

Seth spun through a myriad of possible futures, as if they were photos on a wheel. He'd been right, there was a future in which both he and Miriam survived. But it was only *one* out of the many he saw. And it wasn't one he felt especially comfortable with.

Seth winked at Miriam, who was grinning of all things. He took a deep breath and stepped forward.

"Change of plans, my friend."

42

MIRIAM TOOK ONE LOOK at Seth's face and knew immediately that he was seeing the futures. She knew, just as she knew her father's call had not come by accident.

Faith.

Her knees felt weak with a sudden relief. She'd been here before with Seth, staring into what appeared to be a box canyon without escape. Yet what had once terrified her now delighted her. She stepped back from him and felt a silly grin nudge her lips.

Seth winked at her, took a deep breath, and stepped forward.

"Change of plans, my friend."

Omar lowered the phone. Her father's voice sounded distorted through the small speaker. Seth lifted the knife awkwardly, only mildly threatening. "Phone, please."

"You think your knife threatens—"

Seth reached forward and snatched the phone from his hands before Omar could finish. He brought the device to his mouth.

"I'm terribly sorry, Sheik Al-Asamm, but I have to terminate this call for a few minutes. The prince will call you back momentarily, and I promise you he'll straighten everything out then. Your daughter will be fine. I love her, you know. Crazy but true. And I wouldn't storm the palace if I were you. Not just yet."

He flipped the phone closed.

The sudden silence in the room had a ring to it. Omar stood motionless and unsure. Seth's sudden change had pushed some buttons in the man's head.

"I am seeing things again, Omar," Seth said. "Checkmate." He smiled. "Your thoughts aren't technically futures, so I don't know what you're thinking, but I know dozens of things you would try given the chance. If I'm right, one thing you *will* do is jump me. And although you're slightly stronger than I, I know what your moves might be, and I know exactly how to hurt you despite the fact that I've never thrown a punch in my life. I may even have to kill you."

"You're bluffing," Omar said softly, voice scratchy.

Seth ignored him. "I assume you're hoping that your men will come crashing through that door about now, but I can assure you that there's no possibility of that for some time. You sent them packing, and they fear you too much to question you. Terribly sorry."

Omar began to tremble with rage. His hands gathered to fists. "You think this frightens me? That you can manipulate me with this nonsense?"

"I would be careful," Miriam said, surging with confidence. "I've seen Seth at work and I can promise you that he can defeat you with one hand." The words tasted delicious in her mouth and she could not suppress a wide smile.

Omar glared at her. His face twisted and for an instant she wondered if her taunting had been unwise. What if there were no future in which they survived?

"Miriam," Seth said. "As much as you're enjoying this, we're running out of time. As I see it, we have about thirty seconds. Do you mind turning away? This will get ugly."

Ugly? "You don't want me to watch?"

"Exactly. If you don't mind. I'm not normally given to violence, and I'm not sure I like the idea of your watching." He glanced at her and she saw that he was serious.

The scene felt surreal, Seth facing off with Omar, announcing that he was about to hurt him, taking the time to insist she hide her eyes.

"Just turn around," he said.

She backed up.

"Maybe a quick kiss first," Seth said.

Omar snorted and jerked forward.

"Stay!" Seth said, shoving the knife forward. Omar paused, struggling to maintain his control.

"Kiss, darling," Seth said.

She looked at Omar. Yes, why not? With Seth, nothing was by accident, including a kiss. This was her part in delivering justice. The man who called himself her husband was struggling to maintain his control. She walked forward, broke eye contact with Omar just long enough to kiss Seth tenderly on the cheek, and smiled at Omar. It was a pleasure to play her part.

Seth slipped the cell phone into her hands. "Hit the callback button when I say."

Omar stood immobilized. Miriam took the phone, turned from them, and walked to the corner.

"I don't want to hurt you, Omar," Seth said behind her. "But it's the only way. There's two ways we can do this. You can attack me, or I can attack you. And if you're wondering, I'm talking matter-of-factly like this to unnerve you. It'll work to my advantage, even though you already know that I'm manipulating you. Foresight is such a wonderful thing."

"This is insanity! One call and my men will be here. Do you think you can overcome twenty men?"

"I don't know. It's not in the futures so I haven't seen it. They won't come. Unfortunately, they're in their cars where you sent them. Mercedeses are amazingly well-insulated. I'm afraid you're stranded with me, lover boy."

"You'll never escape this place!"

"One step at a time."

Omar did not respond.

"Well, should I run at you?" Seth said. "Or should I just provoke you into . . ."

A loud snort made Miriam flinch. She glanced around, just long enough to see that Omar had thrown himself at Seth. She knew that Omar was a trained warrior, steeled by hundreds of fights. He looked like a demon descending on Seth, who simply stood, limp. She diverted her eyes, like a schoolgirl caught peeking.

The cabin filled with sounds of heavy breathing and crashing, followed by a tremendous thump and a grunt. Silence.

Miriam could contain herself no longer. She spun around.

Omar was on his belly, face pressed into the floorboards, one arm twisted behind his back. He was gulping for breath. Seth knelt with one knee on Omar's back. He'd bent the man's arm back at an impossible angle with one hand, and with the other he pressed the tip of the knife's blade into Omar's spine, where his neck met his shoulders.

"Now you listen to me, chump!" Seth snarled. The sudden anger in his tone made Miriam consider turning around again.

"The world doesn't need killers like you. Saudi Arabia doesn't need killers like you." Seth bent over so that his mouth was close to Omar's ear. He applied pressure to the blade and the man groaned.

"Miriam doesn't need or want you. And I know it comes as a shock to you, but women are not dogs! You, on the other hand, might be one." Seth pressed the blade again. Omar whimpered. A bead of sweat dropped from Seth's chin and splashed on the man's neck.

"I'm not a violent man, I'm really not, but I swear . . ." He ground his teeth, trembling. "You make me *sick!*"

Seth took a deep breath, calming himself.

"Call your father, Miriam."

She lifted the phone and pressed the callback button.

"You forced Miriam to marry you against her will," Seth said. "Now I'm going to force you to divorce her against your will. As far as we're concerned, she's not married, but we're going to make it official."

He looked at Miriam, eyes glazed. "You aren't supposed to be looking."

She said nothing. She loved him more in that moment than ever before. The phone rang on the other end.

"This blade is very close to your spinal cord, Omar," Seth said. "If you turn or lift, it will sever your nerves and leave you a quadriplegic. Do you want to spend the rest of your days in a wheelchair?"

The sheik answered the phone.

"Father?"

"Miriam! In the name of Allah, what's the meaning—"

"I will never give Omar a child, Father. Never! I have refused him, and if he ever tries to touch me again, I will kill him!" She paused, taken by her sudden fury. She knew where Seth was headed and on impulse she decided to push it forward.

"Omar despises me and wishes to divorce me," she said.

Silence.

"That's right, Omar," Seth said quietly. "You will divorce Miriam now. You will speak it into the phone and the sheik will be your witness. If you hesitate, I will push the knife in. Do you understand? You'll never touch another woman as long as you live."

Omar moaned again and Miriam wondered if he might pass out from the pain.

"Omar cannot divorce you!" Her father had come to himself. "It will ruin everything!"

"It will not ruin me!" Miriam said.

Omar groaned.

Seth nodded at the phone, and Miriam held it to his ear. He spoke quickly to her father.

"If Omar doesn't divorce your daughter, he will leave here an invalid. There will be no son. Either way. Accept the will of God, Abu al-Asamm."

Seth nodded again, and Miriam lowered the phone to Omar's lips. The man's eyes were round with terror. His nostrils flared with each breath, and a string of spittle ran from his mouth to the floor.

"Say it!"

Omar closed his mouth and then opened it, speechless.

"Have it your way," Seth said.

"I divorce you," Omar said in a barely audible groan.

"Again," Seth said. "I divorce you, *Miriam.*"

"I divorce you . . ."

"Miriam."

"Miriam."

"Again. I divorce your daughter, Abu Ali al-Asamm."

Miriam heard her father's voice objecting on the cell phone's speaker.

"I divorce your daughter, Abu Ali al-Asamm."

A wave of relief flooded Miriam. Three times in front of witnesses. The law was fulfilled. She was free. The only way for Omar to reclaim her was to go through another ceremony. She snapped the phone closed on the sheik's protests.

Seth hesitated, staring at the back of Omar's head. He suddenly pulled back the knife, flipped it, and brought the butt down on Omar's head, hard. The man relaxed.

"Sorry about that," Seth said to the unconscious figure.

He jumped up. "We have to hurry! They're coming out of the cars now. When they see me, they'll fire. Wait to a count of five and then run out to our car. They won't fire on you."

"They won't hit you?"

"I have to cover ten feet to the corner—if I move quickly, they won't have the time to properly aim. In three out of four futures they miss."

"The car's out of gas!"

"We have enough. You just keep moving. They'll go for the tires, but that's not where our danger lies. Just do exactly what I say."

"So there is danger? Real danger?"

"There's always danger." Seth leaned forward and kissed her firmly on the lips. "I love you, Princess."

43

SETH JERKED THE DOOR OPEN. "Remember, count to five," he said. He bolted from the hut.

Miriam instinctively dropped to a knee and began to count. Gunfire filled the desert air. Several rifles and at least one automatic weapon. How could he escape that?

In three out of four they miss, he'd said. What about that fourth?

Miriam rushed the last three counts, gathered herself, and then sprinted through the door. The black cars were lined in a half-moon, unmoved. At least six of them had their doors open, weapons trained on the shanty.

"Stop firing!" The driver from the car on the far left ran forward. "It's the woman!" The gunfire ceased.

Miriam slipped at the corner, scrambled to her feet, and tore around the hut. Then she was at the car, panting. Seth sat behind the wheel, frantically motioning her on.

"Hurry! Get in!"

"I am!" Miriam clambered around the back, threw the front door open, and dove in. "Go!"

"When we get to the Mercedes on the far left, I need you to get out," Seth said. "They still don't know that Omar has divorced you. You'll be safe. I won't be—"

"I understand," she said. "It's Omar's car. His driver's in the hut now. Drive!"

"That's right. Don't worry about the tires—"

"Go! Hurry!"

Seth threw the stick into reverse. The car shot backward, throwing sand forward with its wheels. They cleared the shack. A dozen rifles spun their way.

"We're cutting it close," Seth said. "Omar's awake."

He jerked the stick into drive and roared for the abandoned Mercedes on their left. Immediately gunfire popped across the sand. Metal pinged and one of the tires blew. They flew over the sand, and Miriam was sure they would slam into the hood of the car.

Seth slammed on the brakes at the last moment, and they slid to a stop, inches from Omar's car, nose to nose.

Miriam shoved her door open and stumbled out.

Immediately the gunfire stopped. For once, the fear Omar's men had of him worked against him. She leapt to her feet, swung around the open door, and ran for the driver's side of Omar's Mercedes.

Seth ran for the other door, protected by the heavy car.

Miriam slid into the driver's seat. Seth piled in beside her.

The man she'd seen running for the hut spilled out now, followed immediately by Omar.

Beside her, Seth was smiling. "Take us out of here, honey."

She pushed the accelerator to the floor. They slammed into the car they'd just vacated.

"Sorry, I saw that coming," Seth said. "I should have warned you. The other way."

She shoved the shifter into reverse, and they spun backward in a tight loop. Something thumped into the car. Two more. Bullets! Then a whole row along the rear windshield. She glanced at Seth and saw that he was still grinning.

"Any other car, we'd be dead," Seth said. "This one's bulletproof. Literally. Omar's parting gift."

Of course! "Ha!"

"That's right, ha!" he mimicked.

"The tires?"

"No chance."

"Ha!" She slammed the steering wheel in elation. They roared over the sand, leaving the circle of cars behind in their dust.

"Left or right?" she asked.

"Left, back to the highway. Then south, toward Jiddah."

Miriam flew down the road at breakneck speed. For a full minute neither spoke. She glanced at the rearview mirror—a plume of dust rose from the dirt road.

"They're following!"

"Don't worry, we have an ace behind the wheel," Seth said. "I told you your driving would come in handy."

"You're being too casual about this," she objected. "We were nearly killed back there! What if they call ahead and have the road blocked? This is Omar's territory now, not the United States."

"Omar may try to block the road. But your father will withdraw his support now. The coup will crumble. King Fahd will regain the upper hand. Khalid and Omar will be forced to run for their lives. Think about it, Miriam, they have no use for you now. Neither does King Fahd. You are no longer their pawn."

She thought through his analysis. It made perfect sense. He had reason to be casual, didn't he?

"You see all this?"

"No. I don't see anything now. It's gone."

She looked at him, alarmed. "Then how can you be so sure?"

"Because I saw enough when I did see to know how this works. I'm pretty sure my days of seeing are over. We'll have to wander around in the dark now, but I'm not sure that's so bad, are you? Have a little faith." He grinned. "We're free, honey. Trust me, we're free."

Seth pulled Omar's phone from his pocket and dialed a long number. He looked at her and let it ring.

"Clive? Hello, Clive . . ."

Seth listened for a moment.

"Easy, my friend. Omar's divorced Miriam. The sheik is withdrawing his support. The coup is history. I have Miriam now and we're headed for the embassy in Jiddah. Please have it open for us. I'll explain everything later. In the meantime, tell the State Department to call the sheik. He'll confirm everything."

Seth cut the connection.

They drove in silence for several long minutes. The plume of dust still hung on the horizon behind them, but Miriam was driving very quickly, and if she wasn't mistaken, it was further behind than it had been a few seconds ago.

They reached the highway and Miriam turned south toward Jiddah. Seth was right; Omar would have more on his mind than chasing down a woman he'd just divorced. He would be fortunate to survive beyond the night.

It occurred to Miriam that she and Seth had begun their relationship like this, in a car fleeing south over miles of pavement. A Saudi princess and an American outlaw. Bonnie and Clyde. Stranded between two cultures. When would the running stop? Where were they running to? What future awaited them?

Only God knew. Faith.

The emotion swept over her like a tide. The road blurred and she blinked her sight clear.

"I don't think I can live without you, Seth."

"As long as I'm alive, you won't have to," he said. "I swear it. I won't let them take you back. Do you hear me?"

Miriam wasn't sure why, but she began to cry softly. It was the sweetest thing anyone had ever said to her.

"I love you, Seth. I love you very much," she said.

"I love you, Miriam. I will always love you."

epilogue

SAMIR STOOD AT THE MOSQUE'S ENTRANCE, gazing over the floods of men who milled about after prayers, talking in low tones and nodding in agreement. Sheik Abu Ali al-Asamm stood near the front, discussing matters with several lesser Shi'i leaders here in Dhahran. Soon the sheik's day would pass, and one of the lessers would rise up to be the voice of the Saudi Shi'i. And what would be the word of that leader? Would it be a word of love and peace or a word of the sword?

Two weeks had passed since the failed coup attempt. Samir could not have imagined that such gut-wrenching and soul-searching as had plagued him in these last fourteen days was possible.

A lump rose to his throat. He had not discerned the sum of the matter yet, but he was confident the answers would not elude him for long—Allah would never indefinitely withhold the truth from any diligent seeker. In the meantime, several observations had presented themselves to him, none of them particularly welcomed.

The least welcomed of these was that he had lost Miriam's love forever. She had been and still was the only woman he ever loved, and he'd sacrificed her for an ideal that had proven misguided.

"Forgive me, dear Miriam," he mumbled under his breath. He turned from the entrance and walked down the steps to the street.

How could a good Muslim reconcile the militants' ideals for Islam with true love? How could Samir have turned Miriam over to a beast like Omar for the sake of Islam? Would Allah ever do such a thing? No, he didn't think so. You could not swing the sword with the battle cry "Allah is love." The two were irreconcilable—he knew it because he had tried and found nothing but misery.

He held no ill feelings toward the American, Seth—in a strange way he was thankful that a man of such obvious character had saved Miriam from almost certain doom and taken her away to a new life. How many men would have risked what Seth risked to rescue Miriam? The American wasn't Saudi, of course. Nor Muslim. They would endure a host of cultural challenges if they were to wed, but in the end, Miriam would be happy with Seth. If there was anything Samir could do for Miriam now, he could wish her happiness.

"Afternoon, Samir."

Samir turned to the voice. It was Hassan, a fifteen-year-old son of the sheik.

"Afternoon, Hassan."

"God is great."

"God is indeed great."

The boy smiled and hurried off.

Yes, God was great, but those who swung the sword on his behalf were not, Samir thought. Omar was dead, killed trying to escape the day after the coup. Killed by the sheik's men, no less. A kind of poetic justice. Khalid still hid somewhere out of the country. As long as the House of Saud remained in power, Khalid would be on the run. Ostracized, but not powerless. Others expelled from the kingdom had wreaked havoc throughout the world. Samir expected no less of Khalid.

The sheik had not only been spared but commended for his reversal of loyalty in the eleventh hour. Never mind that he'd been one of the plotters—he was still more valuable as a friend to the king than as an enemy. It was the way of the desert.

Islam engaged itself in a great struggle, Samir thought. A struggle between those who wanted to convert the infidels with the sword and those who wanted to convert them with love. The struggle was enough to have moved Miriam away from the faith.

And where did Allah stand on the matter? Was he with love, or was he with the sword? Mohammed had never been clear. He'd embraced both at different times, though he arguably had more success with the sword. To reject the sword would mean to admit the prophet had erred.

Was this so bad? Mohammed had never claimed to be perfect. That was the place of the other prophet. Of Jesus.

It didn't matter. The world had changed. The time for the sword and the militants had passed. Saudi Arabia was divided now, but one day all Muslims would understand that the world was tired of the sword.

Like many of his countrymen, deep in his heart, Samir was a lover, not a fighter. One day, if he were so fortunate, he would find another woman to love. This time he would love her as he only wished he could love Miriam now. With all of his gifts and all of his gratitude. She would be free, and if she was not, he would set her free. Like a bird.

"Fly, my dear. Fly free, dear Miriam."

Samir walked down the street, vaguely comforted.

The Circle Trilogy

Book One
ISBN 0-8499-1791-3

Book Two
ISBN 0-8499-1790-5

Book Three
ISBN 0-8499-1792-1

Only one man can save two worlds from destruction. And he's already been killed. Twice.

Fleeing assailants through a alleyway in Denver late one night, Thomas Hunter narrowly escapes to the roof of an industrial building. Then a silent bullet from the night clips his head and his world goes black. When he awakes, he finds himself in an entirely different reality...a green forest that seems more real than where he was. Every time he tries to sleep, he wakes up in the other world, and soon he truly no longer knows which reality is real.

Never before has an entire trilogy- all in hardcover format- been released in less than a year. On the heels of *The Matrix* and *The Lord of the Rings* comes a new trilogy where dreams and reality collide. Where the fate of two worlds depends on one man: Thomas Hunter

Each book in the trilogy is also available in abridged (CD) and unabridged (CD and cassette) editions.

Discover more at TedDekker.com

Also Available from Ted Dekker

Blessed Child

By Ted Dekker and Bill Bright

The young orphan boy was abandoned and raised in an Ethiopian monastery. Now he must flee those walls or die. But the world is hardly ready for a boy like Caleb. When relief expert Jason Marker agrees to take Caleb from the monastery, he opens humanity's doors to an incredible journey filled with intrigue and peril. Together with Leiah, the nurse who escapes to America with them, Jason discovers Caleb's stunning power. But so do the boy's enemies, who will stop at nothing to destroy him. Jason and Leiah fight for the boy's survival while the world erupts into debate over the source of the boy's power. In the end nothing can prepare any of them for what they will find.

A Man Called Blessed

By Ted Dekker and Bill Bright

In this explosive sequel, Rebecca Soloman leads a team of Israeli commandos deep into the Ethiopian desert to hunt the one man who may know the final resting place of the Ark of the Covenant. But Islamic fundamentalists fear that the Ark's discovery will compel Israel to rebuild Solomon's temple on the very site of their own holy mosque in Jerusalem. They immediately dispatch Ismael, their most accomplished assassin, to pursue the same man. But the man in their sights is no ordinary man. His name is Caleb, and he too is on a quest—to find again the love he once embraced as a child. Tensions sky-rocket as the world awakens to the drama in the desert. The fate of a million souls rests in the hand of these three.

Three

By Ted Dekker

Imagine answering your cell phone one day to a mysterious voice that gives you three minutes to confess your sin. If you don't he'll blow the car you're driving to bits and pieces. So begins a nightmare that grows with progressively higher states. There's another phone call, another riddle, another three minutes to confess your sin. The cycle will not stop until the world discovers the secret of your sin.

Three is a psychological thriller that starts full-tilt and keeps you off-balance until the very last suspense-filled page.

Discover more at TedDekker.com

The Martyr's Song Series

Heaven's Wager

He lost everything he ever wanted—and risked his soul to get what he deserved. Take a glimpse into a world more real and vital than most people ever discover here on earth, the unseen world where the real dramas of the universe—and of our daily lives—continually unfold.

When Heaven Weeps

A cruel game of ultimate stakes at the end of World War II leaves Jan Jovic stunned and perplexed. He's prepared for neither the incredible demonstration of love nor the terrible events that follow. Now, many years later, Jan falls madly in love with the "wrong" woman and learns the true cost of love.

Thunder of Heaven

When armed forces destroy their idyllic existence within the jungles of the Amazon, Tanya embraces God, while Shannon boldly rejects God, choosing the life of an assassin. Despite their vast differences, they find themselves in the crucible of a hideous plot to strike sheer terror in the heart of America.

Discover more at TedDekker.com